Higher Education and Social Class

D0782809

Working-class groups have historically been excluded from participating in higher education. Past decades have seen an expansion of the system towards a more inclusive higher education, but participation among people from working-class groups has remained persistently low. Is higher education unattractive for these groups, or are the institutions acting to exclude them?

This thought-provoking and revealing book examines the many factors and reasons why working-class groups are under-represented in higher education. In particular, the book addresses issues around differential access to information about university, the value of higher education to working-class groups, the costs of participating and the propensity to participate. Issues of gender and ethnicity are also explored and questions raised for those who are currently involved in 'widening participation' projects and initiatives. A unique feature of the book is that its findings are drawn from an innovative study where the views of both working-class participants and non-participants in higher education were explored.

This book will be of interest to students of social policy, educational studies and sociology of education at undergraduate and postgraduate levels. Academics, researchers and policy-makers nationally and internationally will also find it valuable.

Louise Archer is a Senior Research Fellow in the Institute for Policy Studies in Education at the London Metropolitan University.

Merryn Hutchings is Reader in Education in the Institute for Policy Studies in Education at the London Metropolitan University.

Alistair Ross is Professor of Education and Director of the Institute for Policy Studies in Education at the London Metropolitan University.

Higher Education and Social Class

Issues of exclusion and inclusion

Louise Archer, Merryn Hutchings
and Alistair Ross

with Carole Leathwood, Robert Gilchrist and
David Phillips

RoutledgeFalmer
Taylor & Francis Group

LONDON AND NEW YORK

First published 2003 by RoutledgeFalmer
11 New Fetter Lane, London EC4P 4EE

Simultaneously published in the USA and Canada
by RoutledgeFalmer
29 West 35th Street, New York, NY 10001

RoutledgeFalmer is an imprint of the Taylor & Francis Group

© 2003 Louise Archer, Merryn Hutchings and Alistair Ross with
Carole Leathwood, Robert Gilchrist and David Phillips

Typeset in Sabon by
Bookcraft Ltd, Stroud, Gloucestershire
Printed and bound in Great Britain by
The Cromwell Press, Trowbridge, Wiltshire

British Library Cataloguing in Publication Data
A catalogue record for this book is available
from the British Library

Library of Congress Cataloging in Publication Data
A catalog record for this book has been requested

ISBN 0–415–27644–6 (pbk)
ISBN 0–415–27643–8 (hbk)

Contents

Figures

Tables

Acknowledgements

The Social Class and Widening Participation in Higher Education Project was financed by the University of North London's Development and Diversity fund (the University has since merged with London Guildhall University to become London Metropolitan University). We would like to thank the institution, and particularly the Vice Chancellor, Brian Roper, who has continued throughout to show a close interest in the project.

We would like to thank numerous colleagues at the London Metropolitan University who have helped in the production of this book, but in particular we are grateful to Hiromi Yamashita, for compiling the bibliography, and Lindsay Melling and Siobhan O'Hagan for all their help in compiling references.

Thanks must also go to Tim Collier, who did a large amount of work to produce the article and analyses on which Chapter 4 is based, and Simon Pratt, who conducted two of the focus groups for the project.

We would like to acknowledge the helpful assistance of all our colleagues at MORI (in relation to the national survey) and the Office for National Statistics (for facilitating the initial focus groups).

Naturally, we are also very grateful to all our individual friends, colleagues and families who have supported us throughout the writing of the book.

But most of all we would like to thank all the respondents who took part in interviews, focus groups and national survey and the staff at the two FE colleges who greatly facilitated our access. This book is dedicated to those who were kind enough to share their views and experiences with us.

Abbreviations

A levels	General Certificate in Education Advanced Level
AFE	Advanced Further Education
ATTI	Association of Teachers in Technical Institutions
APEL	Accreditation of Prior Experiential Learning
API	Age Participation Index
AS level	Advanced Supplementary Level examination
AVCE	Advanced Vocational Certificate of Education
BTEC	Business and Technology Education Council
CAT	College of Advanced Technology
CBI	Confederation of British Industry
CNAA	Council for National Academic Awards
CSE	Certificate of Secondary Education
CVCP	Committee of Vice Chancellors and Principals
DES	Department of Education and Science
DfE	Department for Education
DfEE	Department for Education and Employment
DfES	Department for Education and Skills
DSIR	Department of Scientific and Industrial Research
FE	Further Education
FEFC	Further Education Funding Council
GCE	General Certificate of Education
GCSE	General Certificate of Secondary Education
GNVQ	General National Vocational Qualification
HE	Higher Education
HEFCE	Higher Education Funding Council for England
HEI	Higher Education Institution
HESA	Higher Education Statistical Agency
NAO	National Audit Office
NCIHE	The National Committee of Inquiry into Higher Education
NCVQ	National Council for Vocational Qualifications
NS SEC	National Statistics Socio-economic Classification
NUS	National Union of Students

NVQ	National Vocational Qualification
Ofsted	Office for Standards in Education
O level	General Certificate in Education Ordinary Level
ONS	Office for National Statistics
PEP	Political and Economic Planning
PCFC	Polytechnic and Colleges Funding Council
UCAS	Universities and Colleges Admissions Service
UFC	Universities Funding Council
UGC	University Grants Committee
UK	United Kingdom

Introduction

Internationally there is a growing concern to increase, and diversify, the numbers of students in higher education (HE) (OECD 2001). These drives to widen participation are motivated by a number of factors, including economic, institutional and social justice concerns, which are framed within the globalization of the knowledge economy/knowledge society. In this book we focus upon the specific UK context, although many of the issues raised will resonate internationally to all those who are engaged in efforts to widen university participation to students from 'non-traditional' backgrounds. Within the UK, the government has explicitly stated one of its aims as being to widen participation in HE to 50 per cent of 18–30-year-olds by the year 2010. To achieve this target of widened (not merely increased) participation, new students will need to be recruited from previously under-represented groups. Currently, almost all young people from middle-class and professional families go on to university. Participation among young people from working-class groups has remained persistently low. Thus young working-class groups are a key target of initiatives aimed at widening participation in post-compulsory education.

In this book we explore issues around social class and widening participation, with particular reference to working-class groups. We discuss patterns of participation, potential reasons for the under-representation of working-class groups in HE and we address the factors and barriers that prevent participation, raising questions and implications in relation to current debates. We supplement and illustrate our arguments with data collected as part of a research study (the Social Class and Widening Participation in Higher Education Project conducted between 1998 and 2001) based at the University of North London (now London Metropolitan University). The book thus draws together research data with theoretical and policy literature in order to address issues around the participation of working-class groups in higher education.

Although education has often been portrayed in terms of its positive and liberatory potential, not least within more recent widening participation and lifelong learning rhetoric, there is also a long history of sociological theorization that has been critical of the ways in which education reproduces and reinforces class inequalities. See for example work by Bowles and Gintis (1976), Bourdieu and Passeron (1977) and more recently by Diane Reay, Stephen Ball and colleagues (for example Reay *et al.* 2001; Ball *et al.* 2000a).

It can be argued that higher education has a particular potential for reinforcing inequalities because, by definition, it is not open to all and is non-compulsory. As Chapters 2 and 3 will discuss, the university system has long played a key role in the reproduction of social-class inequalities.

Indeed, issues of social class and in/equality have never really left the educational agenda. Almost two decades of Conservative rule from 1979 to 1997, combined with the rise of the 'New Right' and an increasing valorization of the market, have contributed to an increasing individualization of society, and have posed renewed threats to equality (Hutton 1996). A Treasury Report published in 1999 noted that

> Over the last twenty years not only has the gap between the richest and the poorest increased, but the amount of movement between income groups has been limited. What is more, damaged life chances perpetuate across the generations.
>
> (HM Treasury 1999: 5, cited in Ball *et al.* 2000)

Critics have thus argued that educational inequalities not only persist, but in some cases have increased. As noted elsewhere (Hayton and Leathwood forthcoming), economic disadvantage is linked with low levels of achievement (Kennedy 1997), and 'since the late 1980s the attainment gap between the highest and lowest social classes has widened' (Gillborn and Mirza 2000: 18). Educational opportunities and achievements reflect not only class, but also ethnicity and gender inequalities with, for example, African-Caribbean boys and Pakistani and Bangladeshi girls and boys performing less well overall than their white counterparts.

This book will analyse, and chart changes in relation to, issues of social class and higher education, with a particular focus on the working class, who have been traditionally excluded from university study. Analyses draw widely on a range of literature and studies from across the UK, but arguments are made particularly by drawing on data collected as part of a research project based at the University of North London (see below).

The research project

The Social Class and Widening Participation in HE research project was conducted in three main phases and utilized a mixture of methods. Focus groups were conducted with inner-city, ethnically diverse working-class respondents, including both 'non-participants' (people who were not in higher education and who were unlikely to apply) in phase 1, and 'participants' (current HE students from working-class backgrounds) in phase 3. In phase 2, the generalizability of focus group findings was explored through a national survey. Details of the methodology used within the three main phases of this project are summarized in Chapter 4 (the quantitative survey) and Chapter 5 (the focus groups).

Overview of chapters

Chapter 1 introduces issues around theorizing social class and higher education. It summarizes some of the dominant theories and debates in relation to conceptualizing 'social class' across the disciplines of sociology and education. These debates are related to the 'widening participation' context. The chapter also addresses how to understand social-class inequalities in participation in relation to other social divisions of 'race', ethnicity and gender. The theoretical position of the book is presented.

Chapters 2 and 3 address the policy context within which debates around widening participation have occurred. In Chapter 2, historical developments in the UK are outlined, leading up to the publication of that important milestone, the Robbins Report. Chapter 3 continues the historical overview, documenting changes in the HE system, such as the effects of the binary policy, and the growth of higher education in the UK to the present day.

Chapter 4 draws upon quantitative data from official statistics and the MORI survey to examine participation and the potential for increased/widened participation in higher education in the UK. Statistical modelling is used to explore the potential to participate among working-class groups.

Chapter 5 looks at the information and knowledge that working-class non-participants and participants may draw upon when making decisions about higher education. The chapter examines the different sources of information which are used and trusted (or distrusted) by working-class groups and it considers the differing constructions or stereotypes of university that were voiced by respondents.

Chapter 6 introduces questions concerning the 'value' of higher education and asks whether participation is actually 'worth it' for working-class groups. The chapter explores the balance between the potential benefits of university study, as compared to the increased risks and costs of participation for working-class groups.

Chapter 7 considers differentially classed entry routes into higher education, discussing the role and impact of different pathways and qualifications upon access to HE. It is argued that the academic/vocational divide within educational institutions, curricula and qualifications has played a key role in the reproduction of inequalities in participation.

Chapter 8 considers issues around student finance and the impact of money and funding systems upon working-class participation in HE. The chapter underlines the complex, and ever-changing, nature of the system for financing HE study and highlights the implications, and experiences, of these factors among working-class groups.

Chapter 9 explores issues of identity in relation to HE participation. Identities and inequalities of 'race' and class are examined in relation to the participation (and non-participation) of working-class women and men from different ethnic groups. Issues around 'changing' identity are discussed and related to resistance or acceptance of university participation.

Conclusions and recommendations are made in Chapter 10. This final chapter also raises a number of questions for policy, theory and practice, such as what are universities, who should they be for and what might the future hold for widening participation?

Chapter 1

Social class and higher education

Louise Archer

Social class has long been a central theme within educational and sociological theorizing, research and analysis. Within sociology, Edgell (1993) has suggested that social class is 'the most widely used concept' although it has undergone fluctuating periods of being in turn either prioritized or dismissed as irrelevant. While the salience of social class may rise and fall within policy and academic discourses, surveys (for example Hudson and Williams 1989) have suggested that recent years have witnessed increases in the gap between broad sections of the population, who have differential access to money, resources, qualifications, life chances and health. As will be outlined later in this chapter, education has always been centrally positioned within sociological theories of class re/production, playing an important role in ensuring either the reproduction of (middle-class) privileges or (working-class) disadvantages.

Within educational research, issues of social class have been predominantly addressed in relation to the compulsory schooling context, where it has been noted that working-class children tend to experience persistently lower rates of attainment and are less likely to follow routes into post-compulsory education. For example, Bates and Riseborough (1993) detail how young people from different social classes do not attend the same types of educational institution, nor do they gain similar levels of qualifications and results, nor follow comparable post-16 routes. They argue that, at all stages within the educational journey, young working-class people experience poorer conditions, receive fewer resources, study for less prestigious qualifications and follow lower-status trajectories. As detailed in Chapters 2 and 3, concerns around class inequalities in access, retention and attainment within higher education have gained in importance in recent years. Internationally, the historical dominance of higher education by better-off socio-economic groups has also become a major cause for concern in the majority of industrialized countries. The intractability of this problem is evidenced by the relatively small changes in working-class participation rates following the mass expansion of higher education in Britain (see Chapters 2 and 3) and in the wake of numerous initiatives and schemes aimed at widening participation.

Various theories and perspectives have attempted to account for working-class groups' generally lower levels of attainment and rates of participation in post-compulsory education, but there remains little consensus as to how to theorize the concept of social class and its relationship to education. It could be asked, however, why it is necessary to attempt to theorize social class and higher education. This question is particularly pertinent because many practical, widening participation strategies could be classed as 'atheoretical' (Archer, Hutchings and Leathwood 2001) in their approaches. We would answer this question by suggesting that the ways in which 'social class' and 'higher education' are conceptualized will have important implications for how research concerned with 'widening participation' is imagined and undertaken. Taken-for-granted assumptions impact upon the solutions advocated and policy recommendations made within particular research projects because the theoretical position adopted by a researcher will frame the terms of his or her investigation (such as the methods utilized, the relationships selected for analysis, etc.). Thus the way in which social class is understood within research on higher education and widening participation is grounded within the researcher's views about the structure of society. This determines the formulation of research questions, the ways in which issues are understood and the subsequent range of recommendations advocated. Questions around class inequalities (or 'bias' in Williamson's words) within higher education are therefore conceptual issues:

> Since answers to them presuppose some further theoretical elaboration about the nature of class inequalities and the way in which these can be related to the structure and functioning of higher education.
>
> (Williamson 1981: 18)

For example, depending upon one's theorizations of social class and higher education, a research project may choose to problematize and investigate widening participation as an issue of either working-class attitudes and aspirations, or institutional cultures within higher education.

This chapter will outline some of the main theoretical approaches that might be drawn on to conceptualize the relationship between social class and higher education. These approaches are organized into two main sections. The first addresses what might be characterized 'categorical' (Williamson 1981), 'modernist' (Bradley 1996) or 'quantitative' (Crompton 1993) approaches. This section largely reviews 'grand theories' and addresses the ways in which such approaches define class in predominantly 'objective', occupational terms. The second section covers what might be characterized as 'process' (Williamson 1981), 'postmodern' (Bradley 1996) or 'qualitative' (Crompton 1993) approaches. This section addresses 'themes' (rather than large-scale theories) in which social class has been conceptualized as subjective and fluid, produced within interactions between social structures and identities. The final part of the chapter outlines the theoretical approach used within this book.

Categorical and modernist approaches

Traditionally, the treatment of social class within educational and sociological research has been dominated by modernist and 'grand' theories, in which class is conceptualized categorically, as comprising groups of people who share particular socio-economic characteristics which distinguish them from other groups (Williamson 1981). Researchers within this tradition have tended to quantitatively study class structures and patterns (Crompton 1993) and share a perception of class as objectively definable and largely fixed/unchanging. We begin by summarizing how such approaches frame the relationship between social class and (higher) education, drawing upon Bradley's (1996) comprehensive work which details the development of sociological literature in relation to social class. The chapter also discusses some of the benefits and limitations of defining social class from categorical/modernist perspectives within widening participation research.

As Bradley (1996) discusses, neo-Marxist and neo-Weberian theorists differ in how they theorize social class, but they share an understanding of capitalist societies as stratified by class, in which the ruling class achieves dominance over the working class through control of property, production and the market. Marx (1976) emphasized the role of alienation and exploitation in the production and maintenance of capitalist power relations, while Weber (1938) emphasized that 'bureaucracy' and 'rationalization' were not only important in producing capitalist societies, but were central to the formation of the middle classes.

Although largely missing from Marx and Weber's original theorizations, the role of the education system has subsequently been stressed by theorists such as Althusser (1971), who posited that, within capitalist society, education is an apparatus of the state, attempting to reproduce the conditions of capitalist production. American neo-Marxists Bowles and Gintis (1976) also proposed that education acts as a class channel, demonstrated through their concept of the 'correspondence principle'. They suggested that although schools may claim to promote equal opportunities for all, they reproduce a capitalist division of labour, preparing children for class-determined careers in the labour market.

These accounts primarily addressed the relationship between social class and compulsory education, but they can be extended to HE, where they can be used to explain working-class under-representation in higher education as a result of the differential channelling of working-class and middle-class children within the school system. From this perspective, differential participation rates appear to be an almost inevitable feature of capitalism; thus for the aim of substantially widened participation in HE to occur, there will need to be fundamental changes within the structure of society. These accounts do not, however, explain the participation (albeit in low numbers) of working-class students. Nor do these theories adequately explain how, and why, some changes in participation rates have occurred over time or why some working-class groups (e.g. black women) appear to participate in greater numbers than others, such as black men (cf. Chapter 9).

Bradley (1996) also documents the thinking of functionalist theorists who have similarly regarded education as a crucial element within the reproduction of class differences. Whereas Marxist and Weberian theorists have emphasized the inequalities inherent within this process of reproducing class differences, functionalist theorists view education as part of a meritocratic sorting process, determining the best people for particular jobs and roles in society. Functionalists have however been criticized for presenting the education system in a legitimating role which hides structural inequalities to the extent that 'upper-class life has been made to look like a reward for educational success and working class life as a punishment for laziness and a lack of ability' (Steven 1983: 291, cited in Bradley 1996: 184). Functionalism echoes Darwinianism in its assumptions that 'natural selection' defines social class within industrialized societies. Applied to an higher-education context, functionalist theories would suggest that low rates of participation among working-class groups are related to lower rates of intelligence, ability and/or application, with the more talented working-class individuals reaching university through their own merit. Thus unequal participation rates are not treated as a social problem requiring action, but as a natural aspect of a functioning society. Indeed, notions of a finite, and stratified, 'natural pool of ability' in relation to higher-education participation have persisted from the 1960s to the present day. However, as Bradley (1996) and others have suggested, functionalist theories can be criticized for being simplistic in their assumptions of meritocratic determinism in the face of a wealth of evidence pointing to structural inequalities such as racism, sexism and classism (discussed later in this chapter). Functionalist theories can also be criticized for overlooking differential patterns of participation between social groups due to their focus upon individual differences. And yet despite these substantial criticisms of functionalist theories, key functionalist themes (such as an unproblematized notion of meritocracy and the assumption that the working-class groups are under-represented in HE due to lower ability levels) underpin some of the more right-wing viewpoints offered within current widening participation debates.

An alternative perspective is offered by 'class–culture paradigm' theorists (Byrne *et al.* 1975), who argue that social classes can be distinguished by their differing 'cultures' which play a role in reproducing particular class positions. For example, Williamson (1981) cites Kelsall, Poole and Kuhn (1972), who suggested that in 1960, working-class students were differentiated from their non-participating peers through their family and educational characteristics. They identified parental encouragement as the key factor determining participation and found that middle-class families were more likely to encourage their children to progress in post-compulsory education. As Edwards and Roberts (1980) also explained, differential class participation rates in HE were regarded as resulting from differential valuing of HE between social classes and contrasting class perceptions regarding the 'cultural accessibility' of higher education. Indeed, this view seems to still have some currency, as it appears to underpin various widening participation initiatives which are aimed at 'raising aspirations', 'increasing awareness' of HE and challenging 'cultures of non-participation' among under-represented groups (for example CVCP 1998). But, as Williamson (1981: 29) notes, the perspective is not unproblematic because 'what such an explanation does is [to] locate the problem [of non-participation] in an aspect of the family or school experience of different groups of children'. Notwithstanding the influence of classcultural theories upon widening participation practice, recently there have been shifts away from 'cultural' explanations towards an emphasis on the role of school/education institutional processes (Foster *et al.* 1996: 139) and towards more nuanced, complex accounts of 'culture' (see later in this chapter). As Williamson argues, this shift may relate to class–culture explanations' inability to explain why some working-class families place more value on HE and/or perceive it as more, or less, accessible than others.

Defining social class within modernist/categorical approaches

Although categorical approaches to defining class are widely used, criticisms have been made of such approaches because 'social class categories are notoriously problematic' (Foster *et al.* 1996: 53). Modernist/categorical approaches define social class primarily in terms of occupation. Occupational classificatory models and scales continue to be influential today, particularly within official agencies, but there is no overall consensus on how to define social class categories and the occupational criteria are being constantly revised. For example, in November 1998 the Office for National Statistics (ONS) announced the government's new social classification, the National Statistics Socio-Economic Classification (NS SEC), which is based on employment conditions and relations and replaces the occupation-based Registrar General's classification system.

The Registrar General's classification system, until recently the main official tool, grouped the population into six classes on the basis of occupation, grouped in terms of skill levels (I, Professional, II Managerial and technical IIIN Skilled non-manual, IIIm Skilled manual, IV Partly skilled, V Unskilled). A similar social grade system is used by the Market Research Society (A, B, C1, C2, D, E). The new NS SEC has seven main classes, with a 'long version' of 30 categories. The seven main categories are:

1   Higher managerial and professional occupations
   1.1   Employers and managers in larger organizations
   1.2   Higher professionals
2   Lower managerial and professional occupations
3   Intermediate occupations
4   Small employers and own-account workers
5   Lower supervisory, craft and related
6   Semi-routine occupations
7   Routine occupations.

Widening participation policy and research have inevitably made use of both the Registrar General's and the Market Research Society classificatory systems. The Dearing Report, for example, uses the Registrar General's system, highlighting the low proportions of social class IV and V students who participate in higher education. In our own research, respondents to the MORI survey were identified as belonging to socio-economic groups C1-E. More recently, HESA and UCAS have begun to classify students in terms of the areas in which they live, using geodemographic profiles (such as MOSAIC).

Inevitably, there are inherent problems within all these approaches to defining the social class of students (and non-participants). In determining the social class of universities' student intake, there are various difficulties faced by researchers using occupational classifications. For example, a decision must be made as to when, and whether, to assign a student's social class according to their own job(s) or that of their parent(s). Currently UCAS uses the age of 21 as a cut-off point; students younger than 21 are classified in terms of their parents' occupations and students over 21 are judged on the basis of their own reported occupation. This method can be problematic in a modern society where people may frequently change job and/or may not live in 'traditional' households. As feminists such as Walkerdine *et al.* (1999) have also emphasized, occupational classificatory models have largely been formulated from a male norm and have particular difficulty defining women's social class positions. Within families, women and men may engage in differently classed employment, complicating efforts to determine a family's social class position. For example, Bradley (1996) cites Braverman (1974) who has suggested that in America a typical working-class couple might comprise a man who works in a factory and a woman who works as a clerk, representing jobs from contrasting classifications.

The move towards identifying students and non-participating groups through geodemographic profiling has been similarly problematic. Although sensitive to the level of an electoral ward (approximately 500 people), the characterization of residential areas can be criticized as being too broad to adequately account for many inner city and urban areas, where there is intense variation of population and housing within very small geographical areas.

Thus conceptualizations of social class which rest on economic factors and employment status are problematic for a number of reasons, not least because of the gendered assumptions upon which such classifications have traditionally been built, the assumptions of homogeneity within class groups, and the changed industrial and labour scene at the start of the twenty-first century (Walkerdine *et al.* 1999). More broadly, there have been serious criticisms of categorical/ positivistic approaches to social class from postmodern and poststructuralist perspectives, which contest the fundamental epistemological basis of the grand theories. These competing approaches have argued that social class cannot be reduced to occupation and that class positions are not homogenous or easily quantifiable. Postmodern theorists have drawn attention instead to how class interacts with other inequalities (such as gender and 'race') and is a 'lived' process that is inextricably tied to 'identity'. Thus it has been argued that categorical concepts of class are lacking because they 'make no reference to questions of identity, or consciousness, or feelings of solidarity' (Williamson 1981: 19). While some, such as Calvert (1982), have argued that the concept of class is so problematic it should be discarded, the following section details some of the attempts made through postmodern and poststructuralist, 'class as process' approaches to theorize a useable concept of social class.

'Class as process' approaches

Since the 1970s postmodern and poststructuralisttheories have provided a substantial challenge to previous, more positivistic ways of conceptualizing social class within education and sociology. There are numerous postmodern and poststructuralist approaches within sociological theorizing, espousing differing epistemological and ontological conceptualizations (Burman and Parker 1993). It is therefore important to note that although the terms 'poststructuralist' or 'postmodern' theory imply a discernible theoretical field, they encompass a varied bundle of approaches (Bradley 1996) that, while opposing 'grand', macro-level theories, do not belong to a coherent movement of work. In this chapter, the term 'postmodern' is used in the broadest possible sense to encompass poststructuralist theories. Postmodern theorists attempt micro-level analyses, attending to particular aspects of social class within defined, local boundaries. Some of the approaches detailed below could be identified as falling within broad theoretical movements and/or academic disciplines (such as feminism, sociology of education, cultural studies), but they broadly share a conceptual stance that understands working-class participation in higher education as constituted by a complex combination of social, structural, economic and cultural factors and enacted through material and discursive inequalities.

Broadly speaking, postmodern theorists draw upon qualitative techniques to explore class formation and consciousness by analysing and deconstructing social categories and concepts (Bradley 1996). Such approaches assume that social 'reality' is not an objective fact or 'real', but is socially, discursively constructed. Thus, postmodern approaches understand social class positions, differences and inequalities as socially constructed processes. Williamson thus argues for the importance of deconstructing the linguistic categories associated with HE in order to understand class inequalities in higher education:

> To gain any understanding of a tradition of higher education ... it is vital to go beyond the terms in which it understands itself. Conventional notions of ability, excellence, scholarship or 'the good mind' have to be relativized ... questions of class cannot really be discussed in an atmosphere of disinterested objectivity for the questions themselves arise out of a larger political problematic.
>
> (Williamson 1981: 20)

Chapters 2 and 3 provide a historical overview to the political and policy context within which concerns about 'widening participation' have developed.

Postmodern, social constructionist (Gergen 1985) approaches are also characterized by a treatment of class not as a fixed, categorical concept, but as produced through interactions between individuals, groups, institutions and policies. Those theorists and researchers who work within postmodern theoretical frameworks have varying views regarding relativism and materiality, with differences emerging, for example, between 'weak' and 'strong/true' relativists (see Gill 1995 for a discussion). As Gill (1995) outlines, 'strong' relativism postulates that there is no 'truth', but rather there are multiple truths, and all competing accounts and views are held to be equally valid.

However, strong relativism has been criticized by feminists and other critical researchers for not enabling them to tackle power inequalities or to mobilize against oppression within such a model, because all accounts are treated as being equally valid (Jackson 1992). Instead, such researchers have sought to adopt weak readings of relativism, espousing theoretical positions which combine poststructuralist thinking and notions of 'permanent partiality' and 'situated knowledges' (Haraway 1988) with 'baseline realities' (Fricker 1994) in order to identify and engage with inequalities of 'race', class and gender. As we have written elsewhere (Archer, Hutchings and Leathwood 2001), by drawing upon a combination of theoretical approaches, as detailed below, critical theorists have been able to forge a 'middle way' between previous methodological divides in class research (Crompton 1993) to encompass lived meanings and patterns of inequality.

The following section will address issues involved in conceptualizing the relationship between social class and education themes within postmodern/social constructionist approaches by examining the following overlapping themes:

- Shifting inequalities: the theorization of classed identities and inequalities as recursively linked and 'in process'; the role of HE institutions in the reproduction of unequal patterns of participation
- Individualism and social class: the relationship between social class and dominant societal discourses, namely the 'hiding' of social-class identities and inequalities by a culture of individualism
- Risk, habitus and capital: the changing nature of social-class identities, characterized by patterns of consumption and taste
- Multiple identities: the inter-relationship of social class with other social divisions, such as ethnicity and gender; the 'lived experience' of these identities and notions of agency and resistance
- Fuzzy definitions: the practical difficulties of defining and identifying social class within postmodern approaches.

Within each section, we try to draw out the concepts that provide the theoretical framework which frames and underpins the subsequent analyses within this book.

Shifting inequalities: linking identities and structures

Whereas categorical, positivistic approaches treat social-class identities as 'given' and objectively identifiable, postmodern approaches tend to treat class identities and inequalities as constantly constructed and asserted through discourse. Discourses (socially and historically located shared patterns of meaning) are drawn on by people in order to construct and defend identities and subject positions. From this perspective, classed identities are never 'achieved' or 'complete'; instead they are constantly 'in process' (Hall 1992), constructed and reconstructed through talk, actions and embodied relations (see for example Gilroy 1993b; Alexander 1996; and Archer, Hutchings and Leathwood 2001 for a fuller account of our theoretical position). Thus, in such models classed identities and inequalities are not fixed structures within society, but are unstable, shifting and subjectively experienced social divisions (see for example Reay 1999; Skeggs 1997; Walkerdine 1990; Zmroczek 1999).

A growing number of theorists, particularly feminists, have also drawn attention to the importance of structural inequalities in defining class positions and identities, and to the recursive link between identities and inequalities (Mama 1995). For example, Mahony and Zmroczek are concerned with 'a search for theory which can begin to describe the relationships between the classed nature of our lives and our positionings within the broader material structures' (Mahony and Zmroczek 1997: 2). As Mahony and Zmroczek stress, researchers need to understand how class both structures people's lives and is reconstituted by them, acknowledging the ways in which material resources and cultural capital continue to shape people's experiences and identities (see also Reay 1997).

As with identities, structural inequalities (for example of class, 'race', gender) are never complete or absolute. They are both material and discursive, shifting and socially/historically constructed, and differently constructed and enacted across time and context for different individuals and groups. These structures are, however, stubbornly durable, and continually reproduced, albeit variously and differently, within a network of multiple, unequal power relations. In other words, any analysis of class inequalities in relation to higher education must take account not only of people's shifting class identities but also the role of the educational institution itself in creating and perpetuating inequalities. These inequalities are not fixed and easily 'discovered', but rather are (re)created across time and context. The recursive link between structures and identities means that aspects of institutional cultures will have implications within working-class individuals' personal identity constructions:

> Higher education, and the universities in particular which have historically dominated it, do play a decisive role in structuring the demand for places and ... many aspects of the social inequalities which are traceable in the decision-making of school pupils have their roots in higher education itself and in the logic of the relationship between higher education and society. What this means is that the relative life-chances for higher education of different social groups cannot be discussed apart from the form, control and social significance of higher education itself.
>
> (Williamson 1981: 30)

Williamson argues instead that universities have excluded working-class groups through financial, social and cultural factors, the result being that 'a demand for such education from this section of society was never cultivated; working-class people were never encouraged to see higher education as something available to them' (Williamson 1981: 35).

Such an approach challenges the basis of numerous existing widening participation approaches which focus predominantly upon 'raising aspirations' among working-class potential applicants, without challenging biased institutional cultures:

> The question of class bias cannot be discussed as if it were in some way concerned only with the social characteristics of those who apply to higher education: a problem, therefore, of the school system or of different patterns of child socialization. It is also a question of the form

of higher education itself, its ethos, organization and pedagogy and social function.

(Williamson 1981: 18)

As we argue elsewhere (Read *et al.* 2003), within the widening participation project it is also important to examine the role of institutional cultures in the reproduction of inequalities in access and participation for different social groups. Working-class (and indeed any 'non-traditional') students may be disadvantaged by institutional cultures that position them as 'others' in contrast to dominant assumptions of student learners as (young), white, middle class and male (Mirza 1995; Grant 1997; Tett 2000).

Individualization and the obscuring of social class

Within some postmodern approaches it has been argued that following technological and social developments, there have been large-scale changes to patterns of re/production of classed identities and inequalities. As detailed in Bradley (1996), the class structures of industrialized countries have changed post-war and in the technology age. There has been an increase in 'individualization' and a shift to a diversification of lifestyles (Giddens 1991) which, it has been argued, has led to a loosening of attachment to social-class identities (Beck 1992) with the result that class identities and inequalities have become obscured and hidden:

> Working together, the ideology of economic individualism and individualization as a reflexive project of identity-formation, mute and obscure the continuing class-based nature of structural inequalities.
>
> (Ball *et al.* 2000a: 3)

However, as Beck suggests, 'class differences and family connections are not *really* annulled ... they recede into the background relative to the newly emerging "centre" of the biographical life-plan' (Beck 1992: 131, emphasis added). In response to the increase in new uncertainties, risks and opportunities of late modernity, collective identities have weakened (Giddens 1991). Thus, Giddens and Beck both suggest that individualization is replacing older traditional social relationships (see Ball *et al.* 2000a for fuller account).

These changes have placed an emphasis upon the role of the family with regard to choosing what is 'best' for their children. But, as Ball *et al.* 2000a point out:

> Some families value more highly or are 'better' at 'choosing' than others and have greater financial and cultural resources to support their children in the post-16 arena, as elsewhere ... Sets of individualized tactics such as moving house, developing church affiliations, skilful networking,

paying for costly cross-city travel, etc are clearly more available to some individuals, families and social groups than to others. Concomitantly, 'bad' choices become a matter of individual responsibility.

(Ball *et al.* 2000a: 4)

Thus, despite the social and economic polarization of wealth and life-chances, Ball *et al.* argue that individuals are more likely to blame themselves for life inequalities.

Beck argues that 'risk' is also an important theme within processes of social-class stratification.

The history of risk distribution shows that, like wealth, risks adhere to the class pattern, only inversely: wealth accumulates at the top, risks at the bottom. To that extent, risks seem to strengthen, not to abolish, the class society. Poverty attracts an unfortunate abundance of risks. By contrast, the wealthy (in income, power or education) can purchase safety and freedom from risk.

(Beck 1992: 35)

Consequently, it could be suggested that within the arena of higher-education choices, participation is an inherently more risky, costly and uncertain 'choice' for working-class groups than for middle-class groups (Archer and Huchings 2000). We will return to this theme throughout the subsequent chapters in this book (for example Chapter 6).

Thus, in relation to widening participation research, these theories suggest that it may be harder to explore class inequalities because these become obscured within the 'social surge of individualization' (Beck 1992: 87). Some respondents may reject and resist class identities because

class identities are submerged identities, pushed out of sight by others which jostle more urgently for public attention. Moreover, people are often reluctant to talk in class terms in a society in which classlessness, though not attained, is seen as the desired ideal. Class becomes a stigma-tized or spoiled identity, rather than one which people acknowledge with pride.

(Bradley 1996: 72)

Working-class non-participants are often the subject of discourses that blame them, rather than social inequalities, for their inability to access higher education. These themes will be taken up and explored further in relation to our data in subsequent chapters.

Risk, habitus, capital and class

The work of Pierre Bourdieu (who works within a neo-Marxist post-structuralist tradition) has been drawn on, and developed, to provide a useful conceptual framework for understanding processes of choice of higher education by a number of researchers (see Ball *et al.* 2000a; Reay *et al.* 2001). Diane Reay, Stephen Ball and colleagues have examined how the concepts of 'habitus' and 'cultural capital' are integral to students' and their families' classed choices of school (Ball *et al.* 1998), FE college (Maguire *et al.* 1999) and university (Reay 1998; Reay *et al.* 1999). Habitus has been described as 'the practical mastery which people possess of their situations' (Robbins 1991:1 cited in Ball *et al.* 2000a: 7). Cultural capital refers to the knowledge, language and culture, differentially accessed and possessed, that guides the decisions made and actions taken. Middle-class and working-class families have differential access to various forms of cultural, social and economic capital and resources, which differentially frames the educational choices that different families can or will make. Middle-class parents can pass on cultural and material advantages that privilege or enable their children to succeed within the education system (Allatt 1993). Working-class families experience more economic and physical constraints and lack the same knowledge of the system and social networks that encourage the /reproduction of privilege (Reay *et al.* 2001). Thus, educational choices operate as a medium of power and stratification, within which there is an interplay of social, economic, cultural capital with institutional and family habitus.

Maguire *et al.* found that for middle-class students, with their increased social, economic and knowledge resources, 'choice is presented as natural, orderly, clear-cut, almost beyond question, very unlike the chancy, uncertain process many working-class students are caught up in' (Maguire *et al.* 2000: 5). Working-class students, on the other hand, experience greater risks and constraints framing their decision-making. For working-class applicants, the importance of 'fitting in' and 'feeling comfortable' within an institution may mean that they are dissuaded from applying to 'prestigious' universities, which transmit a message such places are 'not for the likes of us' through an institutional habitus that alienates 'other' (that is, working-class) students. Maguire *et al.* (ibid.) also found stratifying processes in the marketing strategies of UK universities and in their institutional processes, which encouraged applications from particular class groups:

> The perceptions, distinctions and choices of higher education institutions used and made by students play a part in reconstituting and reproducing the divisions and hierarchies in HE. It is in this way that they 'do' or embody social structures. In effect, this is social class 'in the head'. That is to say, cultural and social capital, material constraints ... social

perceptions and distinctions, and forms of self-exclusion ... are all embedded in the processes of choice.

(Maguire *et al.* 2000: 7)

Thus, social hierarchies are transformed into academic hierarchies (Bourdieu and Passeron 1977) and, as George Bernard Shaw suggested, universities can be viewed as 'shops for selling class limitations'.

These theories will be drawn upon and extended further within subsequent data analysis chapters, for example, to analyse choices and decision-making among non-participants and participants and to explore differential use of information about HE by working-class groups (Chapter 5).

Multiple identities: class, 'race' and gender

Postmodern, feminist and critical researchers have stressed the importance of attending to multiple social identities and inequalities, and the inter-relatedness of inequalities and identities of 'race', class and gender. It has been argued that these cannot be easily separated in their effects and lived experiences, and thus discussions of social-class inequalities must also be considered in terms of their structuring by gender and 'race'. For example, Franklin (1999) stresses that there are differences in black and white class structures, while Reynolds argues that 'many black women in Britain iden-tify "race" as the starting point of any self-definition' (1997: 10). She insists that 'to be a black working-class woman in Britain is construed as meaning something entirely different to being a white working-class woman in Britain' (ibid.: 14–15). Thus, it has been argued that, contrary to Furlong and Cartmel (1997) (who say race is reducible to social class), the meanings and effects of class will qualitatively change across time/space, 'race' and gender. Feminist and critical 'race'/ethnicity theorists have also argued that inequalities generate, and may be met by, resistance (for example Mirza 1992) and attention has been drawn to the psychic, not just material, effects of class (that Sennett and Cobb (1977) term the 'hidden injuries' of class).

In terms of educational research in relation to this theme, sociology of education has long held a particular fascination with working-class young people, but particularly boys (Delamont 2000), which has meant that earlier theories were framed largely from a male, white norm. As summarized below, these have since been taken up by feminist/critical researchers to develop more nuanced accounts of the role of education and the school in the production of gendered, racialized class positions. In other words, these approaches combine 'identity' and 'inequality' (social, cultural and struc-tural) in accounts of the role of education and class. Such research can often be identified as part of a commitment to the important project, identified by Zmroczek and Mahony, as moving class research 'away from a preoccupation with personal identity and towards a commitment to political engagement' (Zmroczek and Mahony 1999: 4).

Paul Willis' seminal study (1977) of a group of young, white working-class boys detailed the social and institutional processes by which the 'lads' were channelled into working-class jobs. His work has since been developed showing the processes through which 'Other' (black) boys are also steered into particular 'non-academic' routes and working-class post-16 routes (for example Mac an Ghaill 1988, 1994, 1996a, b; Sewell 1997). Feminist researchers have also explored the differently gendered and 'raced' processes through which an 'intellectual carnage' (Greed 1991) of working-class girls takes place for white (Skeggs 1997), African-Caribbean (Mirza 1992) and Asian (Shain 2000) girls in Britain.

These studies highlight the complex processes through which institutional, social and economic factors and inequalities interact in complex ways with multiple identities to render particular educational routes 'unthinkable' (Cohen 1988) for diverse young working-class people. But the studies also reveal the ways in which young people respond to, resist and subvert the barriers, options and possibilities open to them. In other words, respondents are not theorized as passive victims and recipients of their class/race/gender positions and destinies. Instead, researchers have highlighted how subjects negotiate various discourses and create spaces 'in-between' competing dominant discourses (Alexander 1996, 2000). For example, Mirza (1992) illustrated how black British working-class girls negotiate strategic 'back door' routes into post-compulsory education.

In this book we will try to apply this theoretical approach to an analysis of discourses of participation and non-participation among diverse working-class respondents. For example, in Chapter 9 we explore how some working-class men may resist higher education as an 'unmanly' option which would threaten the maintenance of racialized masculinities (Archer, Pratt and Phillips 2001).

Defining class: fuzzy class boundaries

Approaches which fall beneath the 'postmodern' umbrella tend to be more interested in exploring and deconstructing the meanings of social-class identities and inequalities within educational research, rather than attempting to define social class. The notions of relativity and subjectivity within such research mean that theorists agree that there is no singular, concrete, definable social-class identity or experience. Yet such a position could imply that the use of such approaches is problematic for attempting to explore issues around widening participation for 'working-class' groups. However, as detailed in Archer et al. (2001a), we would argue that it is possible to adopt a theoretical position which can engage with, and account for, broad patterns of inequality combined with an analysis of people's lived experiences and identifications. From such a position, social class is understood as a fiction, but a politically useful fiction (Bordo 1990). Social divisions, such as class, 'race' and gender, are understood as meaningful categories and identities by many people in their lives. As detailed earlier, class identities and inequalities are shifting and changing, yet inequalities persist and endure (although the exact content and nature of class identities and inequalities will change because they are specifically rooted in socio-historical circumstances). The boundaries of classed identities and inequalities are thus indiscrete, 'fuzzy' and stratified by 'race' and gender. Not all those positioned within the boundaries of particular identities will have equal control over the regulation of boundaries and some groups/individuals will be able to exert more powerful definitions over who is/not included within these boundaries (Anthias and Yuval-Davis 1992; Yuval-Davis and Anthias 1989).

The advantage of this, admittedly complex, approach to the study of classed access to higher education is that it enables researchers to deal with the complexity of the issue and the heterogeneity of working-class groups, who are multiply stratified. While it renders a precise definition of who is, or is not, working class extremely difficult, it enables researchers to grapple with the grey borders of modern class identities and inequalities, while not losing sight of the broad patterns of class disadvantage in relation to HE participation.

For the practical purposes of identifying potential working-class respondents for this study, we drew on a broad range of indicators including occupation (of respondent and/or parents), previous family experience of HE and fee remission for higher education students. We have defined and ascribed social-class positions to our respondents in different ways in relation to the qualitative and quantitative aspects of the research. This was a pragmatic decision, although it also encouraged us to attempt a meta-analysis of research data, reflecting our theoretical commitment to a position 'between' modernism and postmodernism (Archer, Hutchings and Leathwood 2001).

This book will draw upon the theoretical perspective outlined within the preceding themes, examining how racialized and gendered class identities, and the structural inequalities that frame these social positions, interact to constrain working-class participation in higher education in multiple, varying ways. Analyses will also show however the ways in which respondents were able to negotiate and assert spaces between dominant discourses, opening up particular post-compulsory possibilities. We will also argue however that participation in higher education is not an equal or possible 'choice' for everyone.

Chapter 2

Higher education and social access

To the Robbins Report

Alistair Ross

In their analysis of trends in class and gender in access to higher education in the United Kingdom in the twentieth century, Egerton and Halsey (1993) distinguish three key characteristics: it was, they write, a period of enormous expansion, there was considerable movement towards gender equality, and there was very little movement towards social-class equality. This chapter examines these trends over the first two-thirds of the century, in the expansion that took place leading up to the Robbins Report (Robbins 1963a). An eightfold increase in numbers took place over this period – from 25,000 full-time students in 1900 to 216,000 in 1962 (ibid. Table 3) – but who benefited? Which social categories were empowered by this expansion in access to higher education? The period was one in which higher education was still only providing for an elite minority. The age participation index, as far as can be determined from the various forms of data available, rose over the period from about 1 per cent of the age set in full-time higher education in 1900 to about 8.5 per cent in 1962. Going to university was against the norm. In 1962 it was even against the norm for the most socially privileged group, of young males in the higher professional social class (Robbins 1963a: Tables 5 and 21). In this chapter, we examine the growth that occurred and in particular the way in which the social composition of the student population began to change. The expansion noted by Egerton and Halsey began in this period. However, there were only relatively small movements towards gender equality, and still less towards class equality. Chapter 3 will examine participation trends in the final third of the twentieth century, in which there was further growth, this time including a slow but significant element of gender equality (and a factor that was new on a substantial scale, ethnic equality) but again a period of stagnation in redressing class inequalities.

Many of those working in universities in the first half of the twentieth century would have been surprised at questions even being raised about access and equality in admissions to universities. Various purposes have been claimed for universities at different times. One of the most dominant assertions has been that universities exist simply to engage in the pursuit of knowledge and understanding, and to provide the institutional support of the communities of scholars necessary for this. A. N. Whitehead suggested 'the proper function of a university is the imaginative acquisition of knowledge ... . A university is imaginative or it is nothing – at least nothing useful.' (Whitehead 1929: 145). Others have argued similarly, for example, Newman (1873), Schön (1987) and Barnet (1990). But it has also always been the case that the universities have been powerful agents of socialization. Indeed, it can be argued that they were established, organized and supported at different periods to either initiate and sustain social change or to substantiate social inertia. Oxford University was established to counter the potentially subversive influence of a University of Paris controlled by the French monarchy; King's College London was founded in reaction to the godlessness of University College; and the late-nineteenth-century civic universities were created to confer social status on the offspring of local professional and commercial elites. More recently, the polytechnics were created as higher education institutions to rival and challenge 'our snobbish caste-ridden obsession with university status' (Crosland 1966) and to 'democratize higher education' (Crosland 1982: 159).

Access to higher education has always been limited, and has always been intended differentially to empower its recipients: this chapter will explore the events that lead to the recognition, formalized in the Robbins Report of 1963, that exclusive forms of access to the country's universities were incompatible with the meritocratic regime of the mid-twentieth century. But this meritocracy, endorsed by both the Robbins Committee and its successor, the Dearing Report (Dearing 1997), was the 'liberal' conception of meritocracy, not the 'democratic' form advocated by John Rawls (1971). Forms of access to higher education that began to be introduced in the post-Second World War period, which accelerated from the mid-1960s and which persist today, were what Crosland described as the 'weak' meritocratic society 'in which the greatest rewards go to those with the most fortunate genetic endowment and family background' (Crosland 1974: 89).

Beginnings

The relationship between access to higher education and access to power has antecedents that stretch back many centuries. In his description of the changes in the university curriculum and in the recruitment of students in the post-Reformation years, Laurence Stone could equally well have been writing of universities in the late twentieth century:

> This was one of the really decisive movements in English history by which the propertied classes exploited and expanded the higher educational resources of the country. By doing so they fitted themselves to rule in the new conditions of the modern state and they turned the intelligentsia ... into a branch of the propertied classes.
>
> (Stone 1964: 79)

Hugh Kearney (1970) has shown how throughout the sixteenth and seventeenth centuries the universities were not only exposed to political and social pressures but actively reinforced the changing social relationships of the period. Before the Reformation, the universities had in effect been the educational organs of the church; they then began to change to meet the educational needs of the gentry class who had become the country's non-clerical ruling elite. The universities became 'the decisive instrument in transforming England from a society in which the lay military aristocracy left national administration to the clergy, into one in which the laity had the whiphand, thanks to improved education' (Kearney 1970: 24). One outcome of this change was that the universities strengthened the social divisions between the leisured classes and the rest of the population. Their insistence on Latin, their high fees and religious tests all acted as very effective social filters. In the century from 1550, a relatively higher proportion of the age group attended university, 'but the rise benefited the elite, not the non-elite' (ibid.: 168). The sons of the gentry who attended university were exposed to the same system of elitist social values, creating and reinforcing the gentry class and, at the same time, generating social discontent among the non-gentry groups. For those who were above a particular social level – Kearney suggests the level of the prosperous yeoman – the universities could be an instrument for social mobility. But, at the same time, the universities created and reinforced the social division between those eligible and those below this level, who were ineligible. 'The universities, in confining their attention to the powerful few aroused the hostility of the excluded majority' (ibid.: 169).

Exclusion was, and remained, built into the system. Catholics were excluded by statute, but others were excluded more subtly. Until the early twentieth century, the assumption that Latin and Greek were necessary for university admission meant that only those who had attended a particular, and small, set of schools could be considered for entry. The educational system that thus developed in England provided and reinforced distinctions of social class. George Bernard Shaw observed this acutely at the beginning of the twentieth century – at work in both the school and higher educational systems – in the following exchanges in *Man and Superman*:

> TANNER: … But this chap has been educated. Whats more, he knows that we havent. What was that Board School of yours, Straker?
> STRAKER: Sherbrooke Road.
> TANNER: Sherbrooke Road! Would any of us say Rugby! Harrow! Eton! in that tone of intellectual snobbery? Sherbrooke Road is a place where boys learn something: Eton is a boy farm where we are sent because we are nuisances at home, and because in after life, whenever a Duke is mentioned, we can then claim him as an old schoolfellow.

STRAKER: You dont know nothing about it, Mr Tanner. Its not the Board School that does it: its the Polytechnic.

TANNER: His University, Octavius. Not Oxford, Cambridge, Durham, Dublin, or Glasgow. Not even those Nonconformist holes in Wales. No, Tavy. Regent Street! Chelsea! The Borough! – I dont know half their confounded names: these are his universities, not mere shops for selling class limitations like ours. You despise Oxford, Enry, don't you?

STRAKER: No I dont, Very nice sort of place, Oxford, I should think, for people that likes that sort of place. They teach you to be a gentleman there. In the Polytechnic they teach you to be an engineer or such like. See?

(G. B. Shaw, Man and Superman 1903: Act II)

The early expansion of the university institutions: 1900–39

University education in 1900 was provided by a handful of institutions. Oxford and Cambridge, the longest established, were 'where the richest and most influential sent their children' (Gordon *et al.* 1991: 233). Durham University was founded in 1833. London University was formed in 1836, bringing together University College and King's College (each of which was then less than ten years old), who were then joined by Bedford College (the first women's college) in 1849 and by the various medical colleges, some of which pre-dated Oxford. The Victoria University was established in 1880 as a federal university, with constituent colleges in Manchester (based on Owens College), Liverpool and Leeds: these latter two did not become universities in their own right until 1903. In Scotland there were the fifteenth- and sixteenth-century foundations, at St Andrews, Glasgow, Aberdeen and Edinburgh. The newest university was in Wales, where three colleges (the 'Nonconformist holes in Wales': Aberystwyth, Cardiff and Bangor) were federated in 1893 as the University of Wales.

In England, the influence of Oxford and Cambridge on the early development of higher education was strong. Gordon *et al.* suggest that higher education was consequently seen as:

A finishing school for people with wealth and standing … . As many of the students who came were already prosperous, their teachers were little inclined to provide a training for particular professions and consequently presented a view of education which emphasized that diligent study in the older disciplines produced better men [*sic*] with alert minds who would be able eventually to fulfil their proper calling within a governing elite.

(Gordon et al. 1991: 233)

Higher education was for a tiny minority and, moreover, a minority who could pay. Because it was seen as a form of self-improvement, it was held that the expenses of attending university were solely the responsibility of the families who sent their sons to university. In 1900, the concept that universities might have a role in training specialists, or in educating the professions other than clergymen and medics, was an innovation and by no means wholly accepted. State funding of universities was minimal, with a few specialist grants having been paid by government departments from 1889.

Early in the century, the number of university institutions began to increase and with this the number of places available. Birmingham gained a university charter in 1900 for the former Josiah Mason College. Victoria University divided into three. Colleges in Sheffield and Bristol obtained university charters in 1905 and 1909. These Edwardian redbricks all had their origins in older local institutions, such as working-men's colleges and institutes. Very often they were founded and endowed by local businessmen, with the express commitment of providing opportunities for social advancement for young men from the region. Local professionals joined with those from commerce and manufacture to lobby for university status, seeking to establish centres that would serve the particular requirements of the region. The institutions therefore came to university status with teaching styles, buildings and staff already in place. They also came with some commitment to meritocratic advance for those who had ability but who might lack the social attributes seen as necessary for the oldest universities. Most students would be living at home, or have moved a few miles to take temporary lodgings. Even by 1962, only a fifth of the students at these universities (and in London) were living in hostels and halls of residence (Robbins 1963a: para. 60), which was quite unlike the situation in Oxford, Cambridge and Durham, where residence was seen as a necessary condition for university study. But as university status took hold, the nature of the institutions subtly changed. They took on greater national perspective and adopted some of the mores of the long-established universities.

A second wave of newer civic universities followed. Some colleges were established before the First World War, and others just after it: Reading, Nottingham, Southampton, Hull, Exeter and Leicester. These University Colleges first taught University of London External Degrees, and then slowly moved to independent university status (Reading in 1926, the others after the Second World War). They had some origins in local institutions, although not to the same extent as the Edwardian foundations. These newer civic redbricks accepted the tutelage of an older institution, and, after an apprenticeship, re-emerged as universities: not quite an amoeba-like fission, more an engulfment, reshaping and disgorgement. Keele, founded as a university college in 1949, was slightly different, being the first university to be founded on a greenfield site; it still, nevertheless, underwent a 13-year apprenticeship under the tutelage of three local established universities. This set of universities had, from their inception, a less well founded local base than the establishments of the 1880–1914 period. They took a wider view of their role, recruiting students more widely from across the country, as can be seen from the fact that about half their students were in university-provided residential accommodation in 1962 (Robbins 1963a: para. 62).

The growth in student numbers: 1920–50

This expansion made more places available. There was an expanding professional class, able to take advantage of this growth and many of them had lobbied for local university status. There was also a growing realization that some opportunities for university education should be provided for those of ability who could not otherwise afford it. The colleges of Oxford, Cambridge and, to a lesser extent, Durham were able to fund some scholarships for poorer students from their private endowments. Scholarships made by local authorities were provided from the late nineteenth century, albeit in very small numbers. State scholarships followed in 1919. Initially there were just 200 state scholarships available. The Geddes Axe on public expenditure in 1921 reduced the 200 to zero, but this number was restored in 1924 and gradually rose to 400 in 1939. Local authority scholarships were greater in number (there does not appear to be a central compilation of what was available); these made fees and some element of maintenance support available through a competitive process. Systems were locally determined – the number, scope and limitations of the scholarships varied from area to area and according to local political and economic circumstances.

The state was beginning to make other kinds of demands on the functions of universities. The First World War revealed national deficiencies in particular scientific areas, such as in the supply of chemicals and in the munitions industries. A Department of Scientific and Industrial Research (DSIR) was established to promote scientific research, in both the government departments and in the universities. Specific scientific research scholarships were established in this first wave, in a series of moral panics about national scientific and technological competitiveness that were to be a characteristic of policy interventions throughout the century.

What was the extent of the growth of universities up to the Second World War and who were taking up these new university places? Figure 2.1 shows the growth of full-time higher education over the period.

A study by Political and Economic Planning (PEP) in 1950, quoted by the University Grants Committee (1952), estimated that 38 per cent of undergraduates at university in 1938 had scholarships or assisted places. This would suggest that there were about 3,000 entrants to undergraduate study each year receiving some kind of financial support, with perhaps 5,000 entrants who were supported entirely by their families. Blackburn and Jarman (1993) estimate that by 1938 the age participation index for women was about 0.5 per cent and 3.5 per cent for men. Glass (1954) examined the

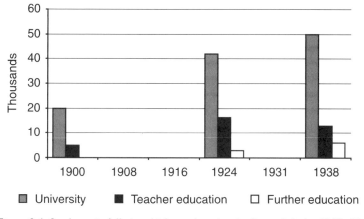

Figure 2.1 Students in full-time higher education in Great Britain, 1900–38
Source: from Robbins 1963a: Table 3
Note
This table is of all years, and includes postgraduates

class backgrounds of boys entering university between 1928 and 1947: 8.9 per cent of all boys from non-manual backgrounds entered over this period, compared with 1.4 per cent of all boys from the much larger group from manual backgrounds. However, this was a twofold improvement for working-class boys compared with the situation prior to 1910 (Moodie 1959). The survey undertaken for the Robbins Committee in 1962 shows an increase in participation rates, although there was very little improvement in the ratio of manual to non-manual background for males (the non-manual to manual ratio shifted from 3:7 to 3:5.5) and a much worse ratio for women, who were not included in Glass' study (Table 2.1).

By 1922 women were obtaining 23 per cent of all the first degrees awarded (House of Commons 1999). Women were not allowed to receive degrees at Cambridge until 1948, although they were able to undertake undergraduate studies (attempts had been made to rescind the rule preventing them from being awarded degrees from 1919 onwards).

The significant expansion of the first half of the century, in both the numbers of universities and students, was virtually over by the early 1920s. The period from then to the outbreak of the Second World War was charac-terized, in the words of Gordon and his collaborators, as 'not … a period of confidence and growth, and for some of the redbrick universities and univer-sity colleges mere survival proved difficult' (Gordon *et al.* 1991: 236). Access clearly had improved but was still very inadequate, though we know rela-tively little about the changing social composition of the student body in the period to 1939, or of the effects of university life on the 'new' students.

Table 2.1 Annual entrants to higher education by father's occupation: 1928–47 and 1961

(a) percentages

Father's occupation		Full-time higher education		
		1928–47 *degree*	*1961* *degree*	other
Male	non-manual	8.9	15.7	4.2
	manual	1.4	3.1	2.1
Female	non-manual	u/k	9.4	10.4
	manual	u/k	1.0	2.1

(b) numbers

Father's occupation		Full-time higher education		
		1928–47 *degree*	*1961* *degree*	other
Male	non-manual	5,600 (est)	10,950	2,900
	manual	2,400 (est)	5,900	3,950
Female	non-manual	u/k	6,600	7,300
	manual	u/k	2,050	4,100

Sources: 1928/47: Glass 1954; 1962: calculated from Robbins 1963a: Tables 6 and 21

As had happened in 1914–18, the exigencies and demands of the Second World War led to very significant effects on the nature of university teaching and admissions. Figure 2.2 shows the changes in total student numbers in the period from 1922 to 1951. Students following scientific and engineering courses, and medical students, were helped to complete their training; arts students largely had their studies interrupted. University academics, particularly in technological and scientific fields, were brought into government service.

Science and technology in higher education

As in the previous war, there was a sudden realization that the country lacked highly skilled scientists and technologists and a recognition of the role that the higher education system should have had in the 1920s and 1930s to produce them. The Percy Committee, established in 1943 to report on higher technical education (Percy 1945), set out the case for upgrading regional colleges of technology to teach Diplomas in Technology. The Barlow Committee's report on *Scientific Manpower* (Barlow 1946) argued for locating scientific growth in the universities, and proposed funding them to double the output of scientists within a decade. There were even proposals to move the universities from direct Treasury control to the Ministry of Education: these were resisted, and

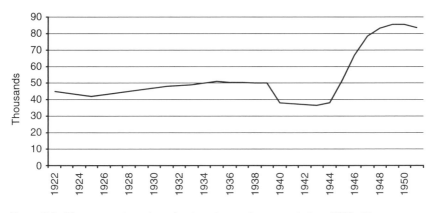

Figure 2.2 Changes in size of total university student population, 1922–51
Source: from UGC (1953)

the sector continued the advantages of direct Treasury funding, on a generous quinquennial basis. The University Grants Committee (UGC) revitalized itself, and set up sub-committees to consider the supply of scientists and other professionals, marking an acceptance of the more instrumental demands being made on the university sector by the government. The UGC even began its own attempts to match graduate output to careers, noting in 1948 that 'it is doubtful whether the future demands for arts graduates will be sufficient to absorb the entire output of the universities at its present rate' (UGC 1948: 19).

This debate over the location of scientific training and research continued through the 1950s. There was resistance by the University Grants Committee to any suggestion that the increased resources they were receiving should be channelled to education and training in the applied sciences and technology. The reaction to this by some politicians was that if this attitude persisted, science and technology would never be adequately resourced. Alternative institutions should be established, that would be separately and generously funded, be able to award degrees and that would gather an eminence and reputation to match the prestigious technological institutions of the United States and some European countries. Gordon *et al.* (1991) quote a memorandum from Lord Woolton, a senior member of the 1951 Conservative government, to R. A. Butler, then Chancellor of the Exchequer and formerly the Education Minister who had driven through the 1944 Education Act:

> We should establish for industry a school of university standing equivalent in prestige to the schools of medicine … a separate and national institution which establishes a course of training of university standing around a degree in technology.
>
>   (PRO, April 1952, quoted Gordon *et al.* 1991: 237–8)

The significance of these proposals for access is that these Institutes of Technology would be at the pinnacle of a hierarchy of regional colleges, with lower level, sub-degree and evening courses feeding into the technological education network. This would draw in students from a potentially much wider range of backgrounds and interests: where, apropos the earlier G. B. Shaw quotation, they would teach people to be 'an engineer or such like' rather than a gentleman.

Other politicians argued as strongly against this. Butler asserted that the notion of liberal education should encompass the education of the scientific elite. He therefore expanded Imperial College and the Manchester College of Technology, already within the university ambit. C. P. Snow's influential Reith Lecture series and paper, *The Two Cultures* (1959), argued that a *rapprochement* between the sciences and the humanities was both urgent and possible through broad-based university traditions.

A further compromise was reached in the White Paper, *The Organization of Technical Colleges* (Ministry of Education 1956), which promoted a group of ten regional colleges to become Colleges of Advanced Technology (CATs) with degree-awarding powers. There were in 1956 some 22 Regional Colleges of Technology and a further 731 area and local Technical and other Colleges. The White Paper led to a number becoming Colleges of Technology, with a wider regional remit. All remained within local authority control, though the elevation of the CATs led to problems in relation to the university system, only resolved when the CATs became universities in their own right, including Salford, Aston, Battersea (Surrey), Brunel and Loughborough (Venables 1978).

These changes had a particular significance in the growth of the non-university higher education sector, which will be returned to in Chapter 3.

Patterns of university recruitment 1945–58

As the war ended, there was a widespread move towards university expansion. Special arrangements were made to take on those men and women returning from the armed services who had deferred their admission. Financial support arrangements for these students was assured. The egalitarian spirit of Attlee's Labour administration was echoed in the Barlow Committee's comments on access to scientific training in universities: 'the scales are weighted today in favour of the socially eligible' and those with 'athletic prowess and pleasant manner and address' (Barlow 1945: 35). The UGC also commented on the changing nature of admissions and access in their 1948 report: 'A pecuniary test of fitness is obviously unsatisfactory and it is offensive to the social consciousness of our day'. They noted that the number of students who were from poorer homes had been growing rapidly in the inter-war period and was continuing to accelerate (UGC 1948: 34).

The number of students who had scholarships and assisted places rose substantially in the post-war period, from 38 per cent in 1938 to 73.8 per cent in 1951. Whereas before the war, the UGC calculated that one person in 60 was admitted to university, in the early 1950s the ratio was one in 31 (PEP 1950; UGC 1953). This can be translated to a change in the age participation index from 1.7 to 3.2, which approximately corresponds to the figures reported in Glass (1954) (in Table 2.1 above). These figures need to be interpreted in the light of the low participation in secondary education at this time. The school-leaving age had only just been raised to 15 and the UGC reported that only 28 per cent of 15-year-olds were attending school in January 1952, with just 6.5 per cent of 17-year-olds still in education (UGC 1953). Those staying on would almost all be in private schools or in grammar schools. Access to grammar schools was, following the 1944 Act, generally determined by an entrance examination at the age of 11. Depending on the level of local provision, only between 10 and 25 per cent of pupils could be admitted to the grammar schools. Given this, half of those attending school to the age of 17 were securing university entrance. But, as Himmelweit had argued, 'success within the grammar school is partly determined by ... social class membership' (Himmelweit 1954: 159).

What were the effects of this policy of that made access rather more possible for those from working-class backgrounds? The report of the University Grants Committee in 1953, on the quinquennium 1947 to 1952, is revealing of the attitudes of senior university staff at the time. Discussing the expansion that had taken place (see Figure 2.2), they noted the much higher proportion of entrants who were:

> Young men and women who have few cultural interests and attainments beyond those which they have acquired at school. The presence in the universities of relatively large numbers of students who lack the advantage of a cultured home background has forced upon the universities a number of problems of teaching and the organization of university life.
>
> (UGC 1953: 24)

Fortunately for academics confronted with such difficulties, help was at hand. The Committee went on to note that because 'now more [university] staff are drawn from the same social strata of society as the students' there were now lecturers available who could offer these students 'a more sympathetic understanding of their difficulties' (ibid.: 24).

The UGC was equally unwilling to recognize the potential financial difficulties of these new students. They noted the increasing propensity of these kinds of students to undertake paid work in the vacations and concluded 'to spend whole vacations, particularly in the summer, in clerical or manual occupations indoors is thoroughly bad' (ibid.: 25).

The attitude that seems displayed through these comments appears almost colonialist. Taking on a selected minority of students from non-professional backgrounds, the universities appeared to see their purpose as being to enculture these individuals and to foster in them the social and cultural attributes of the ruling classes, rather in the way that Frantz Fanon observed French colonialism in North Africa giving the indigenous people white masks in *Peau noire, masques blancs* (Fanon 1975). This loss of identity (the contemporary context of which will be examined in Chapter 9) was noted in the 1950s: Richard Hoggart's *The Uses of Literacy* (1957) examined the various cultures of the working classes, which he argued were being diluted and lost as working communities 'lost' their most able young people to university and cosmopolitan life.

After experiencing the consequences of expansion in the immediate post-war period, the universities themselves seemed to become more conservative at the moment that the Conservative Party returned to power in 1951. The UGC interim report in 1952 claimed that there could be 'no further substantial increase … without affecting standards' (1952: 8). This assertion was repeated in their full report in the following year; there could be no increase that might lead to employment problems for graduates and might reduce university standards (1953: 26).

But there was a growing realization that the educational system – secondary schooling as much as university education – was creating major questions about equality of opportunity and social exclusion. Not only was there rising affluence but expectations of social change were developing. The pattern was emerging in the late 1940s and early 1950s that a fair proportion of those being educated in grammar schools would move into higher education. Consequently, the tripartite system of secondary schooling introduced by the 1944 Act, with its increased numbers of selective grammar school places, would inevitably create greatly increased demands for university places as the new cohorts of pupils moved towards their eighteenth year. The tripartite system (of grammar, modern and technical secondary schools) itself was under scrutiny for its recruitment patterns at age 11, where it rapidly became clear that the 11-plus examination was a fairly effective social class filter (for example Glass 1954; Crosland 1956; Benn and Simon 1970). The university vice-chancellors, stung by the criticism that they were administering a socially exclusive entry policy, commissioned an enquiry into admissions applications. This pointed out that 72 per cent of the adult population were manual working class, and that just 9 per cent of Cambridge admission and 13 per cent of Oxford admissions were of students from manual family backgrounds, that 31 per cent of provincial universities' students were of manual-class origin. But, the report went on, the percentage of applicants who were not admitted, when compared with the percentage that were admitted, showed no bias; and, that 'with the possible exception of Oxford and Cambridge, the universities themselves bear no responsibility for the continuing inequalities' (Kelsal 1957, quoted in Moodie 1959: 4). Despite the continuing concerns that 'so many new students are handicapped by limited backgrounds in getting full advantage from their university' (UGC 1958: 8), further expansion was inevitable.

This growth began in the mid-1950s, with the establishment of a new wave of universities. These foundations were quite unlike the former waves of creations. Six universities were agreed in 1959, and set up on greenfield sites, in smaller cities. These were the 'new universities' of the 1960s, sometimes referred to as the 'Shakespearean universities', as they sound rather like the *dramatis personae* from Richard III – York and Lancaster, Warwick and Sussex, Essex and Canterbury. Springing up without local or regional ties or philanthropic endowments, they were national institutions from the start. They were also given university charters from their inception, without the need for a lengthy apprenticeship.

The case for expansion: student recruitment in the late 1950s

There were three parallel drivers for expansion. The first was purely demographic. The birth rate had been depressed during the Second World War and there had been a very sharp increase in the birth rate in 1947; the number of 18-year-olds would leap in 1965 from 747,000 to 963,000.

The bulge would only last three years, but after a fall, would resume its underlying upwards trend from 1970 onwards. If no additional places were available, then the age participation ratio for university education would plummet from around 4.3 per cent to 3.4 per cent. Moreover, it was already clear in 1959 that the proportion of those with university entrance qualifications who were being admitted was beginning to fall, because the proportion of the age group obtaining the minimum entrance qualifications was rising very quickly. Through the 1950s to 1958, between 72 per cent and 75 per cent of all those 18-year-olds who had acquired the entrance qualifications would be able to take up university places. Figure 2.4 shows what would have happened if the expansion of the early 1960s had not taken place, and the growth in places shown in the late 1950s had continued. Combining this projected growth rate with the faster rising numbers of those achieving qualifications, and the population bulge of 18-year-olds that would peak in 1965, only 40 per cent of those with qualifications would find university places that year (Figure 2.4).

The reason for the acceleration in the proportion of pupils with university entrance qualifications was almost certainly the success of the 1944 Education Act in establishing a widespread pattern of selective secondary grammar schools, in which sixth forms had been strongly promoted (Gordon *et al.*: 239). The first pupils to pass through the full seven-year cycle of the new schools would have been achieving entrance qualifications in the mid-1950s. The grammar and private schools were effectively the only source of university applicants in the 1950s, and the combination of the General Certificate

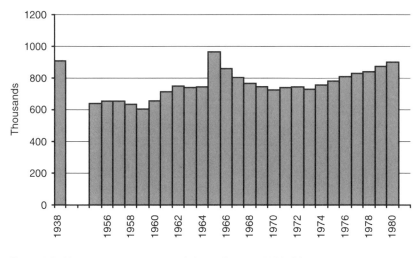

Figure 2.3 18-year-old population of Great Britain, 1959–80
Sources: from Registrar General, in Robbins 1963a: Table 25

of Education (GCE) examinations system O (ordinary) and A (advanced) levels, introduced in 1950 in England and Wales, was seen as the appropriate filter (Kelsall 1962). There is a more extended discussion of these and other qualifications in Chapter 7. A range of five to ten O levels (sometimes specified by subject), taken at around the age of 16, demonstrated the applicant's general proficiency, while the A level (in two to four subjects, taken at around the age of 18) acted as a test of attainment in the subjects of specialism. Scotland persisted (and still persists) with the system of Highers, which takes the 'general proficiency' test to a higher level of attainment in a broader range of subjects.

This increase in the percentage of those achieving the entry standard contributed to the second pressure for expansion: the government's desire to meet the rising expectations of the new affluent society. Economic growth in the 1950s fuelled a new consumer society, and with this came greater expectations for the younger generation to achieve educationally and economically. As Brian Simon (1985) has suggested, the Conservative administration found it politically impossible not to acquiesce in university expansion. Harold Macmillan led the party to its third successive victory in 1959 with the slogan 'You've never had it so good!' The wave of reports from the Central Advisory Council on Education added to the pressure for higher levels of participation in all post-compulsory education. For example, the Crowther Report 15–18 (Crowther 1959) set out a 20-year programme to ensure that half of all 18-year-olds would stay in full-time education. The report also argued that pressure for places in higher education was distorting the secondary school curriculum. The Campaign for Education, which Geoffrey Crowther led shortly

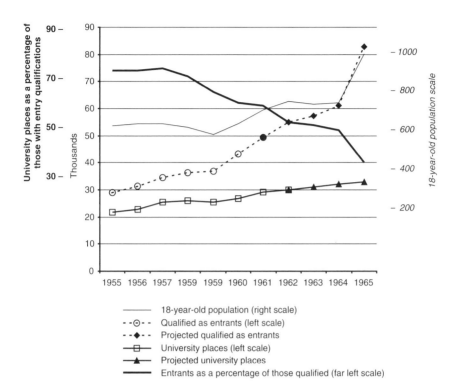

Figure 2.4 Robbins' dilemma: numbers of university entrants and of 18-year-olds qualified for entrance (with the total 18-year-old population and the percentage
of qualified applicants who achieve entrance) each year from 1958 to 1965
(actual figures 1958–61; projections if no action was taken for 1962–65)

Sources: As Figure 2.3, and Robbins 1963b Part IV: Tables 10, 12, 14 and 23

Note
Actual numbers (shown with hollow markers) are derived from percentages, and the trends of
1958–61 are projected using a parabolic trendline for 1962–5 (using solid markers), and the
projected percentage of entrants to those achieving the standard is calculated from this

after his report had been published, used the slogan 'all to sixteen, half to eigh-
teen and a fifth to twenty-one' (Smith and Eddison 1963: 12).

The third pressure for expansion was the desire for social justice and
equality in education. Anthony Crosland, a leading Labour Party theoretician,
published *The Future of Socialism* in 1956. Although much of the attention
this was given focused on his critical assessment of Morrisonian nationalized
industries (which led to Crosland being branded a revisionist), this was a
careful examination of the social and economic inequalities of the period,
which – drawing on a range of sociological studies of educational disadvantage, such as Glass (1954) and Halsey and Gardner (1953) – concluded that

'the school system in Britain remains the most divisive, unjust and wasteful of all aspects of social equality' (Crosland 1956: 141). He argued that the only way to break down barriers to equality was to fundamentally reform the educational system; in particular, the comprehensive system should replace the tripartite system of the 1944 Act, and entry into the public schools should be democratized. These two reforms would ensure that 'all schools will more and more be socially mixed; all will provide routes to the Universities and to every type of occupation … then, very slowly, Britain may cease to be the most class-ridden country in the world' (ibid.: 207). Crosland, to become Secretary of State for Education in 1965, had a very clear sense of the class-based injustices in all aspects of the educational system.

The Trades Union Congress was also pushing for universities to expand: greater numbers, they argued, would mean a better chance of equality of opportunity and social justice: there should be 'unrestricted access to Higher Education for all children who are capable of benefiting from it' (TUC 1956: 15). The Fabian Society suggested a Royal Commission on Higher Education in 1959: expansion would allow broader access, arguing 'some or all of the universities are bastions of privilege and "the establishment" (Moodie 1959: 3); 'University education should not, any more than other types of education, be a privilege of wealth or class' (ibid.: 5).

The case for expansion: the Robbins Report

The first step was to reform the system of student fees and maintenance. In 1956–7 some 75 per cent of students were receiving some form of scholarship or assistance to attend university, although the system was under strain as numbers overall were rising (Figure 2.4). A committee was established under the chairmanship of Sir Colin Anderson, which reported in 1960. This set out a system of grants for university fees and for student maintenance, based on the principle that these should be available for all, on a scale that was tested against parents' means. Anderson estimated that this would allow all qualified students who wished to go to university to do so, and estimated that this would mean the student population would eventually rise to 175,000 students. The Anderson system covered all student fees (including those of overseas students) and had a scale of maintenance allowances for home students that reflected local living costs and length of the study year. The new system was broadly welcomed across the political spectrum: 'equality of opportunity really does mean something in this context' (Prest 1963: 15). The payment of overseas fees was the only area that attracted some criticism; it was argued by some that it was no more than a 'subsidy to the scions of wealthy families from anywhere in the world' (ibid.: 14).

The calls for a Royal Commission were heeded. There was a broad bipartisan agreement on the need for immediate expansion; the Robbins Committee was established not to argue the case for further growth but to calculate its necessary size: 'to review the pattern of full-time higher education ... and to advise ... on what principles its long-term development should be based' (Treasury minute of 8 February 1961, Robbins 1963a: para. 1). They were asked whether new types of institutions were needed and whether the planning arrangements for higher education needed modification. The committee did more than this.

Robbins examined the whole pattern of provision, commissioning research into the structure and arrangements by which the universities conducted research and teaching, the pattern of student recruitment and the changes in this, the staffing structure, the capital and buildings necessary for universities, and comparative studies of higher education in a range of other developed nations. They particularly examined the way in which the potential demand for higher education was emerging: not the demand from employers and industry – they largely avoided issues of manpower planning – but the demand for access from young people: who was qualified, who was enrolling, analysed by both family and school background. In doing so, they took evidence on the idea of a 'pool of ability': was there a group of people able to take advantage of higher education but not coming forward for reasons of lack of educational attainment or a lack of financial or other means? If so, was this pool limited in size? How large might it be?

The Report made some 178 recommendations, the principal of which are summarized in Table 2.2.

What the Committee did not recommend was anything about the kind of student that might be attracted (with the sole exception of para. 515). However, the extensive analysis of the data that the Committee commissioned did document the inequalities that existed in detail; these related to both gender (where women were noticeably under-represented) and social class, which has been documented above. Setting this in their context of their definition of the aims of higher education, the direction they urged was clear.

The four essential objectives for higher education were:

- instruction in skills suitable for work (para. 25);
- the promotion of the general powers of the mind (para. 26);
- the advancement of learning (para. 27); and
- the transmission of a common culture and common standards of citizenship.

> This function, important at all times, is perhaps especially important in an age that has set for itself the ideal of equality of opportunity. It is not merely by providing places for students from all classes that this ideal will be achieved, but also by providing, in the atmosphere of the institutions in which the students love and work, influences that in some measure compensate for any inequalities in home background.

(Robbins 1963a: para. 28)

Table 2.2 Principal recommendations of the Royal Commission on Higher Education
(Robbins 1963)

Area	Summary of recommendations	Paras
Future demand	• The growth in full-time student numbers to rise from 216,000 (1962–3), to 390,000 (1973–4) and 560,000 (1980–1) [although greeted on publication as ambitious, this turned out to be a fairly large under-estimate]	179
Influence of Oxbridge	• Further capital investment in universities outside Oxbridge	216
Selection for HE	• Improve information sources for schools and parents	225
	• Extend the centralized Admissions Council (UCCA, now UCAS)	227
	• Supplement A levels with aptitude tests	232
Co-operation with schools	• Develop links with schools on transition	236–40
First degree courses	• Develop broader-based courses	262
	• Flexible courses to ease changes of student's plans	264, 271–2
Postgraduate courses	• Increasing the proportion of postgraduate places (for 30% of graduates, rather than 20%)	301
Education and training of teachers	• Teacher Training Colleges to be renamed College of Education	351
	• Increase the size of colleges	319
	• Develop a four-year BEd degree	329
	• Removed colleges from LEA control (and fund by a Grants Commission)	354–6
	• Place under academic aegis of local university's school of education	351–2
Technological education in universities	• More postgraduate work in science and technology	380
	• Proper emphasis on technology in this	381
	• Large departments encouraged	382
SISTERs and CATs	• Special Institutions for Scientific and Technological Education and Research to be designated at Imperial College, UMIST and Glasgow and an unidentified CAT (and a new one created) and generously funded.	383–8
	• Remaining CATs to become universities, with full degree-awarding powers	393–7
Regional and local authority colleges	• Regional Colleges of Technology should take on more full-time advanced students	422–4
	• Remain under LEA control	422

Academic awards	• National Council for Academic Awards was proposed to award all non-university degrees, and oversee the quality of courses, teaching and examination in all the non-university colleges	433–5
Pattern of higher education, planning and institutions	• Planning for higher education should be on a ten-year rolling basis	457
	• Directed to providing places for all qualified students who wished to enrol in higher education	465, 491
	• Existing universities should expand to at least 8–10,000 places	471
	• Six new universities should be established	476
Areas of study	• Expansion to allow proportion studying science and technology to increase	507
	• Adult education to be encouraged	513–14
	• Special grants for adult women to enter higher education	515
Staffing	• University staffing ratios to be maintained	527
	• National patterns of service and pay, sabbaticals, etc.	540–5
Teaching and learning	• Teaching and research are complementary, should be in balance and should be in all universities	354, 355
	• More teaching in small groups, fewer lectures	567–58
	• Personal tutors for all students	570
	• Review examination methods	574
	• Monitor wastage rates	580–4
	• Two-thirds of all new places for students should be residential	594
Finance	• Loans for students inappropriate: maintain grants	647
	• Tuition fees should be 20% of current institutional expenditure	654
Internal government	• Universities should have a broad-based internal government with staff representation	665–75
	• LEA colleges should have full governing bodies with academic representation	679
National government	• A single Grants Commission for all autonomous institutions	744
	• Ministry for Arts and Science for the Grants Commission and the Research Councils	784
	• Ministry of Education for the LEA colleges	783

Source: Summarized from Robbins 1963a: 277–91

Robbins' message for access to higher education is spelt out in the detail of Appendix 1 of the Committee's Report (Robbins 1963b). This analysis of the demand for places first examined the existing pattern of entry, gathering together data on the 1961 entry cohort. The under-representation of particular groups – women and the working classes – was identified in having 'its origins long before the age of entry to higher education' (1963a: para. 50).

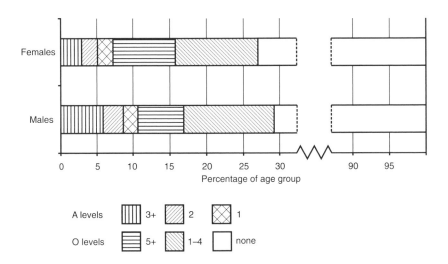

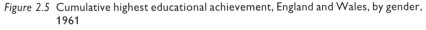

Figure 2.5 Cumulative highest educational achievement, England and Wales, by gender, 1961

Source: Robbins 1963b Part I: Table 2

Robbins suggested different reasons for these two kinds of differential representation. The reasons for the gender difference were relatively obvious and uncontroversial. The report examined the highest educational qualifications of boys and girls in 1961. Figure 2.5 shows this in graphical form: the bars show the size of each group by highest qualification. Thus 27 per cent of girls obtained at least one O level, and 15.4 per cent obtained more than five; however, only 2.9 per cent obtained three or more A levels, compared with 5.9 per cent of all boys.

There was a progressive widening in the difference between the performance of males and females. The numbers achieving O-level passes was almost identical, but a far smaller proportion of women moved on to take A-level examinations. Taking only those with five or more O levels, some 82 per cent of males attempted three A-level papers, and only 60 per cent of the females. The pass rates were identical (58 per cent of both male and females passed all three papers). And, as the Report noted, almost half of those with good O levels never attempted any A-level examinations (1963b: para. 12). In Scotland, the differences were far less marked. In terms of the school population, this was the reason for girls' lower rates of entry into full-time higher education.

Figure 2.6 shows the gender ratio of admissions to various forms of higher education provision. In full-time education, the gender ratio replicated the difference in terms of A-level achievement. But there were, within the various types of institution, marked differences: for university education, 71 per cent

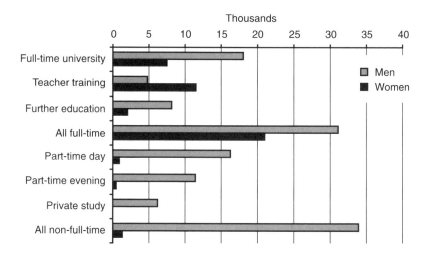

Figure 2.6 Entrants to higher education, 1961: by institutional type, mode and gender
Source: Robbins 1963b Part I: Table 9

of entrants were men, and only 29 per cent women. But in the teacher training colleges, this ratio was nearly exactly reversed. In the full-time technical college sector – then only about 20 per cent of the whole full-time provision – 80 per cent of entrants were male. So, although the overall full-time entrance rates reflected the attainment rate at 18, the institutional destinations were highly gendered, with a much greater proportion of qualified males going to the more prestigious university institutions. The part-time higher education situation was overwhelmingly male: only 3.7 per cent of entrants were women. Figure 2.7 (a and b) show the distribution of men and women respectively in institutions in part-time and full-time higher education, showing the distortion that was taking place.

The evidence on social class and educational achievement was more complex to analyse, but Robbins was unequivocal that this was the result of social deprivation:

> It might be held that superior innate intelligence was the only reason why a greater proportion of middle-class children than manual working-class children reach higher education. But this is not the case.
>
> (Robbins 1963b, Part II: para. 8)

Part of Robbins' analysis was based on an examination of children of all social classes born in 1940–41 who attended maintained grammar schools (or senior secondary schools in Scotland). In England and Wales, these schools were already under scrutiny in terms of their selective admission procedures (the 11-plus examination), which was suspected of acting as a proxy for social class

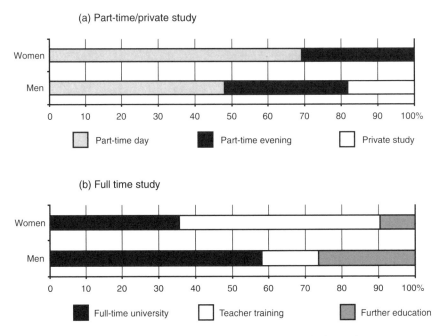

Figure 2.7 Distribution of the male and female population in higher education
Source: As Figure 2.6

(for example, Floud *et al*. 1956). But they did admit sufficient working-class children to allow for an analysis of their destinations.

The population of these schools was divided into three groups by intelligence quotient, as measured at age 11 (in 1951–2), and into two groups based on the fathers' occupations. Table 2.3 gives an abbreviated set of data on the highest course of education undertaken by each of these six groups.

Children of equal levels of measured ability, in the same school settings (and thus with theoretically the same access to examinations), were achieving differentially on the basis of social class. Children from manual backgrounds, of the same level of ability and in the same educational environment as children from non-manual backgrounds, were less than half as likely to attend university. Of all children from manual backgrounds in the sample, 20.3 per cent obtained no school qualification, while only one seventh (2.9 per cent) of children from non-manual backgrounds obtained no qualifications. As these children progressed through the secondary school system, the gap in educational attainment between the manual and non-manual widened at each stage – O level, A level and university entrance. Another survey, made by the Ministry of Education of over 100,000 school leavers from maintained grammar schools in 1960–1, confirmed the same findings. Analysis of this suggested that if working-

Table 2.3 Highest course of study by children (born Great Britain 1940–1) in grammar schools/senior secondary schools, by IQ at 11 and by father's occupation, percentages

IQ	Father's occupation	Higher education			A level/ highers	O level	not O level	Total
		degree	other	part-time				
130+	non-manual	37	4	10	7	41	0	100
	manual	18	12	10	14	45	1	100
115–129	non-manual	17	17	4	17	41	3	100
	manual	8	7	9	10	53	13	100
100–114	non-manual	6	11	8	8	64	4	100
	manual	2	4	7	7	50	31	100

Source: Robbins 1963b Part II: Table 4

class children stayed in schooling to the age of 18, then they would perform as well as their counterparts of equivalent ability. Figure 2.8 demonstrates this graphically: each group of four bars represents a third of all pupils, rated by ability, and each of the four bars represents a different social class. The shaded elements of the bar are the proportion staying on to 18 and the black elements of this are those who leave, at 18, with two A levels. Taking just those who stay on to at least age 18, the proportion of these who get at least two A levels is related to the ability band, not to social class. Thus, in the most able third (rated by 11-plus entry), 81 per cent of semi-skilled and manual workers' children get two A levels, and 79 per cent of professional and managerial workers' children; in the least able third, the corresponding figures are 53 per cent and 43 per cent.

The Robbins Report laid out a challenge for expansion, to schools and to universities. The tasks, in an age of equality of opportunity, were to redress the inequalities and imbalances in the higher education population, in terms of gender and social class. In the context of the great expansion that Robbins foresaw and planned for, these were tasks that may at the time have seemed within reach. Two social trends in particular seemed to support this ambition. First, the predicted increase in school attainment at age 18 meant a higher and higher proportion of young people would become eligible for university admission. Second, there was a growing consensus that the grammar school system needed to be reformed so that it no longer reflected and reinforced the prevailing class structure, and this should have made it more possible for children from working-class backgrounds to stay at school till 18. The following chapter will examine the fate of Robbins' proposals, how far the expansion went and whether the increases in provision were able to redress the imbalances.

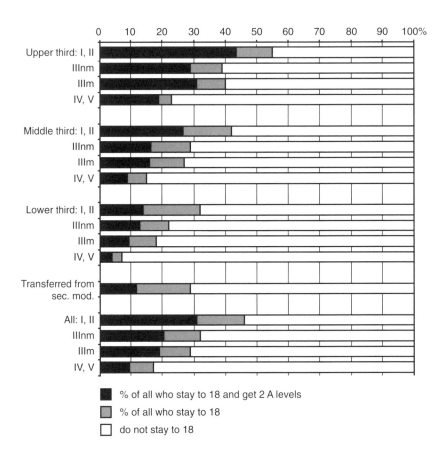

Figure 2.8 A-level performance and age of leaving maintained grammar schools, by ability band and father's occupation, 1960–1

Source: Based on Robbins 1963b Part II: Table 7

Chapter 3

Access to higher education
Inclusion for the masses?

Alistair Ross

The Robbins Committee reported in October 1963. This was not a good moment for a policy report to attract sustained government action. The Conservative government, in power for 12 years, had spent the summer rocked by a succession of political scandals and had just changed leaders from Macmillan to the Earl of Home (who had to renounce his peerage in order to become prime minister). He was a stop-gap leader; an election had to be held in a year and it was widely anticipated that Labour would win. The reform of higher education was not going to be an immediate government priority.

The plans for an expansion of the existing system, necessary to avoid a catastrophic fall in the age participation index as those born in 1947 became 18, were already in place. Robbins' other proposals were largely ignored. The main thrust of the administrative arrangements he suggested were to consolidate the position of the university sector within higher education – the sector which he really knew and understood. Tyrrell Burgess (a Labour Party and public-sector college activist and adviser) saw Robbins' view of higher education 'as a kind of club, with the universities as full members, the colleges of education as associate members, and regional colleges on a gratifying waiting list' (quoted in Crosland 1982: 158).

Robbins had argued for a separate ministry, represented in the Cabinet, for university and higher education. This was denied, after some internal argument, by the Conservative government (Salter and Tapper 1994). Instead, the Department of Education and Science was created in April 1964, bringing together the universities and the school system. The new department 'contained officials who regarded the universities as over-protected and over-resourced in comparison with other [education] demands' (Gordon *et al.* 1991: 242). This unification of the two sectors accorded with Labour Party policy at this time, of breaking down barriers in education. The party's Taylor Committee recommended in *The Years of Crisis* (Labour Party 1963) that a unitary system of higher education be established by incorporating all technical and regional colleges with the existing universities into 45 new institutions; as Robinson pointed out, the committee hardly seemed aware that any further education students were over 18, or that unifying higher education 'would effectively be the unification only of the education of the professional classes' (Robinson 1968: 59). Taylor's recommendations were not accepted as party policy, but the Shadow Education and Science spokesman, Richard Crossman, wrote (in his diary, in September 1965) that 'When I was shadow science minister I became more and more convinced that one of the biggest jobs for the next Labour Secretary for Education was to break down the rigid division between higher and further education' (Crossman 1975: 236). A single department responsible for both sectors would assist in this.

Labour came to power in October 1964. Richard Crossman did not become Secretary of State for Education, possibly because he was too strongly – and publicly – committed to a unitary system that would antagonize universities and local authorities alike (Robinson 1968). In January 1965, Tony Crosland became Secretary of State. His biographer and wife records that

> when he first arrived at Curzon Street [the location of the main offices of the DES] the Robbins Report was on the table. Robbins held that higher education was synonymous with university education. Other forms of high education were beyond the pale.
>
> (Crosland 1982: 158)

She also reported his comment – after an evening in which 'the Vice Chancellors … went on and on as if their precious universities weren't already rich and successful' – that he was 'not frightfully interested in the universities' (ibid.: 147).

His priorities were firstly to reform the school system – 'the most divisive, unjust and wasteful of all aspects of social equality' (Crosland 1956: 141). To this end, he vowed first 'to destroy every fucking grammar school in England' (Crosland 1982: 148), issuing Circular 10/65 requesting local authorities to replace the tripartite system with comprehensive schools.

The endorsement of the binary system

However, higher education was not neglected. If the universities enshrined elitism, then alternative forms of higher education needed to be explored. Robbins argued for the Colleges of Education to be taken from the local authorities to become part of the university system, almost as mini-university colleges. This was rejected: not only did the local authorities resist the wholesale removal of 'their' institutions, that produced their own teachers, but the ministry/department was also loath to lose their control over this significant sector of higher education. 'We thought it unwise,' Crosland rationalized later, 'to change horses in the middle of a turbulent stream of expansion' (Crosland 1967, in Robinson 1968: 251).

Robbins argued for the establishment of yet more universities; this too was denied, other than the upgrading of the Colleges of Advanced Technology. One of Crosland's first acts was to announce that there would be no more new universities, for at least ten years (and no colleges were to be allowed to join existing universities). But his proposals for a National Council for Academic Awards (CNAA) were adopted. A Royal Charter created the Council with degree-awarding powers and this became one of the powerful engines for further expansion of higher education (Silver 1990). Robbins intended the CNAA to have rather limited functions, to focus on institutions that were en route to university status. But it demonstrated that it had very much greater potential than this (Robinson 1968).

The origins of the system

Crosland combined an initial suggestion from one of his Department of Education and Science officials, Toby Weaver, with proposals from the Association for Teachers in Technical Institutions (ATTI 1965). In a speech at Woolwich Polytechnic in April 1965, he put forward a proposal to create a separate set of higher education institutions. He detected and rejected 'our snobbish caste-ridden hierarchical obsession with university status' (Crosland 1982: 159).

> On the one hand we have what have come to be called the autonomous sector, represented by the universities, in whose ranks, of course, I now include the colleges of advanced technology. On the other hand, we have the public sector, represented by the leading technical colleges and the colleges of education. The Government accepts this dual system as being fundamentally the right one, with each sector making its own distinctive contribution to the whole. We infinitely prefer it to the alternative concept of a unitary system, hierarchically arranged on the 'ladder' principle, with the universities at the top and the other institutions down below.
>
> (Crosland, Woolwich, 27 April 1965, quoted in Becher and Kogan 1980: 23)

The binary policy was thus launched. The following year a White Paper (*A Plan for Polytechnics and Other Colleges*, DES 1966) designated 30 proposed polytechnics, created by the local authorities out of some 70 colleges of technology, art and commerce, to become 'major institutions of higher education'. The newly created Council for National Academic Awards would accredit the degrees of the new institutions, in what was described as 'as symbiotic relationship' with the new institutions (Hall [Assistant Director of Hatfield Polytechnic] 1969: 5).

The binary system in one sense already existed, as Crosland himself admitted in a speech at Lancaster University in 1967 (designed in part to mollify the university sector for the bruising he had given it at Woolwich) – 'a plural system already existed' (Crosland 1967, quoted in Robinson 1968: 249). The Woolwich speech set out a policy for higher education in selected technical colleges because there was, he argued, a dichotomy of purpose between the academic education of the universities and the vocational education of the colleges. Comprehensive higher education institutions, in the public sector, responsive to local community needs through the local education authorities, would better serve the nations' needs and the demand Robbins had predicted for places in higher education. Indeed, teacher education in the colleges of education might eventually be more properly realigned with the public college sector than the university sector. The new sector was to be separate but equal to the universities, he announced.

The ATTI had argued that, rather than seek the promotion of a small number of colleges into universities, there should be the maximum expansion of colleges outside the university system.

Weaver's contribution to the policy, as deputy secretary at the DES, was probably significant; he certainly recalls his influence as being significant. He was given responsibility for higher education when the Department was created in 1964:

> I was at once confronted with the Robbins Committee Report on Higher Education of 1963, and was told that it was my business to analyse it and explain to Ministers what it was all about and make recommendations as to what should be done. The Government had already decided to accept – about the only major feature of the report that in the end they accepted – the numerical expansion over the first few years recommended by Robbins. Apart from that it was all to play for.
>
> The main feature of the report was that all higher education should be virtually under the aegis of universities, [and] that it should not be controlled by the Ministry … . By then … I had reached the conclusion that there must be some more general and empowering thing that education could do for the great majority of the population (not excluding the comparatively small minority who had the good fortune to get higher education). There must, I felt, be some way of making higher education more accessible and more helpful to the great run of intelligent young men and women who did not want primarily to become scholars ….
>
> I advised Ministers not to accept the major proposals of the Robbins Report. I was very doubtful whether we wanted gradually to create another 40 universities because that would have meant tremendous pressure on regional technical colleges to cast aside all the vocational work they were doing at sub-degree level and with sandwich courses in order that they might join the race to become universities. And so, rightly or wrongly, I advised Ministers to declare that there would be,

with one exception, no new universities, that none of the regional colleges would be promoted and that the teacher training colleges would remain under the aegis of local education authorities who had the main responsibility for the supply of teachers to the schools. That more or less disarmed the main thrust of the Robbins Report, leaving a vacuum.

What was to fill that vacuum? I suggested first to Edward Boyle, the Secretary of State, [*sic*: Boyle was actually a Minister of State at the DES] and later to his successor Anthony Crosland, that we ought to build up 30 of the regional and other large technical colleges aspiring to become polytechnics with the mission to put much more emphasis on the practical side of education, to expand the system of sandwich courses, to offer wider access to mature and part-time students rather than to concentrate on the standardized 18–21 undergraduates, and to emphasize the value of vocationally-oriented courses without sacrificing proper academic standards.

(Weaver 1994: 14)

The purposes of the system

Weaver here highlights the significance of the binary policy: the polytechnics were expected to offer access to a different form of higher education, and to offer it to different kinds of students. Moreover, the sector was to be locally and democratically controlled. It would be provided in a comprehensive setting: at Lancaster Crosland set out the 'great educational advantages from … the universities, of more broadly based higher education institutions in which full-time, sandwich and part-time students at all levels of higher education work together' (quoted in Robinson 1968: 253). He was not defending the status quo, but creating a counter-force to the hegemony (that Robbins had sought to extend) of the university sector. According to his biographer, Crosland

had to struggle with the intellectual cohesion with which he defended the binary policy to democratize higher education; he succeeded in altering the terms of the debate – the Robbins attitudes had lost their dominance. The polytechnics – related to the needs of technology and industry – were to stand alongside the universities, not inferior, but different.

(Crosland 1982: 159)

Reaction to the binary system

The university sector's reaction to the binary policy was mixed. There was some disdain for the concept that institutions other than universities might award degrees. In November 1964, for example, the Director of Oxford University's Department of Education explained to an American audience that the CNAA 'is empowered to grant "degrees" ... as a sort of national accrediting agency to validate courses in ... what are at present "sub-university" institutions' (quotation marks as in original text; Peterson 1966: 231). The Vice Chancellor of Liverpool University referred to polytechnics as offering 'a cheaper way of getting degrees', and of producing 'second-class citizens in the graduate world' (quoted by Brosan 1971: 62).

Lord Robbins professed himself confused by the government's binary policy. On the one hand, he complained, they were:

> trying to introduce the comprehensive principle into schools, which I think is the right thing to do provided it is done with good sense and prudence. At the same time they are deepening the existence of lines of division in higher education and actually announcing, as a matter of policy ... that these divisions are to be permanent. They are making the system more hierarchical than ever before.
>
> (Robbins and Ford 1965: 6–7)

On the other hand, Gordon and his colleagues suggest that the university sector very soon came to welcome the establishment of the polytechnic sector. It 'ended once and for all the scramble for university recognition by aspiring bodies', and the universities saw that the polytechnics and the CNAA, who were

> less expensively endowed and less prestigious, would serve as a filter, allowing the universities to continue to draw in the more able academic students, to maintain their style of teaching and research, and to claim that they were centres of excellence in higher education.
>
> (Gordon *et al.* 1991: 241)

The effects of the binary policy

What was the effect of the binary policy on access to higher education? There were several. First, the sector as a whole increased in size much faster than the Robbins Committee had predicted. Second, the rate of increase was particularly marked for women students, who were staying on in sixth-form education, achieving two or more A levels, and entering university at a higher rate of increase than male students (though it would take a quarter of a century to catch up). Third, the public sector, particularly the polytechnics, expanded at a very much faster rate than had been predicted or planned. However, at the same time, they were changing in orientation and mission from Crosland and Weaver's vision towards a rather more conventional form of higher education; 'academic drift' (Pratt and Burgess 1974) set in fairly rapidly after designation. The consequence of this was that the student populations and the courses in the university sector and the polytechnic sector were not as distinctive as they might have been. Fourth, thus, the proportion of students of working-class origin did not substantially change over the following 25 years. Certainly there were many more such students and a greater proportion of the working-class age sector participated, but the increase only matched the general (and enormous) increase in the age participation index. Finally, although there was much more evaluation and monitoring of the changes in higher education (for example, the collection of much more detailed statistics on students), there was relatively little interest shown in the social composition of the student body in comparison with the population as a whole. Compared with gender and ethnic minority inclusion, social class fell off the agenda.

The growth of the higher education system

Taking first the size of the higher education sector, Robbins had estimated a growth from 216,000 full-time students in 1962–3 to 390,000 in 1973–4 and 560,000 in 1980–1. The actual numbers in these two years were 575,000 and 620,000, respectively. The under-estimation by Robbins was matched again and again in successive government projections.

It is not easy to be certain of the figures of students. The basis on which data were collected changed and some socio-economic information about student backgrounds was never collected. Statistical runs variously include or exclude students in some kinds of institutions and variously refer to England, Great Britain and the United Kingdom. Part-time students, in particular, were included in statistics on a very irregular basis. Although postgraduate student data are generally available, it was never possible to tell if a 'new' student enrolling on an undergraduate course had enrolled before, or was embarking on a second undergraduate degree. Figures for age participation indices were particularly difficult to calculate, as students would begin higher education at various ages, usually from 17 years onwards, so the notion of a single cohort disintegrates into an age cohort and a cohort based on year of enrolment. Further, age participation indices that relate to participation of a particular social class can only be regarded as indicative, because the size of each social class shifted greatly over the period, with classes IV and V in particular shrinking in size. Whether class participation indices always reflected these, or whether they are based on the class distribution of the age group (as opposed to the class distribution of the population as a whole) is rarely clear. Class membership of post-21 students has generally been based on the economic activity of the individual, while the pre-21 student is categorized by their parents' occupation.

Notwithstanding all this, Figure 3.1 shows the number of full-time students in the United Kingdom over the period from 1960 to 1994.

There are two periods of particularly rapid growth, from 1963 to 1970, and from 1988 to 1993. Of the first wave of growth, Halsey *et al.* (1980)

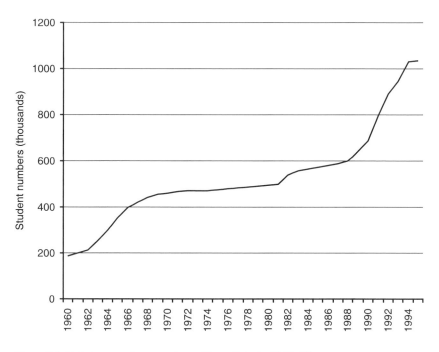

Figure 3.1 Full-time student numbers, Great Britain 1960–95
Source: Derived from Dearing 1997

has pointed out that, while the fastest rate of growth went to the lower socio-economic groups, the absolute incremental growth went to the higher socio-economic groups. The result was to more or less maintain the ratio of classes participating in higher education: about three-quarters of the students were middle class, and one-quarter working class. The changes in the class structure of the population, as occupations shifted from manual to non-manual, offers only a partial explanation. It also seems that the members of the higher socio-economic groups are better able to take advantage of the expansion in size, and to continue to take up a disproportionate share of the places available.

In 1972, the White Paper *Education: A Framework for Expansion* (DES 1972) set a new target of all students of 750,000 for 1982: the actual number was 877,000.

In 1978, a DES discussion document (*Higher Education into the 1990s*) (Oakes 1978) put forward three variations of potential growth, revising the 1972 target for full-time undergraduates downwards (Table 3.1).

The 1985 White Paper *The Development of Higher Education into the 1990s* (DES 1985) made two projections for full-time degree students on their first undergraduate course (Table 3.2).

Table 3.1 Projections of growth in higher education, 1978 (000s)

	Estimates		
	1978	1986	1994
Low projection	521	546	463
Central projection	522	603	528
High projection	524	656	593
Actual	520	582	1030

Source: DES/Scottish Office 1978

In 1987, yet another White Paper, *Higher Education: Meeting the Challenge* (DES 1987) proposed an age participation index by 1999 of between 15.8 per cent and 18.5 per cent – between 630,000 and 720,000 full-time students. The actual age participation index achieved in 1999 was 33 per cent – 1,150,000 students.

Higher Education: A New Framework (DfE 1991) projected a 32.1 per cent age participation index by 2000, with 921,000 full-time undergraduates and 490,000 part-time students. By 1998, there were in fact 915,000 full-time undergraduate students and 627,000 part-time students, so the 1991 projections were more accurate than most. Layard and Williams (in Brosan *et al.* 1971) examine the beginnings of this trend of consistent under-estimation.

The inclusion of women

The expansion that took place shows how much successive policy makers in part underestimated the pool of qualified school-leavers. This was becoming evident very soon after Robbins reported. In 1969, the statistical team that had worked for the Robbins Committee reassessed the developments since their work in 1963 (Layard *et al.* 1969) and noted the upsurge in the proportion of pupils achieving the two-A-level standard at 18, necessary for higher education admission. Where they had projected in the Robbins Report that,

Table 3.2 Projections of growth in higher education, 1985 (000s)

	Actual	Estimates	
	1983/4	1989/90	1996/7
X projection	565	612	525
Y projection	565	566	492
Actual		739	1,024

Source: DES 1985

as a percentage of the age group, 8.8 per cent would reach this level by 1967, in fact 10.9 per cent did so. The increase was particularly marked for girls, where it was projected that 6.3 per cent would reach the qualification level: in fact, 8.6 per cent did so (all the more remarkable an increase, as only 2.9 per cent had done so in 1954). However, the percentage of those with the necessary qualifications entering university remained constant, at 44 per cent (1962 and 1967), as did the boys' percentage (68 per cent). Nevertheless, this meant that the numbers of females entering higher education was rising faster than the number of males. The proportion of females entering higher education remained a major policy preoccupation for the next 20 years; by 1979 the male:female ratio was 60:40, and by 1985, 56:44 (DES 1987).

The principal reason for the slowness of this growth is the decline in numbers of places for teacher education in the mid-1970s. As has been noted in Chapter 2 (Figure 2.6), a disproportionate number of women entering higher education in the early 1960s were going to the then teacher training colleges. The number of places available for professional teacher education courses was controlled closely by the Department for Education and Science (the only area where there is any central control), and the need for teachers fell sharply in the mid-1970s. The rapid contraction affected both the size of the whole public higher education sector (Figure 3.2) and the age participation ratio for women as a whole.

The extraordinary growth of the 'other' sector within public higher education shown in Figure 3.2 (a 330 per cent increase between 1962 and 1976) is masked by the expansion and decline of the teacher training

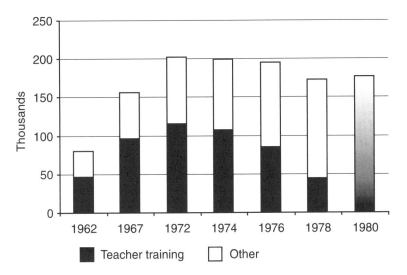

Figure 3.2 Full-time student numbers in public-sector higher education (England and Wales)

Source: House of Commons 1980, pp. 5–9; Robbins 1963b: 9a, 10

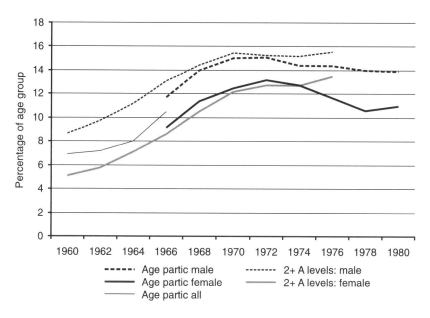

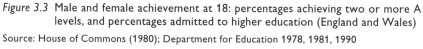

Figure 3.3 Male and female achievement at 18: percentages achieving two or more A levels, and percentages admitted to higher education (England and Wales)

Source: House of Commons (1980); Department for Education 1978, 1981, 1990

element. The effects of this on women's participation in higher education are shown in Figure 3.3.

The females gaining two or more A levels can be seen to be rapidly closing the gap with their male peers. But the age participation indices show that, while women narrowed the gap between 1966 and 1974 (from 2.5 per cent down to 1.6 per cent), by 1978 it had widened again to 3.4 per cent. This was almost wholly the result of the contraction of the colleges of education.

The growth of the public sector

The expansion in size was very largely achieved by the polytechnic sector. This was not by design. It was partly an outcome of the peculiarities of financing the sector in the 1960s and 1970s and partly the result of the university sector's response to the funding strictures imposed by the government in the early 1980s. The method of funding what was called the Advanced Further Education Pool in the 1960s was variously described as 'remarkable' (Layard *et al.* 1969: 71) or 'unbelievable' – the response of Anthony Crosland, as incoming Secretary of State, when it was described to him by his civil servants (it apparently took several days before he accepted that he was not the subject of an elaborate leg-pull). The Colleges of

Technology, Education, Commerce, Art and the Polytechnics were all controlled by individual local education authorities (LEAs) (or, in the case of some polytechnics, by joint committees of neighbouring LEAs). All expenditure by these institutions was met by each respective LEA and apportioned into Advanced Further Education (AFE) or Non-Advanced Further Education. AFE broadly covered degree- and Higher National-level work. Not all LEAs had institutions covering AFE work, so to make the coverage of these costs equitable, at the end of each year the expenditure of all the local authorities for such work was pooled. The liability for the costs was apportioned between all local authorities on a formula based on a combination of the school population (representing the demand for higher education) and the non-domestic rateable value of the local authority (representing its degree of capacity to bear such costs). The result of this was that, if an LEA decided to increase the level of provision on advanced work at its polytechnic (thus creating additional demand for local services, construction, and so on), it could do so at a very small marginal increase in its overall budget. Expansion of the local polytechnic also brought prestige for the local area. The consequences of this system were that there was no overall control or cap on expansion; that it was in each local authority's interests to expand their higher education provision as much as possible; and that there was a concentration on the courses that would generate the highest full-time equivalent higher education numbers. There was therefore a political and economic pressure on polytechnics to move away from the provision of the part-time and lower-level vocational courses that they had originally been intended to provide, in favour of courses more similar to those provided by the university sector.

Coupled with this was a form of inferiority complex on the part of the polytechnics. In order to demonstrate their equivalence to universities in terms of parity of esteem, they felt that had to develop postgraduate work, to develop degrees in a wide range of subjects (in the academic and not merely the directly vocational sector) and generally to demonstrate an academic standing that would give their students and their students' qualifications the esteem that they deserved. The polytechnics were given very little in the way of governmental guidance on this. The DES, for all the energy that had been put into establishing the sector, had not laid out with clarity or authority the nature of the higher education that they were to provide. The White Paper of 1966 was, observed one commentator, little more than a statement of intent 'and was inadequate in both educational and institutional terms' (Nixon 1987: 58). But the DES lacked the power to complete its policy objectives (Salter and Tapper 1994: 134). Some polytechnic directors sought to establish a particular philosophy: for example, Brosan at East London (aided by Tyrrell Burgess), Lindop at Hatfield and Eric Robinson in his manifesto volume, *The New Polytechnics*. All tried to consolidate a polytechnic ethos that maintained a plurality of levels of further and higher education provision, delivering a range of vocational and applied studies through a variety of modes of delivery. But without the DES giving a lead on academic planning, it was argued by Pratt and Burgess, the polytechnics would inevitably 'undermine the policy that they are meant to express' (1974: 109). An academic drift, as Pratt and Burgess termed it, was perhaps inevitable, as polytechnics moved towards replicating the universities. As Hughes points out:

> The official statements in the 1960s contain only general aspirations which governments in the 1970s and 1980s did not then elaborate or develop. Notoriously, the higher education policies of British governments have been characterized by pragmatic responses to political purposes, and not by logic, clarity and educational vision. So, the polytechnics can be seen as an attempt to rationalize and strengthen the higher education then provided in a large number of different kinds of local authority colleges by concentrating that provision in a few academically stronger and more efficient institutions ... crucially [these] would remain under local, and latterly, national government control. It is only recently that government has attempted to define the purposes of higher education, and then tentatively and, some would say, incoherently.
>
> (Hughes 1998: 89)

There was, however, one strong directing force that was able to impose some coherence and distinction to the public sector provision. The CNAA was not subject to the pressures of the individual polytechnics and local authorities. It was able to establish a clearer set of principles for course direction and management and for access to courses, than was the DES (Silver 1990).

The AFE pool persisted to the late 1970s, at which time the government set up a committee of enquiry chaired by Gordon Oakes which recommended a National Advisory Body (Oakes 1978). The pool was now to be cash-limited by the Treasury. However, the incentive to expand student numbers remained: the only way to get more cash now was for an institution to increase in size faster than other institutions. Meanwhile, the spending cuts of the early 1980s not only capped the AFE pool: they also gave 15 per cent less money overall to higher education. The university sector, through the UGC, was to exercise its prerogative of semi-independence and to maintain 'the unit of resource' – the hypothetical sum spent on each student – by cutting the number of students recruited. The argument – that this was the only way to maintain quality – met with government disapproval and meant that the polytechnic sector moved to become the major provider in higher education.

Expansion of the higher education system took place at twice the rate in the polytechnic system as it did in the university sector. By 1978 the division between the universities and the polytechnic sector was 52:48. By 1985, this had shifted to 48:52.

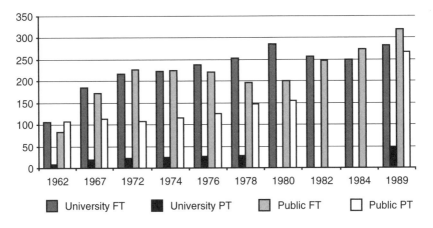

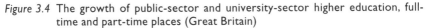

Figure 3.4 The growth of public-sector and university-sector higher education, full-time and part-time places (Great Britain)

Source: From Department for Education 1991

Note
Part-time data not shown for 1980, 1982, 1984

Figure 3.4 shows this graphically. Note the decline in the public sector provision in the 1976–80 period (noted above as being the result of the rapid contraction of the colleges of education in this period). This is followed by a period of dramatic growth for the public sector, while at the same time the universities, through their policy of maintaining the unit of resource, contract in size in the early 1980s.

Finally, note the position of part-time students: almost all have always been concentrated in the public sector institutions. At the time of Robbins (1962), they form more than half the students in the sector: in the dash for academic growth that followed the establishment of the CNAA, the numbers of part-time students stagnate until the late 1970s. From this point, they begin to grow in numbers substantially – being located in the 'other' (non-college of education) institutions, the part-time numbers are unaffected by the closures and contractions in teacher education, and they gradually regain their significant position in the sector by the late 1980s.

Class imbalance in the recruitment of students

The logic of 'the pool of ability' might have suggested that the only way that this expansion might have been accomplished would have been through a system-atic expansion of the groups known to be under-represented in the sector – women, and students from manual backgrounds. If there was some innate pool, surely the non-manual male pool would by now have been fully utilized, and the enormous, unexpected and unplanned-for increase that was taking place must have been tapping into those pools of ability that had not yet been exploited? A policy for increased access for under-represented groups did take form in the late 1970s; however, its roots were not egalitarian but financial.

Education: A Framework for Expansion (DES 1972) set out ambitious plans for the age participation index to rise to 22 per cent by 1981. Despite a large planned fall in teacher education recruitment (because of the over-supply of teachers), from 114,000 student places to between 60,000 and 70,000, it was estimated that the total student body could rise to 750,000 within a decade, with the increase divided equally between the university and the public sector. 'The only problem was that the department did not have the direct power to implement its proposed policies', as Salter and Tapper observed (1994: 134). But the birth rate was now falling, and the number of 18-year-olds would fall fairly dramatically after 1982.

This was to present a particular problem, as a DES discussion paper set out (Oakes 1978). The age participation index had been stagnant at around 14 per cent from 1971 to 1978: the rising number of 18 year olds had, to an extent, obscured this. The DES set out three possible projections for the next 15 years, based on achieving, by that date, age participation indices of 15 per cent (the low variant), 21 per cent (the high variant) or 18 per cent (the median). Each of these would mean a fall in student numbers – even the high variant would lead to a fall after 1988 of 70,000 places. The low variant would see the fall beginning in the early 1980s, with numbers falling to 1972 levels by 1992. This, the discussion paper observed, assumed that existing recruitment policies continued: these might change – for example 'the system itself might reach out to embrace different types of students and to meet fresh needs, such as that of recurrent or continuing education' (ibid.: 3). The problems of expansion in higher education to be followed by contraction would be great. Buildings would in time need to be disposed of, or made redundant, and 'public money would inevitably be spent on capital provision for some short-term purposes'. More difficult would be issues of staffing: the age profile of the higher education teaching force was skewed towards the under 35-year-olds and there would inevitably be very heavy redundancy costs. Even if significant numbers could be shed over a short period of time, the impact on career development and promotion prospects would make recruitment difficult.

The discussion paper suggested some solutions: there need not be a fall in student recruitment 'if social and economic requirements brought significant changes in the pattern and composition of the student body' (ibid.: 8). There was, it suggested,

> the possibility of taking positive steps as a matter of social policy to encourage participation by children of manual workers to approach more closely the level of participation by children of non-manual workers ... while it may be difficult to point to any particular measures

> which would have a swift and significant impact on participation ... it is
> at least possible that participation by this group will by the 1990s be as
> much affected by the gathering impact of policies in the fields of housing,
> health and the social services generally as much as by educational poli-
> cies. ... . Comprehensive reorganisation [in schools will mean] ... no
> children will be educated in institutions which, by their status, nature
> and organisation, are apt to cut off their pupils from higher education
> opportunities. In the climate which reorganisation will have created,
> higher education may be made a more attractive proposition for young
> people from poorer home backgrounds.
>
> (DES 1978: 8–9)

The proposition was being put to the higher education institutions that if
they wished to avert the severe disruptions that a fall in student numbers
would entail, they would have to consider 'what measures might be found
to extend participation on a broader social basis so as to avert a demo-
graphically-linked decline in student numbers at the end of the 1980s?'
(ibid.: 10).

The CNAA offered the public-sector colleges a particular coherent set of
policy options to increase access along the lines suggested by the DES. The
Council

> consistently emphasized the importance of the development of provision
> for non-standard and mature students, and has emphasized the need for
> its institutions to take advantage of the opportunity offered by the
> CNAA's liberal regulations on mature students.
>
> (Silver 1990: 261)

These principles and regulations were explicitly formulated to extend access
to a much wider range of students. Most polytechnics took advantage of this,
admitting mature students (post-21) without two A levels, or developing
Access courses for students to lead them into specific higher education
programmes. Part-time courses, the recognition of experiential or prior
learning as a qualification for admission and the recognition and acceptance
(through credit accumulation schemes) of work-based learning: all contributed to widening participation. By 1976, a third of all students admitted to
the CNAA degree courses were over 21.

The effects of this on the class distribution were noticeable, though not
great. Halsey *et al.* (1980) have pointed out that the middle classes tend to
take up a greater number of higher education places as the system expands,
even though their rate of growth is somewhat lower than that of the working
class. Figure 3.4 shows the distribution of the social classes for 18-year-olds
in 1971 in the first bar, followed by the distribution of the classes in the 1961

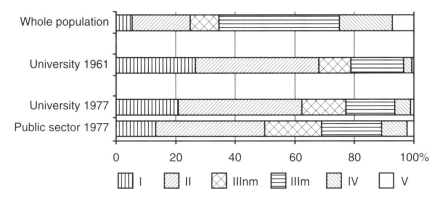

Figure 3.5 Social-class distribution in universities (1961 and 1977) and public-sector higher education (1977), compared with distribution in population

Source: Robbins 1963b, Appendix 1 pp.39–40; UCCA (1979); OPS (1978)

university population (bar 2). The overwhelming domination of social classes I and II is very evident.

The third and fourth bars show the social-class distribution in higher education in 1977. The university sector shows very distinct moves towards a more balanced intake (though it is still very far from replicating the distribution in the population as a whole). The public-sector colleges show that they have recruited, compared with the university sector, more students in social classes IIIn, IIInm, IV and V, and fewer in classes I and II. But half the public-sector student population is still from the upper two classes, who comprise only 25 per cent of the population as a whole (Figure 3.5).

Was this the result of the CNAA and polytechnic sector's access policies? This is impossible to answer directly; however, we can gain some insight by examining the class composition of the public-sector colleges before the post-Robbins developments and comparing this to the distribution later. It is also possible to differentiate the polytechnic students by mode of course. Figure 3.6 does this: the first bar again shows the distribution of the 18-year-old population by social class, and the second bar the distribution by class of those studying for A levels at age 18 in 1974 (England only): 60 per cent of them are in social classes I and II.

The next set of four bars shows the distribution by social class in the various sectors of higher education in 1961. It is noteworthy how very different the distributions are for the three non-university groups. Full-time courses were more likely to be middle class (I, II and IIIn), and part-time courses were very distinctly dominated by social class IIIm. Teacher training was somewhat between the two. The final set of three bars shows the social-class distribution in the polytechnic sector in 1972. There had been a distinct incursion by middle-class students into the sector, for degree-level work,

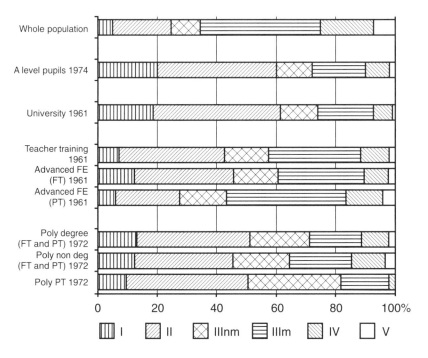

Figure 3.6 Social-class distribution in public-sector higher education (1961 and 1972), compared with distribution in population

Source: As Figure 3.5

non-degree level work and for part-time study. Of course, at the same time there had been a very large growth in the overall size of the sector, so that the 1972 college population was much larger than the 1961 population. More working-class students were in public-sector higher education (and university education) in 1972 than in 1961, and the participation ration for these social classes had also increased – but not at the same rate that the middle classes had increased.

Academic drift in the early stages of the development of polytechnics was also accompanied by social-class drift: they were moving towards a university social profile, while, at the same time, the universities were moving towards a polytechnic social profile. Social convergence was matching the academic convergence.

Changes in higher education structures

The government rhetoric on access changed as the Conservatives gained power in 1980. Discourses of disadvantage and social exclusion were largely muted: virtually silenced in the case of social class and in terms of the ethnic minorities addressed on a sporadic basis in response to outbreaks of urban unrest, such as in Brixton in 1980. Gender discrimination was more openly acknowledged and addressed. *The Development of Higher Education into the 1990s* (DES 1985) had generally rather different preoccupations: the relatively poor level of comparative national economic growth, which was ascribed to the low numbers of students qualifying in science, engineering and technology, the alleged anti-business bias of the higher education institutions (particularly the universities), and the lack of links between higher education and industry, business and commerce. Even so, the White Paper found it necessary to recommend the need for greater access for mature students: 'some universities should be making a more extensive commitment' (ibid.: 18). There was also some commendation of steps to allow non-standard entry. There should be 'a reasonable degree of openness for late developers, and for those who for whatever reason did not enter higher education earlier, while ensuring that academic rigour and standards are maintained' (ibid.: 27). Both of these were widespread in the polytechnics, less so in the university sector.

The eclipse of the local authorities

Two years later, in 1987, the public higher education sector was removed from all local authority control. A Polytechnic and Colleges Funding Council, in parallel with a Universities Funding Council, was to provide public funding for what would from now on be independent institutions, owning their own assets. The government commended the polytechnics' contribution to the growth in higher education over the previous eight years – the growth had been at three times the rate of the 1970s, and 'virtually all of this major increase in full-time student numbers has taken place in the polytechnics and colleges sector of higher education' (DES 1987: 5). The age participation index was to rise to between 15.8 and 18.5 per cent by 1999, and this increase was based on the continued increase in women students and also access students. Numbers in this latter category were 'to accommodate students with a wider range of academic and practical experience than before, many of whom will not have the traditional qualifications for entry' (ibid.: 9).

Pratt suggests that 'if there was a failure of the polytechnic policy, it was in the arrangements for the governance of the institutions' (1997: 303). Local control was central to the idea of polytechnics at their inception, but LEAs did not – or could not – direct and shape their polytechnics' academic direction. The National Advisory Body removed one swathe of local authority control and the 1988 incorporation under the Polytechnics and Colleges Funding Council completed this. Free of the direct academic control of the CNAA and of the interference of LEAs, nationally funded, university status was inevitable.

The end of the binary policy

In 1991, yet another White Paper, *Higher Education: A New Framework*, was published. The binary policy was ended: all polytechnics, and a number of other colleges, were to be granted university status, and would have the power to award their own degrees. The CNAA was to be wound up, its mission accomplished.

What did the polytechnics achieve? Robbins held that they moved selection into tertiary education at the same time that comprehensives began phasing it out of secondary schooling. The binary policy institutionalized a division between academic knowledge and vocational competence. The protagonists of the polytechnics suggested that they were populist institutions, that democratized higher education and made it accessible, linked to the real world and to local communities and their needs. And while on the one hand advocates such as Tyrrell Burgess could warn of polytechnics' 'academic drift' towards the universities, he also pointed out that the universities had also undergone vocational drift, to the point that they had become polytechnics (Burgess 1999).

On the other hand, some have argued that there was from the outset a degree of commonality between the two sectors. Fowler (1982; quoted in Pratt 2001: 3) suggested that although there were nominally two sectors 'with distinct purposes, served by different methods of funding and control', the division did not correspond with reality. Universities had vocational courses, while fine arts courses – distinctly un-vocational – were largely located in polytechnics. There was no real functional distinction between the institutions: unlike the system of other countries, both offered undergraduate, postgraduate and doctoral degrees. From the start, polytechnics were more like universities than their overseas equivalents.

Pratt suggests that 'The British polytechnics were a success, yet the binary system was dismantled. In Britain, as in many other [countries], there has been convergence of sectors, "blurring the boundaries" as the OECD (1991) put it. Non-university institutions acquire the characteristics of universities, universities acquire some characteristics of polytechnics' (Pratt 2001: 1).

The polytechnics expanded student numbers at twice the rate of the universities. They were highly successful in recruiting mature women students and students from ethnic minorities, less so in widening opportunities for those from working-class backgrounds (Blackburn and Jarman 1993). The proportion of students on part-time courses fell from three-quarters in 1969 to one-third in 1991. At their inception, two-thirds of polytechnic students were on courses of below degree standard; at their ending, only one-quarter were on such courses. With the CNAA, the polytechnics made major curriculum transformations in higher education: honours degree subjects in vocational disciplines, modularization, credit accumulation, franchising and access courses.

Toby Weaver, one of the original architects of the binary system, reflected on its demise:

> I have been amazed that a policy which I helped to establish in 1965 survived almost unchanged in the face of continuous opposition, and disparagement, largely from vice-chancellors and from all the traditional higher education folk. ... In order to cope with modernism and the technological revolution most of the universities have already taken on many of the defining characteristics of the polytechnics in order to compete with them. They are slowly understanding how to provide access to mature students and to students without proper A-level qualifications and they are introducing a wide range of vocational courses.
>
> (Weaver 1994)

The changes that took place between 1988 and 1993, when the new universities were incorporated, committed the government to another wave of expansion in higher education, on a scale not seen before (see Figure 3.1). The age participation index rose in a dramatic fashion (Figure 3.7).

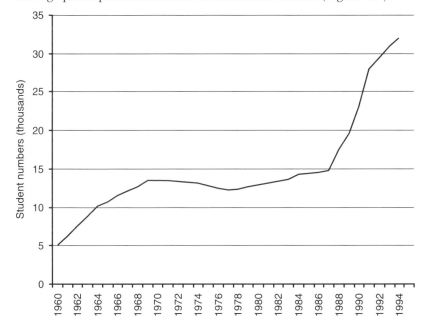

Figure 3.7 Higher education age participation index

Source: From Dearing 1997: Chart 3.5

Note
Initial entrants to full-time higher education courses for the first time (a number of caveats apply to the definitions used over various periods)

There was no apparent consideration of the long-term funding implications of such an expansion: there had been some changes in student support funding, where a proportion of the means-tested maintenance grant was replaced by student loans, at a low rate of interest, repayable on an income-contingent basis. Although this probably had an effect on some potential students' decisions about entering higher education, the fiscal effects on the total costs of higher education were negligible (see Chapter 8 for a more extended discussion of this). Universities were expected to absorb some of the increased costs, through what were termed 'efficiency gains' and student income per head fell over an extended period of time (Figure 3.8). The funding mechanisms imposed by the Funding Councils (directed by the Secretary of State) did not allow for universities or polytechnics to maintain the unit of resource by cutting numbers.

Cynics might suggest that the Conservative government of the early 1990s had no expectation of winning the election due in 1992 and, thus, had no real interest in a strategy to secure the funding needed for the inevitable additional costs of this expansion.

Unexpectedly returned to office in May 1992, the Major government eventually recognized the need for some longer term investigation into the nature and funding of higher education, and of what size it might eventually become. There had been no overall review of the sector since Robbins, more than 30 years before. Moreover, there was a dearth of information about students in higher education: there were no consistent data about all students from the 1960s to the 1990s (Dearing 1997: para. 3.4). The 1991 White Paper had led to the establishment of the Higher Education Statistics Agency

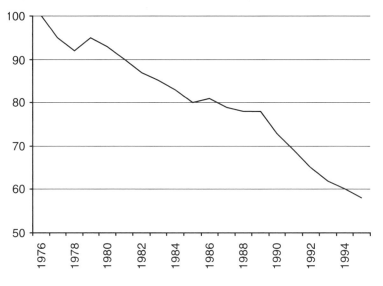

Figure 3.8 Index of public funding per student in higher education 1976–95
Source: from Dearing 1997: Chart 3.16

(HESA). National data on individual students, who were assigned unique student identifier numbers for the first time, was beginning to become available from the mid-1990s (Ramsden 2001). The Higher Education Funding Council for England (another outcome of the Act following the White Paper) reported in 1996 that data on the socio-economic background of students was consistently poor, 'difficult to collect and full of caveats' (HEFCE 1996: 23). Robertson and Hillman, commissioned by the Dearing Inquiry to report on widening participation from lower socio-economic groups, admitted

> We know practically nothing system-wide about part-time students, nor about the socio-economic profile of older students. In short, the data contains material absences on 33 per cent of the total HE population which studies part-time, and on 50 per cent of the HE population which is now entering at ages above 21.
>
> (Robertson and Hillman 1997: para. 1.1)

A committee of inquiry was appointed in 1995, to be chaired by Sir Ron Dearing. It was to report on how to maximize participation in higher education, while maintaining diversity and equality, enhancing teaching and learning, and recommend a student support system that was 'fair and transparent'. The terms of reference were both wide-ranging and vague: one of the key requirements was that the report was to be made in the summer of 1997, significantly after the last possible date for the general election that was due that year. Both major political parties had agreed that it would be in their mutual interests not to have to respond to such a major review of higher education in the period immediately preceding an election.

As part of their work, the committee commissioned studies on a wide range of topics, including on access for students from lower socio-economic groups (Robertson and Hillman 1997) and on ethnic minorities and women (Coffield and Vignoles 1997). Table 3.3 summarizes the principal conclusions of the inquiry.

The committee's report set out what it called 'a vision of the learning society'. The Robbins Committee principles were broadly endorsed again, but there was also a significant move towards defining an instrumental relationship between the higher education institutions and society and the economy.

> At the heart of our vision of higher education is the free-standing institution, which offers teaching to the highest level in an environment of scholarship and independent enquiry. But, collectively and individually, these institutions are becoming ever more central to the economic well-being of the nation, localities and individuals. There is a growing bond of interdependence, in which each is looking for much from the other. That interdependence needs to be more clearly recognized by all the participants.
>
> (Dearing 1997: para. 1.22)

Table 3.3 Principal recommendations of the National Committee of Inquiry into Higher Education (Dearing), 1997

Area	Summary of recommendations	Chapter: recommendation
Long-term strategy	• Respond to increased demand for HE • Expand sub-degree work: lift cap on full-time sub-degree at once • Lift cap on full-time degree places in 2–3 years	6:1
Access	• Prioritize funding to widening participation • Explore low expectations and achievement in progress to HE • Pilot enrolment projects in disadvantaged localities	7:2 7:3 7:4
Student funding	• Allow students access to social security benefits • Double access funds • Fund institutions to support disabled students	7:5 7.6
Lifelong learning	• Collect data about progress on this	7:7
Teaching and learning	• Focus teaching strategies on promoting students' learning • Examine staffing roles as ICT develops	8:8 8:9
Staff development	• Train teaching staff • Establish an institute for teaching and learning for staff development	8:13 8:14
Course development, student monitoring	• Review courses to balance breadth and depth • Increase work experience opportunities • Chart individual student achievement and progress • Introduce framework for HE qualifications	8:16 8:17, 18 8:19 10:22
Quality assurance	• Quality Assurance Agency to monitor franchising arrangements • QAA to introduce National Codes of Practice • QAA to benchmark threshold standards for qualifications	10:23 10:24 10:25
Research	• Establish an Arts and Humanities Research Council • Introduce postgraduate training in professional skills • Evaluate and fund inter-disciplinary research • Include international members on RAE panels	11:29 11:31 11.32 11:33
Local links	• Institutions should adopt a regional and local role with local enterprises	12:36–12:40
ICT	• ICT should play a major part, with careful management and development • Copyright should be simplified for teaching purposes	13:41 13:43

	• All students should have network access, and their own portable computer by 2005	13:46
Staff pay	• An independent review committee for staff pay and conditions	14:50
Mission	• A diversity of institutional mission ... should continue to be an important element ... [and be] reflected in the funding arrangements for institutions	16:61
Titles	• Maintain existing criteria for university status	16:63
	• Control use of title 'University College'	16:65
Growth	• Priority of growth in sub-degree work should be in FE colleges	16:67
Students' maintenance and fee support	• Review student support levels annually relative to prices and to earnings	17:70
	• Target funding on following students, rather than block support	17:72
	• Waive tuition fees for part-time students who are seeking work or caring for families	20:76
	• Introduce income-contingent repayment of support for fees and living cost support	20:78
	• Students should pay c. 25% of costs of HE through income-contingent repayments	20:79
	• Establish a Student Support Agency to assess, means-test, give support to students and pay tuition changes to institutions	20:83
Further reviews	• A further review of HE in 2002, and then 2012 and every ten years	22:88

Source: Dearing 1997 (Summary of recommendations)

The four main purposes of education, defined by Robbins in 1963 (see Chapter 2) were elaborated:

- For individuals to develop capabilities to the higher potential throughout life, so they grow intellectually, are equipped for work, contribute to society, and achieve personal fulfilment
- To increase knowledge and understanding, for its own sake and to apply beneficially to the economy and society
- To serve the knowledge-based economy, locally and nationally
- To play a major role in shaping a democratic, civilized, inclusive society.

(Dearing 1997: para. 5.11)

How inclusive had the higher education system become since Robbins? Figure 3.9 shows the changes in middle-class and working-class participation in higher education since the 1940s. Participation rates for both have shifted substantially. Halsey (1993) again observed that, just as he and his colleagues had shown of the growth in the 1960s (Halsey *et al.* 1980), the incremental growth in numbers was greatest for the middle class.

The particular growth of the early 1990s was highlighted by Robertson and Hillman (1997). Within the five years 1991–95, those in socio-economic class I had increased their participation rate from 55 per cent to 79 per cent – a growth of 43 per cent. The growth of the other socio-economic groups was also great – the increase for socio-economic class V, from 6 per cent to 12 per cent, was a doubling in size, for example. In terms of expectations, higher education had now become the normal rite of passage of a social class I young person, and was still only the exceptional route for just an eighth of those in social class V. Pratt (1997) had claimed that the polytechnic contribution had been to open up higher education to disadvantaged students. This may be true for certain minority ethnic groups, but has become increasingly less true for those from the lower socio-economic classes. Figure 3.10 shows the moves of the early 1990s in more detail.

The data collected for the Dearing Inquiry show that the polytechnics (now the '1992 universities') had, by the early 1990s, achieved a smaller proportion of working-class students than ever before. Figure 3.11 brings together some data shown above in Figures 3.5 and 3.6 (adjusted to show both degree and non-degree advanced courses) with data in Robertson and Hillman's (1997) report for the inquiry.

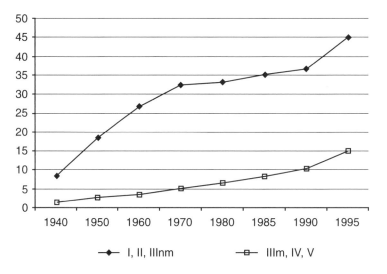

Figure 3.9 Changes in participation indices by different socio-economic groups, 1940s–
90s

Source: Robertson and Hillman 1997 (based on Halsey *et al.* 1980 and evidence to Dearing 1997 from DfES)

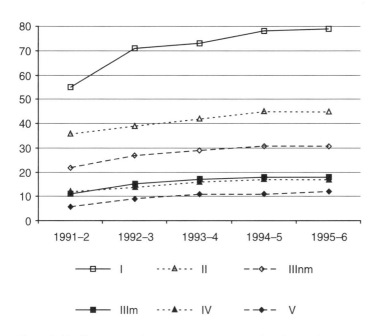

Figure 3.10 Changes in the age participation index for each socio-economic class, 1991–5 (England)

Source: Based on Robertson and Hillman 1997: Table 1.2

As the evidence to Dearing concluded, it is hard to claim that the former polytechnics were materially influencing patterns of under-representation of the working-class groups.

> Despite their roots in many inner cities, and their traditions of catering for locally-based and 'second-chance' students, the achievements of the 1992 universities lend little support to the view that these institutions can be left to get on with the job of widening participation to the groups in question. While such institutions will no doubt continue to fulfil the terms of their Missions by addressing the *individual* representation of students from lower socio-economic groups, they do not seem to be able to make inroads into improving the *collective* representation of these particular groups.
>
> (Robertson and Hillman 1997: para. 1.16)

The Dearing Committee report was published in June 1997, just after a general election had returned a Labour government to power. The immediate reaction of the new government to Dearing's major recommendations

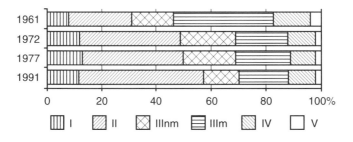

Figure 3.11 Public-sector higher education: changes in social-class composition 1961–91

Sources: As Figure 3.6 and Robertson and Hillman 1997

on student finance was to reject them. Instead, they proposed that all students would be eligible for a loan for all their subsistence needs (maintenance grants would end) and that all students would be liable for a tuition fee (some poorer students only paying a fraction, or none of this). These proposals were subsequently radically revised for Scotland by the Scottish Executive. These changes, and their implications, are discussed further in Chapter 9.

The other responses to Dearing, particularly as they affect student recruitment and finance, are traced in the chapters that follow. But a major exposition of the new government's policy on higher education was made by the Secretary of State, David Blunkett, some months into office. He gave this address at the University of Greenwich: an institution which had developed out of Thames Polytechnic in 1992, which had in turn developed out of Woolwich Polytechnic in 1969. Woolwich was where Tony Crosland had announced the binary policy. Blunkett outlined that he thought that universities must adapt and change to stay ahead in the global market and how the government wanted to combine greater diversification with excellence. He further suggested how the role of higher education in sustaining economic competitiveness and social justice should be developed:

> A new national initiative is needed to maximize Britain's chances of success in this global environment. The Higher Education Funding Council for England will bring forward proposals for a new collaborative virtual venture – a consortium of 'e-universities'. We want to create a new partnership between universities and the private sector which will develop a novel means of distance learning and exploit the new information and communication technologies … .
>
> If we are to become a leading knowledge based economy we must create new routes into higher education and new forms of provision.

Our historic skills deficit lies in people with intermediate skills – including highly-qualified technicians. We have to develop new higher education opportunities at this level, orientated strongly to the employability skills, specialist knowledge and broad understanding needed in the new economy. We therefore intend to create new two-year Foundation Degrees to help meet our objective that half of all young people benefit from higher education by the age of 30. Last year some 80,000 students with two or more A levels, or the vocational equivalent, did not enter higher education directly. That's more than one in three of those who gained qualifications at this standard.

The Foundation Degree will offer a new vocationally-focused route into higher education. It will be academically rigorous and will provide an accessible and flexible building block for lifelong learning and future career success, drawing together further and higher education and the world of work. .... . For students wishing to continue their learning, there will be the opportunity to progress to an honours degree with only one-and-a-third extra years of study.

Blunkett (2000)

There is a fearful symmetry in all this. Both Robbins and Dearing were established by Conservative governments, with bipartisan agreement, towards the end of long periods in office – in Robbins' case, for 13 years, in Dearing's for 18 years. In both cases, a report was published within ten months of the election that brought about a Labour administration. In both cases, the Labour governments, fairly swiftly, rejected the principal recommendations of the reports. And in both cases, the Secretary of State set out their alternative vision of higher education at Woolwich/Greenwich.

Chapters 2 and 3 have traced the growth of higher education in the UK from the point in 1900 when it was only pursued by a tiny minority of young people, to the point in 1999 when over a third of all young people were already participating in higher education, and this proportion was planned to shortly rise to a half. Through all this expansion there has been a persistent, consistent and continuing tendency to recruit students from the middle classes. The size of the middle class has itself increased, but this is a relatively minor explanatory factor. Over the same period, it has become acknowledged that possession of higher education qualifications confers powers and privileges. Graduates are differentially incorporated into civil society, and benefit materially and in status.

There are many possible causes for this phenomenon. In the past, first women, and then minority ethnic group members, were largely excluded from higher education. Both categories are now much better represented in higher education as a whole, albeit rather unevenly across the various institutions and subjects in higher education. But the disproportionate recruitment of middle-class students, and the parallel comparative exclusion of those from working-class origins, remain. The change has been that the social differentiation has now become so marked, because of the increase in the overall proportion going into higher education, that we now risk universities becoming a major fault line across our society.

Chapter 4

Participation and potential participation in UK higher education

Robert Gilchrist, David Phillips and Alistair Ross

Who participates and who does not?

Chapters 2 and 3 have charted the marked increase in participation in higher education in the United Kingdom over the past half-century. This increase has been particularly great since 1990. The data of the Universities and Colleges Admissions Service (UCAS) (UCAS 1999 and UCAS 2002) show a 23 per cent increase in full-time home acceptances to degree courses in the period 1994–2000, with a corresponding 19 per cent increase in HND acceptances. This is despite the reductions observed in 1997–8 of 3.5 per cent and 1.5 per cent, for degree and HND courses respectively, this being the year prior to the introduction of fees. Part-time students have also increased in number, from 131,000 starting courses in 1994–5 to 196,000 starting in 1999–2000. The overall age participation index (API) – the percentage of the age cohort who take part in higher education – has increased steadily over the last six decades, from 2 per cent in 1940 and 8.5 per cent in 1962, to 32 per cent in 1995 (Dearing 1997) and 36 per cent in 2000.

One approach to understanding the nature of participation is to identify the social characteristics of those who do not participate and then to explore why they might not be represented in the higher education population.

First, consider gender. Women now appear to participate at the same overall rate as men. Yet certain subjects, for example, physics, engineering and chemistry, appear to have an over-representation of men, while other subjects such as nursing and education have an over-representation of women. It is only in some subjects and in the higher education population as a whole that we have a gender balance that broadly represents the overall population. This balance is itself relatively recent; it was only in 1992 that men and women were recruited in equal numbers. The division between subjects is not static. In medicine and dentistry, for example, there were only 10 per cent women students in the 1960s; now there are 53 per cent (HESA 1999 entry).

Second, there is the influence of social class. Table 4.1 shows the percentage of 21–30-year-olds from each social class who have achieved

Table 4.1 Percentages and numbers of 21–30-year-olds by social class who have higher
education qualifications as their highest level of attainment, 2001

Social class		% of each socio-economic group with HE qualifications	Numbers of each socio-economic group having HE qualifications (000s)
I	Professional	87.2	382
II	Intermediate	57.1	1,092
IIInm	Skilled non-manual	23.6	430
IIIm	Skilled manual	8.4	99
IV	Partly skilled	10.7	102
V	Unskilled	6.1	12
Total		28.3	2,117

Source: Quarterly Labour Force Survey, December 1996–February 2001 (OPS)

higher education qualifications (note that these will be lower than the
percentages who have enrolled for higher education due to withdrawals).
The participation rate is seen to vary greatly according to social class.

The most precise measure of socio-economic group on admission is
provided by the data UCAS collect on admissions to universities. UCAS only
records full-time and sandwich students (we refer to both of these as full-
time, for convenience). The UCAS data (Table 4.2 and 4.3) clearly show that
particular social classes appear to take advantage of full-time higher education opportunities at different periods in their lives. Taking the 2000 full-
time entry figures of UK-based students, Table 4.2 indicates the percentage
of students starting their degree or HND course by age, by social class at the
point of application and as a cumulative percentage.

Table 4.2 Percentage of total of full-time higher education participants from each social
class who are enrolled in higher education at different ages

Social class		Age on admission											N	
		<18	18	19	20	21	22	23	24	25–29	30–39	40+	Total	(000s)
I	Professional	3.7	60.1	24.5	6.6	1.0	0.5	0.3	0.2	0.7	0.9	0.6	100	42.1
II	Intermediate	2.9	54.1	23.8	7.2	2.5	1.0	0.7	0.6	2.4	3.2	1.7	100	122.3
IIInm	Skilled non-manual	2.3	43.9	20.9	7.2	4.7	3.4	2.3	1.7	5.5	5.9	2.1	100	40.3
IIIm	Skilled manual	2.7	49.8	24.9	8.7	3.1	1.4	0.9	0.7	2.9	3.6	1.3	100	45.1
IV	Partly skilled	2.4	42.2	21.9	8.4	4.6	3.1	2.0	1.7	5.4	6.2	2.2	100	30.5
V	Unskilled	1.9	43.0	26.0	11.3	4.6	1.8	1.7	1.3	3.5	3.6	1.4	100	5.5

Source: UCAS 2000

Table 4.3 Cumulative percentage of full-time students admitted by each age

Social class	Cumulative percentage admitted up to and including age										
	<18	18	19	20	21	22	23	24	25–29	30–39	40+
I Professional	3.7	63.8	88.2	94.8	96.7	97.2	97.5	97.7	98.5	99.4	100
II Intermediate	2.9	57.0	80.8	88.0	90.5	91.5	92.2	92.8	95.2	98.3	100
IIInm Skilled non-manual	2.3	46.2	67.1	74.3	79.0	82.4	84.7	86.3	91.8	97.7	100
IIIm Skilled manual	2.7	52.4	77.3	86.0	89.2	90.6	91.5	92.2	95.1	98.7	100
IV Partly skilled	2.4	44.6	65.5	74.9	79.5	82.6	84.6	86.3	91.7	97.8	100
V Unskilled	1.9	45.0	71.0	82.3	86.8	88.6	90.3	91.6	95.1	98.6	100

80% admitted   90% admitted

Source: UCAS 2000

Entrants from the professional and intermediate classes take up higher education very largely by the age of 20, while those from skilled non-manual and partly skilled origins tend to enrol significantly later, some taking into their mid-20s to begin.

The question remains as to how many of those with standard university entry qualifications in each social class group actually go to university. The standard admission criterion to UK universities for students below 21 has basically been the possession of two A-level grades. The following table gives an estimate of the percentage of 21-year-olds (England and Wales) with A/AS level or higher qualifications in 2000 (Table 4.4).

The next table is an approximation to the current situation, based on the Quarterly Labour Force Survey (the QLFS is a large sample of the adult population). In Table 4.5, data have been used for the cohorts who are 21–30 years of age in 2001. The derivation of the table assumes that all the different cohorts participated in HE in the same proportions from 18

Table 4.4 Percentage of those with qualifications at level 3 or above at age 21

Socio-economic group	% of group with degree, A or AS level as highest qualification level at age 21, 2000
Managerial/professional	69
Other non-manual	65
Skilled manual	46
Semi-skilled manual	39
Unskilled manual	33

Source: Department for Education and Skills (2001c)

Note
The data do not differentiate between numbers of A levels achieved

onwards as do current 18–30-year-olds. Full cohort analysis is not possible with the available data, and this table is included to demonstrate the scale of the situation, not the precise size. Column 2 is an approximation of the starting rate of young entrants to higher education (under 21 on entry). Column 4 shows an estimate of the residual population: those who have not started higher education by the age of 21, and who are therefore theoretically 'available' for higher education – though many may not be qualified (formally or informally) or wishing to study at this level. Column 5 then shows an esti-mate of the percentage of each social class who take up higher education opportunities in their 20s. Again, it is stressed that these figures cannot be seen as other than rough guides as the data for a proper cohort analysis are not available.[1] However, the non-numeric descriptions of the situation – in column 3 for the under-21s, and in column 6 for the 21–30-year-olds – reflect the situation in a general way, indicating the potential scale and location for further increasing entry and access to higher education.

Table 4.5 Approximate estimates of the potential for mature student participation in higher education by socio-economic class

Social class	Under 21		21–30		
	% of group starting HE (nearest 5%)	Level of participation	% group 'available' for HE (nearest 5%)	% of group starting HE (nearest 2%)	Level of participation
I Professional	90	Virtually saturated	10	6	Minimal entry – none left
II Intermediate	55	Fairly well saturated	45	10	Large potential
IIInm Skilled non-manual	20	Poor take up	80	10	entry, with entry qualifications
IIIm Skilled manual	10	Very poor take up	90	2	Very large potential
IV Partly skilled	10		90	4	entry, but largely without 'traditional' qualifications for entry
V Unskilled	5	Minimal take up	95	2	

Sources: See note 2 for detailed explanation of computations

Thus, taking as an example the intermediate group: about 55 per cent of the entire socio-economic group are currently enrolling in higher education before they reach the age of 21. The residual group – 45 per cent of the class at age 21 – is thus 'available' for education (though they might not be qualified to participate, nor might they wish to participate). Some 10 per cent of the socio-economic group will enrol in higher education by the age of 30 – so about 35 per cent will not have engaged in higher education by the age of 31.

The expansion of participation in higher education has been achieved by differential enrolment from different social classes. While all groups have increased their level of participation, the higher groups have substantially increased their participation, with the participation of other groups being more modest. Currently, most of those who will become students, in all social classes, start their higher education studies before 21. The percentage of those with A/AS level qualifications at age 21 achieving higher education qualifications by age 30 from social classes IIInm, IIIm, IV and V is between 18 per cent and 36 per cent (Table 4.6). This contrasts with social classes I and II, of whom nearly 90 per cent of those with entry qualifications at age 21 end up with a higher education qualification by age 30.

Socio-economic groups IIInm, IIIm, IV and V thus form the largest potential for expansion in the mature (i.e. over 21 years old) higher education sector. A greater proportion of these groups already enters higher education at 21 or over, although the numbers are still relatively very low. One noteworthy aspect for these social classes, with respect to the potential expansion of mature students, is that after reaching the age of 21 entry qualifications for higher education become considerably more flexible.

The differences in entering university before 21 can be partially explained by differences in levels in attainment between different social classes. There is evidence in the UCAS data of lower rates of application to higher education from those with standard A-level qualifications from

Table 4.6 Achievement of higher education by achievement at 21

Social class		% with at least A or AS levels at 21 (Table 4.4)	% of 21–30-year-olds who have achieved HE qualifications (Table 4.1 Col. 2)	% of those with entry qualifications at 21 who obtain HE qualifications by age 30
I	Professional	69	63.7	92.3
II	Intermediate			
IIInm	Skilled non-manual	65	23.6	36.3
IIIm	Skilled manual	46	8.4	18.2
IV	Partly skilled	39	10.7	27.4
V	Unskilled	33	6.1	18.5

Table 4.7 All subjects: acceptance rate variation by social class

Social class		Percentage of applicants to higher education by social class	Percentage of acceptances by HEIs by social class	Percentage by which number of acceptances exceed or are less than number of applications
I	Professional	13.0	15.4	18.5
II	Intermediate	36.6	37.6	2.7
IIInm	Skilled non-manual	15.6	14.0	−10.3
IIIm	Skilled manual	12.3	11.9	−3.3
IV	Partly skilled	8.6	7.9	−8.1
V	Unskilled	1.9	1.6	−15.8
	Unknown	12.0	11.5	−4.2

Source: House of Commons (2001c) Written Question 148702

socio-economic groups IIInm to V. There is a higher rate of rejection by universities of applicants from these socio-economic groups, particularly in certain subjects (Table 4.7). However, this may be entirely or partially due to differences in entry qualifications, so any conclusions in this respect must be viewed with caution. Indeed, elite universities would claim that they accept as high a percentage of applicants from maintained schools as from the independent sector and that any 'access problem' essentially reflects the lower proportion of suitably qualified applicants from the state sector.

Similar observations may be made of students of minority ethnic background (Table 4.8). The proportion (14.5 per cent, 2000 entry) of minority ethnic students in higher education now exceeds their proportion in the age group as a whole. But this conceals three kinds of significant variation. First, as with the male–female distribution, the proportion of minority ethnic students is not evenly distributed across different subjects of study. Certain subjects appear to attract students of a minority ethnic background – pharmacy, for example – while others appear either not to attract such students, or not to recruit such students. Second, this distribution is not neutral in terms of gender; as in the population at large, a higher proportion (52 per cent) of minority ethnic higher education students are female (HESA 1999 entry). For part-time mode, 54 per cent of minority ethnic undergraduates are women, with a corresponding proportion of 64 per cent for postgraduates. Third, and perhaps most importantly, the various minority ethnic groups are not evenly represented in higher education. Certain groups are over-represented: for example, those of a Chinese, south-east Asian or an Indian background, while others are under-represented, such as those of a Bangladeshi, Turkish or Pakistani background.

Table 4.8 Minority ethnic groups in the British population of normal university age and enrolments in higher education full-time undergraduate courses

| | Total population GB (15–24) | | HE full-time degree 2000 | |
	000s	%	number	%
Black Caribbean	60	0.89	2,609	0.93
Black African	48	0.71	4,604	1.63
Black Other (non mixed)	51	0.75	1,697	0.60
All Black	*159*	*2.35*	*8,910*	*3.16*
Asian Indian	143	2.12	12,253	4.35
Asian Pakistani	115	1.69	6,486	2.30
Asian Bangladeshi	41	0.61	2,051	0.73
Asian Chinese	29	0.43	2,746	0.97
Asian other (non-mixed)	26	0.39	3,453	1.23
Other (non-mixed)	53	0.79	5,112	1.81
All Asian	*354*	*5.24*	*26,989*	*9.58*
All minority ethnic	*580*	*8.57*	*41,011*	*14.55*
White	6351	93.92	222,046	78.79
Total population	*8010*		*18,752*	

Sources: UCAS admission data 2000; Population data for 15–24-year-olds based on QLFS data (as analysed by Schuman 1999)

Who might participate?

The preceding discussion points to marked variations in HE participation between different social groups and by key social characteristics. We have previously indicated how differential participation of males and females has diminished considerably in recent years, although there remain significant pockets of academic subjects which remain dominated by one or other gender. Again, increasing participation rates for students from minority ethnic backgrounds point to some acceleration in representation, though absolute rates remain unequal. Notable, however, is the persistence of a strong and relatively unchanging link between participation and social class, with extremely low numbers of students from the lower socio-economic groups being accepted onto university courses.

The context, then, is one of apparent educational 'exclusion' linked to socially located forms of disadvantage in terms of economic and educational background. How is this situation to change? UK government policy is committed to increasing participation rates to 50 per cent. The aim is to enhance access by widening participation in ways that specifically target potential students from disadvantaged groups, in particular from poorer backgrounds. For such policies to succeed, it becomes important to develop a fuller understanding of factors which may influence the educational choices of potential working-class applicants and their decisions about whether or not to apply to study at university.

The following section explores the role played by such factors, through a statistical modelling of potential working-class participation.[3] We draw on our research over the period 1998–2000 as part of the *Social Class and Widening Participation in Higher Education Project*, based at the University of North London.[4] That study sought to develop a model of potential working-class participants in higher education, through analysis of future plans in relation to HE entry and how planning intentions might be linked to a range of potentially influential factors including demographic characteristics, motivation, attitudes and beliefs about education, and educational qualifications. Data were gathered from a nationally representative quota sample[5] of 1,278 'lower-middle' and 'working-class'[6] adults in England and Wales, interviewed during June 1999, over three consecutive weekly waves of MORI's Omnibus survey. Respondents aged between 16 and 30 years, from social class categories C1, C2, D, E, were asked about their plans and intentions, and their attitudes towards higher education. Information was also gathered on their educational qualifications, sources of encouragement (or discouragement) for continuing with education after the age of 16, as well as standard demographics. A fuller analysis of the data obtained from the survey is presented in Collier *et al.* (2002); we here discuss the main conclusions.

The full UK sample consisted of 44 per cent male and 56 per cent female respondents; 91 per cent were white, with 9 per cent from black and other minority groups. Social class composition was 33 per cent 'lower middle' (C1), 28 per cent 'skilled working' (C2), 21 per cent 'semi- and unskilled working' (D), and 17 per cent 'lowest subsistence level' (E). Within the full sample one in six (17 per cent) had already been or were still attending university. Another one in six respondents (17 per cent) had either applied, was currently applying, or planned to apply to go to university at some time in the future. This left almost six of every ten (59 per cent) who had no plans to go to university and a further six per cent quite interested in going but not likely to apply.

The following discussion focuses on the plans of those respondents in the MORI survey who, as yet, had not participated in higher education. The 'plans' response variable was grouped into the three categories: (i) planning to apply (i.e. firm/definite plans), (ii) may apply and (iii) not planning to go. Eliminating all those respondents who had either participated or were currently attending university, as well as those who had not responded to each of the questions of interest, reduced the number of cases available for analysis to 871.

Table 4.9 Cross-tabulations of 'plans' with social demographics, qualifications and mothers' encouragement (percentages in brackets)

		Plan to go		May go		Not going	
Social class	C1	55	(22.9)	48	(20.0)	137	(57.1)
	C2	38	(13.8)	33	(12.0)	204	(74.2)
	D	20	(9.6)	38	(18.3)	150	(72.1)
	E	15	(10.1)	26	(17.6)	107	(72.3)
Ethnicity	White	107	(13.2)	134	(16.6)	568	(70.2)
	Black	8	(34.8)	3	(13.0)	12	(52.2)
	Asian	11	(34.4)	8	(25.0)	13	(40.6)
	Other	2	(28.6)	0	(0)	5	(71.4)
Gender	Male	53	(14.1)	60	(16.0)	263	(69.9)
	Female	75	(15.2)	85	(17.2)	335	(67.7)
Age	16–18	69	(28.0)	56	(22.8)	121	(49.2)
	19–20	17	(16.2)	15	(14.3)	73	(69.5)
	20–30	42	(8.1)	74	(14.2)	404	(77.7)
Qualifications	≥2 A levels	51	(33.6)	30	(19.7)	71	(46.7)
	HND/≥5 GCSEs	50	(16.7)	61	(20.3)	189	(63.0)
	<5 GCSEs	26	(7.3)	48	(13.4)	283	(79.3)
	No formal	1	(1.6)	6	(9.7)	55	(88.7)
Mothers' encouragement	Strong	91	(29.3)	52	(16.7)	168	(54.0)
	Some	21	(9.6)	53	(24.2)	145	(66.2)
	None/discouraged	16	(4.7)	40	(11.7)	285	(83.6)

Social characteristics

Table 4.9 summarizes relationships between 'plans' and a number of key social characteristics. There is a pronounced association with social class,[7] with a distinct gradient across the social categories and the 'lower middle-class' C1 respondents standing out in terms of potential HE participation. Almost one in four (23 per cent) in the C1 group definitely plan to apply, with a further one in five (20 per cent) saying that they may apply. Of social class C2, only 14 per cent have definite plans to enter HE with another 12 per cent who may go. Social classes D and E are similar with around 10 per cent planning to go, 18 per cent who may go and 72 per cent who say that they are definitely not going.

A clear difference appears between the plans of black and Asian respondents compared with whites, with whites displaying a lower propensity to participate (though numbers of non-white respondents are small and further analysis indicates this difference is largely accounted for by other underlying influences, notably social class). Around one in three black (35 per cent) and

Asian (34 per cent) respondents plan to enter HE, compared with just over one in eight of white respondents (13 per cent).

There is virtually no evidence of an association with gender, with males and females across the sample as a whole reporting similar propensities towards participation and non-participation.

Predictably, participation 'plans' of those outside HE are linked strongly to age, with the 16–18-year-olds showing greatest interest and over 50 per cent indicating they plan definitely or possibly to enter HE. Interest falls away in the older groups, with comparable potential participant figures of 30 per cent for 18–20-year-olds, declining to only 22 per cent among the older 21–30 group.

The importance of prior educational qualifications emerges clearly, with one in three definitely planning to go among those who have two or more A levels and another one in five considering participation as a possibility. There is a sharp contrast here with for respondents who have no formal qualifications, where almost nine out of ten say they definitely plan not to participate. The proportions planning to go decrease consistently from those who already possess appropriate HE entry qualifications (two or more A levels) through to those with no formal qualifications, where only 1.6 per cent plan to participate. It is of interest that even among respondents with two or more A levels (those most likely to participate), there are more who say they will definitely not participate (47 per cent) than who say they plan to go (34 per cent).

Analysis revealed consistent and strong associations between 'plans' to go to university and different sources of encouragement to continue in education past the age of 16. Parents are the most frequently cited source of encouragement, with nearly 40 per cent of those who responded reporting strong encouragement from mothers and 35 per cent from fathers. This compares to 32 per cent for teachers, 25 per cent for career advisers, 15 per cent for friends and 13 per cent for employers. As the figures for 'plans' by 'mothers' encouragement' show, almost 84 per cent of those receiving no encouragement (which includes any who were actively discouraged) are planning not to participate in HE compared to only 54 per cent of those who received strong encouragement. Close to one in three of those who received strong encouragement from mothers plan to participate in HE, dropping to one in ten among those who received mild encouragement and only one in 20 for those who received no encouragement. Of the group actually planning to go to university, 71 per cent reported strong encouragement by mothers and 66 per cent strong encouragement by fathers. Mothers' encouragement and fathers' encouragement are highly correlated, though as 'mothers' encouragement' has the higher incidence it was selected to represent parental effects of this kind in subsequent modelling analysis.

Attitudes to higher education

To explore attitudes towards HE participation, the survey included a series of 15 five-point (strongly agree/strongly disagree) items covering attitudes towards study, the potential value of a degree, perceptions of students and universities, the implications of studying, including potential debt and managing their other responsibilities, and the trade-off between doing a degree or earning money. A further six three-point (agree/disagree) items covered views about their abilities and qualifications, and their experience of accessing information about university courses.[8]

Factor analysis was used to investigate the underlying dimensionality of attitude responses, which enabled definition of a reduced set of attitudinal indicators to be included in subsequent statistical modelling. Six statements were selected to broadly represent attitudes towards HE participation:

- 'I enjoy studying' (referred to as 'enjoy study')
- 'I would rather earn money than go to university' ('rather earn money')
- 'I could better myself by having a degree' ('betterment')
- 'I am sure I have the ability to pass a university degree' ('belief in ability')
- 'My responsibilities would make it difficult for me to do a degree' ('responsibilities')
- 'My school or college gave me information about going to university' ('information').

There is evidence of strong statistical associations ($p < 0.001$) between 'plans' and each of these six indicators. Table 4.10 shows the cross-tabulation of 'plans' with these variables (the five-point items have been reduced to three levels by combining the strongly agree/agree response and the disagree/strongly disagree responses). They reveal very clearly the power of educational beliefs and attitudes as motivational influences upon potential HE participation. Almost half of respondents either planning to apply or who may apply report that they enjoy studying, reflecting positive orientations towards – and presumably experiences of – education and learning. They are more likely to value studying for a degree over earning money, while conversely those who would rather earn money are four times more likely to plan not to go. Potential participants are more likely to view degree study as a source of betterment and personal development, while self-belief in having the required ability to pass a degree is important. Only three out of ten disagreed that their responsibilities would make it difficult for them to study for a degree, and the presence or absence of competing responsibilities is a key factor in decisions. Prior access to information about university is clearly important, with over half disagreeing that their school or college gave them adequate information. Overall, a pattern seems to emerge that combines idealism and valuing of

Table 4.10 Cross-tabulation of 'plans' and attitudinal variables (row percentages in brackets)

		Plan to go		May go		Not going	
Enjoy study	Agree	96	(25.8)	85	(22.9)	191	(51.3)
	Neither agree/disagree	16	(11.5)	31	(22.3)	92	(66.2)
	Disagree	16	(4.4)	29	(8.1)	315	(87.5)
Rather earn	Agree	35	(5.7)	87	(14.0)	498	(80.3)
money	Neither agree/disagree	27	(24.3)	23	(20.7)	61	(55.0)
	Disagree	66	(47.1)	35	(25.0)	39	(27.9)
Betterment	Agree	113	(19.8)	124	(21.7)	334	(58.5)
	Neither agree/disagree	7	(5.1)	14	(10.2)	116	(84.7)
	Disagree	8	(4.9)	7	(4.3)	148	(90.8)
Belief in ability	Agree	121	(23.3)	107	(20.6)	291	(56.1)
	Neither agree/disagree	5	(3.8)	22	(16.5)	106	(79.7)
	Disagree	2	(0.9)	16	(7.3)	201	(91.8)
Responsibilities	Agree	31	(6.3)	79	(16.1)	380	(77.6)
	Neither agree/disagree	14	(13.0)	13	(12.0)	81	(75.0)
	Disagree	83	(30.4)	53	(19.4)	137	(50.2)
Information	Agree	92	(25.1)	68	(18.6)	206	(56.3)
	Neither agree/disagree	1	(2.7)	4	(10.8)	32	(86.5)
	Disagree	35	(7.5)	73	(15.6)	360	(76.9)

education, with important factors of confidence and self-belief, combined with practical considerations involving trade-offs in areas like income and other commitments.

At the same time, the figures underline very clearly the considerable potential that exists for widening participation still further among those respondents who currently say they have no plans to apply to university. Just over half of those who report they enjoy studying have no plans to go, as do close to 60 per cent who believe a degree would be a source of betterment. Again, well over half believe they have the ability to successfully pass a degree yet do not plan to apply; interestingly separate analysis shows that this level of self-belief is present among respondents who actually lack the required HE entrance qualifications.

Discussion so far has focused on simple two-variable associations and one needs to be cautious about reading too much into such results, separated as they are from the much more complex and multivariate process of HE decision-making as a whole. Apparently strong findings can reflect the indirect or accumulated effects of other variables in combination. The next step is to consider how these indicators might work together with other key variables.

Statistical modelling

The primary aim of statistical analysis was to develop a comprehensive model of potential HE participation which explored these multiple background, attitudinal and other key factors, such as qualifications and parental encouragement, working in combination. The method used was that of multinomial logit regression (Aitkin *et al.* 1989) where 'plans' to enter HE is the main variable of interest, with three levels of response category: those with definite plans to apply, those who may possibly apply, and those who have no plans to enter HE. Based on prior analysis, an initial pool of 14 explanatory variables had been identified as potentially significant predictors of 'plans'. These included four background variables, 'social class', 'ethnicity', 'gender', 'age', plus 'qualifications', three 'encouragement' variables (mothers', friends' and teachers' encouragement) and the six attitudinal indicators derived previously.

Because respondents differ systematically in their relationship to the 'standard' age of application and entry to HE (usually 18 in the UK context), two separate modelling exercises were undertaken (i) for the 16–18-year-old age group, who had not yet reached this decision point, and (ii) for the 19–30-year-olds who will have passed this initial entry stage and whose decision-making is of a different order. A further reason for separating the two age groups was the differential relationship each would have with 'qualifications', with many respondents in the younger group not having completed their careers in secondary education and not yet attaining their highest educational qualifications (such as A levels), whereas almost all the older group would have completed this educational stage.

Essentially, the method proceeds by computing log odds ('multinomial logits') for comparing the different levels of the 'plans' variable modelled in terms of all the linear permutations of the explanatory variable categories, a technique which can generate a very high level of dimensionality. Through refinement of the analysis it was possible to reduce the number of predictor variable levels (desirable for computational efficiency) and to eliminate those marginal factors which had no effects on 'plans' for both age groups. These included 'ethnicity' whose effects were largely subsumed by other variables, notably social class.

The strength and direction of the relationships between 'plans' and the various explanatory factors are quantified by their odds ratios. Table 4.11 shows the odds ratios for planning to apply to university as opposed to planning not to go, comparing the extremes of each factor. Thus, in all cases, the odds ratios compare categories (i) and (iii) of the plans variable with the extreme levels of the other factors. For example, the odds ratio comparing 'planning to apply (i)' to 'not planning to go (iii)' for 'mothers' encouragement' for 16–18-year-olds, shows that those who receive strong encouragement are 5.8 times more likely definitely to plan to apply than

Table 4.11 Odds ratios comparing 'Planning to apply' (level i of plans) against 'Planning not to go' (level iii of plans)

Factor	Levels compared	Odds ratio	
		16–18-year-olds	19–30-year-olds
Qualifications	≥2 A levels/No Formal	7.0	5.3
Social class	C1/E	3.8	
Age	16, 17, 18 19–20, 21–22, … , 29–30		
Gender	Female/male		
Ethnicity	White/black/Asian/other		
Mothers' encouragement	Strong/none	5.8	3.0
Friends' encouragement	Strong/none	2.7	
Teachers' encouragement	Strong/none		
Belief in ability	Yes/no	12.1	9.3
Rather earn money	Disagree/agree	27.2	5.0
Enjoy study	Yes/no		10.6
Betterment	Yes/no		11.1
Responsibilities	No/yes		2.7
Information	Yes/no	2.9	

those who receive no encouragement. The absence of an odds ratio indicates no significant effect (equivalent to an odds ratio of 1.0).

Interpretation of the models

Results of the modelling exercise for the 16–18-year-old group are displayed[9] in Figure 4.1. Considering first the background and other non-attitude items, the important role of prior educational qualifications as an influence upon potential HE 'plans' is registered very clearly, even within this largely pre-A-level group. Those with better qualifications are seven times more likely to have firm plans to apply to university (as opposed to not applying) than those with little or no formal qualifications. The determining influence of previous educational achievements is unsurprising, especially given the emphasis that the UK HE entry system currently places upon formal qualifications, and echoes findings from previous research cited, for example, in the Dearing Report on UK higher education (Dearing 1997).[10]

The model confirms the presence of a systematic social class gradient (even within a sample, remember, constrained to the lower middle-class C1 and working-class grades C2, D and E), with the highest propensity to enter higher education amongst social class C1. Respondents from this group are 3.8 times more likely to have definite plans to apply than those

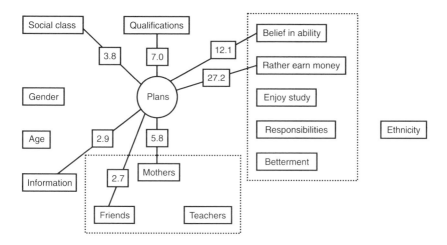

Figure 4.1 Odds ratios for 16–18-year-olds comparing levels as in Table 4.11

from social grades D and E. It is useful to mention at this point that the odds ratios on which this type of model are based operate cumulatively. Thus, for example, a 19–30-year-old respondent from a C1 background with good qualifications is 26.6 (3.8 x 7.0) times more likely to have firm plans to apply to university than someone from a D or E position with no formal qualifications, provided all other factors are at the same levels. Of the other social background factors, age and gender display no separate effects, any influence they may appear to exert being accounted for by more powerful indicators in the model, as is also the case with ethnicity.

Parental encouragement (here represented by mothers' encouragement) emerges as influential, as does the lesser influence of friends' encouragement. Taken together a respondent who receives strong encouragement from both mother and peers to continue their education is over 15 times more likely to plan to enter HE than a young person lacking this sort of encouragement. Access to information about universities provided by schools and colleges is also important for this age group.

While our selection of attitudinal indicators is essentially exploratory, the model reveals the very significant effects that core beliefs and orientations towards education can have on future plans. Two items in particular registered strong effects. Those with the confidence to believe they had the ability to pass at degree level, whether founded on previous educational achievement or not, were 12 times more likely to apply than those who lacked this self-belief.[11] An even stronger influence is the trade-off respondents are prepared to make between earning money or postponing this for degree study. Those with a preference to earn money were 27 times more likely *not* to plan to enter higher education, an effect which by itself is as strong as the combined influences of social class and qualifications upon 'plans'. Clearly the competing financial implications associated with the decision to go to university are of great significance among younger potential entrants from lower middle- and working-class backgrounds.

Who, then, among the 16–18-year-old group is most likely to apply? The profile of a potential HE participant would be someone from the lower middle class, with good educational qualifications, receiving encouragement from family and peers, with access to information on HE at school or college, who believes they have the ability to succeed in degree study and who positively chooses university over earning money. Though purely illustrative, the figures in the model suggest that, if such people existed, then someone who combines these attributes is almost 57,000 times more likely to apply than someone who lacks them all.

The picture that emerges for the 19–30-year-old respondents, who are at a later phase in their educational or working career paths, is somewhat different (see Figure 4.2). Prior qualifications again display a strong influence on potential HE plans; respondents with educational qualifications are over five times more likely to consider applying than those with no formal qualifications. However, the social class effect found with the younger group is no longer statistically significant here, which suggests that the determining influence of class background (considered again, it should be emphasized, only across the narrower range of lower middle C1 and working-class C2, D, E grades) appears to become weakened within the older group. It may also be possible that this initial effect diminishes as potential applicants grow older and more detached from the initially formative contexts of family and school background.[12]

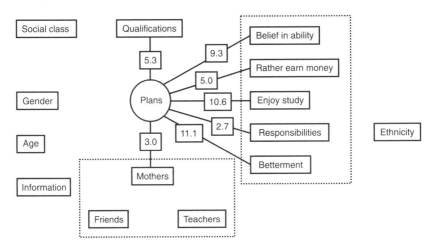

Figure 4.2 Odds ratios for 19–30-year-olds comparing levels as in Table 4.11

Again, there are no direct effects for any of the other social background factors, age gender or ethnicity. Further analysis shows that among the older group it is the attitudinal factors which largely account for variations in propensity to enter HE among members of different minority ethnic groups, with belief in one's ability playing a particularly stronger role within black and Asian groups. Mothers' encouragement remains a significant factor, while encouragement from friends is no longer influential. Even among these older respondents, those who report receiving strong encouragement from mothers are three times more likely to plan to apply to HE than those who received no encouragement or who were discouraged.

The main difference lies, however, in the attitudinal area where underlying beliefs and values about education come more strongly into play among this older group. Belief in one's ability to pass a degree and relative preference for earning money over studying remain significant if somewhat reduced influences. However, other attitudinal indicators also register significant effects and older respondents who believe they could better themselves through having a degree or who report that they enjoy studying are much more likely to consider HE. Taken together, older respondents who both see degree study as a source of betterment and enjoy studying are 117 times more likely to be potential HE participants. Additionally, views about the possible difficulty of combining HE study with competing responsibilities exert an influence among older respondents, with those who do not endorse this as a problem 2.7 times more likely to apply.

The model for 19–30-year-olds appears, then, to place greater emphasis upon attitudinal factors: subjectively carried beliefs about one's ability, positive orientations towards education, confidence, motivation to study or at least the absence of impeding responsibilities. The profile of a potential HE participant in this older group is someone who sees degree study as a source of personal betterment, who enjoys studying, is confident about their ability to pass a degree, is prepared to postpone earning in order to study, has the qualifications, has received parental encouragement to continue in education, and does not see their responsibilities as an obstacle. Again hypothetically, the figures indicate that a lower middle- or working-class person with all these attributes is 200,000 times more likely to apply than someone who lacks them all.

Discussion

The predictive (odds ratio) models outlined above were developed using multinomial logit regression to identify links between plans to go to university and a pool of key indicator variables. It is important to stress that such models are essentially exploratory and tentative, dependent on support from other evidence, and alternatives could well have been developed from these data: in a wellknown statistical variant of the uncertainty principle, 'All models are wrong, but some are useful' (Box 1976). Given these caveats, what usefully emerges here?

The factors common to both models reveal the enduring importance of educational qualifications, parental encouragement, belief in one's ability to complete a degree, and a preparedness to postpone earning for entry into study. These factors appear to exert a consistent influence upon propensity to enter HE for this sample of lower middle- and working-class respondents irrespective of age group. Additionally, some important differences were noted between the 16–18- and the 19–30-year-olds, considered separately because of the different stages they occupied in relation to HE decisions and educational career paths. For younger respondents, access to information about university is another important influence, one that is presumably more relevant given their more recent closeness to school or college information sources. The determining influence of social class on educational choices is seen even within this group, which is drawn, remember, from the relatively narrower lower middle- to working-class range, with those from lower middle C1 backgrounds markedly more likely to consider university. Among the older group, this particular social class effect is not seen. What seems to count more are attitudes towards studying and the potential for personal betterment through education, combined with the presence or absence of competing responsibilities which might make degree study difficult.

It is of interest that once allowance is made for the effects of the factors listed, that neither gender or ethnicity appear to exert any additional influence upon plans to enter HE. However, if the attitudinal factors are removed from the models, an ethnicity effect is observed for the 19–30-year-olds but not for the 16–18-year-olds. Thus, the attitudinal factors can, to some extent, be used to explain the ethnicity effect, or vice versa, at least for the older respondents. A not dissimilar phenomenon occurs with gender. Hence, for the 16–18-year-old respondents, if no allowance is made for the attitudinal factors, then there is some weak evidence of a different propensity to enter HE for males and females. However, no such gender effect is noticeable for the 19–30-year-olds, even without having allowed for attitudinal factors.[13]

As we concluded in our original paper reporting this analysis:

> It is notable that several of the influences are concerned with confidence and self-belief, and attitudes and motivation towards university study. While this combination of educational values and commitment may be the norm in more middle-class contexts, it is not typical among potential entrants from socially deprived backgrounds, where opportunities are more limited for the development of educational ambitions and where the intrinsic value of a university education must compete with more pressing material priorities. The models imply that an effective strategy for widening participation in higher education may require rather more than increasing the number of available degree places for suitably

qualified candidates. It points to the importance of earlier formative experiences, primarily in educational contexts but also within the family, in developing self-belief in one's capacities and abilities, positive attitudes towards education and studying, and the fostering and encouragement of personal motivation to continue in education.

(Collier *et al.* 2002)

Summary

We have emphasized that the most significant group missing from higher education are members of the socio-economic classes IIInm, IIIm, IV and V. Why might working-class students in particular not be represented in higher education? Our models above, together with a broad consideration of the literature, suggests that there are five groups of possible explanations, which may operate in combination or individually. The first three of these can be derived both from our models and from the literature.

First, it could be hypothesized that *working-class young people lack information about higher education opportunities*. Parental experience and knowledge of higher education are greater among the middle-class population, and these parents are aware of the nature of higher education, and how to prepare for and apply to higher education. While schools and further education colleges may supply information and assistance to potential first generation university applicants, this is relatively weak support compared to parental aspirations and guidance. These issues are discussed further in the next chapter.

Second, working-class students *may not feel that higher education has sufficient value* to be worth the effort and time. Three years of study represents three years of loss of earnings, and three years less progress in any profession or trade. The potential for later higher earnings with a degree may not be believed in, may represent a risk, and may be insufficient an incentive to be worth deferring more immediate entry into the labour market. We return to this in Chapter 6.

Third and perhaps most importantly, working-class young people *may lack the necessary normal entry qualifications*, and thus feel that they are unable to apply, or will not be accepted, or will not succeed if they apply and are accepted. There is an apparent correlation between A-level success and social class, and relatively poor working-class A-level results would therefore seem to be a contributory factor in the low take-up of higher education. Also linked to this are questions of self-confidence and a belief in one's ability to succeed in an academic environment. Chapter 7 explores these issues in more detail.

Fourth, the *financial commitment to study may be seen as too great, too risky, or* (related to the first point) *insufficiently understood* (or, some would argue, understood only too well). For further discussion, see Chapter 8.

Finally, there is the possibility that some students *may perceive higher education as a threat to their class identity*. Both higher education study and qualifications are likely to lead to different social perceptions, and ones that working-class students may feel will undermine their social position and solidarity. This last explanation is investigated more fully in Chapter 9.

Notes

1 The available data are for those who complete, not those who enter; thus the estimates of Table 4.5 have utilized an estimate of retention rates for those who had entered HE, to facilitate calculation of estimates of those who enter at various ages. It may also be noted that this omits consideration of those who have withdrawn from HE but might re-enter later.

2 Details of computations in Table 4.5:

Column 2: percentage of each socio-economic group who start higher education before the age of 21, derived from the percentage of those who have achieved higher education qualifications in 2001 (Table 4.1, column 1), divided by the approximate retention rate for this SEG, multiplied by the percentage of the group who enter higher education before 21 (Table 4.3, column 5). For example, 57.1 of socio-economic group II have higher education qualifications; 88 per cent of those in SEG II who attain higher education qualifications have enrolled by 21, and about 85 per cent do not withdraw, so about 55 per cent of the whole group enrol as pre-mature students.

Column 4: the residual percentage from column 2 in this table: the percentage in each socio-economic group who has not enrolled by age 21.

Column 5: percentage of the total number in each socio-economic group who start full-time higher education between 21 and 30, from the 2001 percentage of those who will achieve higher education qualifications (Table 4.1, column 1) multiplied by the percentage of the group who enter higher education between 21 and 30 (Table 4.3, columns 6–10), divided by the approximate retention rate for that SEG.

Note: Estimates for retention rates by SEG are based on the overall retention rate for the sector (HEFCE Performance Indicators for 1998–9) mediated on the basis of unpublished research carried out by the authors using national data.

3 A detailed account of this analysis and the associated statistical modelling, described here in summary form, was first presented in Collier *et al.* (2002).

4 The Social Class and Widening Participation in Higher Education Project was based at the University of North London, and supported by the university's Development and Diversity Fund over the period 1998–2000. The project was directed by Professor Robert Gilchrist and Professor Alistair Ross. The Principal Research Fellow was Dr Louise Archer. The University of North London merged with London Guildhall University in 2002 to form London Metropolitan University.

5 Respondents were interviewed across 198 constituency-based sampling points. Interviews were carried out using CAPI (Computer Assisted Personal Interviewing) face-to-face in respondents' homes on the following dates: 10–15 June 1999, 18–21 June 1999, 24–29 June 1999.

6 We recognize that the concept of 'class' is problematic and contested (Rose and O'Reilly 1997) and its definition remains unresolved within this research. However, we understand 'working-class' as broadly comprising people from manual, partly and unskilled occupational backgrounds, who experience some degree of economic and social disadvantage within society. The measurement

of class is also problematic. This survey utilized the social class definitions used by the Institute of Practitioners in Advertising, namely the social grade classifications to denote 'lower middle-class' (C1) and 'working-class' (C2, D, E) backgrounds, and which are standard categories on all surveys carried out by Market and Opinion Research International Limited (MORI). This classification coincides with the social-class system adopted by IES/CVCP/HEFCE/UCAS (1999), which provided a compelling pragmatic reason for its adoption.

7 That is, there is a significant marginal association ($p < 0.001$) in the two-way table between plans and social class, but not allowing for the effect of other factors.

8 With some exceptions, these items were confined to those respondents not currently attending or having been to university.

9 The diagrammatic representations of the modelling results are purely schematic, with predictor variables of similar types (for example social background, sources of encouragement, attitudinal items) grouped for convenience. No statistical significance should be read into the physical arrangement of elements and their relative contiguity or distance.

10 For further references, see the Dearing Report (1997) and its bibliography or, for example, Parry (1997).

11 It might be conjectured that belief in ability is a proxy for qualifications; however, belief in ability and qualifications is not highly correlated and our model indicates that these two factors are additive, with both needed in the model. One is not a proxy for the other.

12 It may be noted that the pattern of social-class effects applies even when the models are fitted without the attitudinal factors; thus the attitudinal factors are effectively orthogonal to the social class effect (or lack of it).

13 For a further discussion on how some discourses and attitudes may possibly be racialized or gendered, the reader is referred to Chapter 9.

Chapter 5

Information, advice and cultural discourses of higher education

Merryn Hutchings

Lack of information is one of the major explanations put forward for low participation in HE by working-class groups: 'certain groups in society lack information about the opportunities that are available' (Thomas 2001: 135). As a result, provision of information is a central aspect of most widening participation initiatives.

The assumption that the possession of information is central to individual decision-making is a key aspect of the way that the market is represented in government education policy (Gewirtz 2001). The most rational decisions are assumed to be those that, in the long term, maximize the economic position of the individual. An example of this is the Dearing Report's claim that if information about the long-term financial benefits of higher education were widely known, more people would decide to enter (Dearing 1997).

There are several problems with this view. First, for the majority of people there is no 'moment of decision' about entering higher education. Some (generally middle-class) have long taken for granted that they would go to university: this has been a clear expectation in their families (Allatt 1993, 1996). Which universities to apply to may be more of a decision, but again institutions are ruled in or ruled out on the basis of 'what people like us do'. Other people (more often working-class) have never considered higher education; it simply has not been on the agenda. Probably only a minority of people reach a point where they make a decision about whether or not to apply. From the point of view of widening participation, this is a group to target, because it may be possible to inform and/or influence their decisions. But from the point of view of social justice, the focus must also be the larger group who never even consider the possibility of higher education. Thus it is important to research their perspectives.

Second, decisions are not always made on 'rational' grounds, but are often based on hunches, feelings or emotions (Gewirtz *et al.* 1993); this has been linked to social class. Hatcher (1998a) argues that middle-class educational decisions are almost uniformly rational choices in terms of a cost–benefit–probability calculation. But he considers that there is no single working-class orientation to decision-making; those who aspire to middle-class destinations may make choices on economic grounds; others may aim to achieve educational qualifications that will give access to more desirable working-class jobs (see Brown 1987) (possibly the most economically 'rational' course) or may elect to remain within the working class (for example, the lads described by Willis 1977). This last course may not offer long-term economic benefits, but is linked to cultural identity construction. Thus decisions about higher education are not simply to do with economic prospects, but also with emotion and identity (see Chapter 9). And in that such decisions are made within the context of a family, they may involve a range of contradictory emotions. In view of these considerations, some theorists have rejected rationalist approaches to choice; for example, Gewirtz *et al.* prefer to use the metaphor 'landscapes of choice', allowing for the possibility that decision-making is more 'amorphous, processual, tentative and intuitive' (1995: 6).

Third, information is not neutral. The person presenting the information does so from a specific perspective and with a particular purpose in mind. Equally, the person receiving the information selects, interprets and constructs it in a way that fits their own perspectives (Burr 1995). This implies that the distinction between information (seen as unbiased fact) and advice or guidance (seen as context- and person-specific) becomes rather artificial. All information incorporates an element of advice; therefore in this chapter we do not attempt to distinguish between information and advice. This approach contrasts with the distinction that Connor and Dewson (2001) make between 'information' and 'influencers' in their analysis of issues affecting decisions about participation by lower social class groups.

In the light of these arguments, the relationship between information and decision-making appears much less straightforward than is assumed in the Dearing Report. People having access to identical information about higher education may construct it to come to entirely different decisions about whether or not to apply to university. These reflect their perceptions of the providers of the information, as well as a whole range of contextual and identity factors.

This chapter will consider the argument that working-class young people lack information about HE, and will identify possible reasons for this. Next it will focus on how information is perceived and what sort of information is trusted, drawing on Ball and Vincent's (1998) distinction between 'hot' and 'cold' knowledge. This leads to a consideration of cultural discourses of higher education.

This and the following chapters draw on data from focus groups with young working-class people in their first term of university and with non-participants. The next section explains how the data were collected.

The qualitative data

The advantage of focus groups for this research lay in the opportunity they afford to tap into the jointly constructed discourse of the young people. Morgan (1997, 1998) pointed out that interaction with others makes people more aware of their own perspectives because they have to explain or defend them to other group members who 'see the world differently' (1997: 46). The discussion in each group centred around two broad themes: respondents' own education, and their perceptions of higher education.

Sixteen focus group discussions involved non-participants: a total of 118 working-class[1] people aged 16–30 living in north and east London. Approximately one-third of the sample identified themselves as 'black' (black African, black Caribbean, black–mixed race), one-third 'Asian' (Pakistani, Bangladeshi and Asian-mixed) and one-third 'white' (white British, white Italian and white Turkish).[2] Ten groups took place in further education (FE) colleges, where respondents were attending courses from which they were considered to be unlikely to progress to higher education (for example NVQ Level 1). Six further groups were recruited from the general public according to gender and ethnicity (African-Caribbean, Bangladeshi, white); these included people who were not participating in any form of education (many of whom had left school at 16 and were now working or unemployed), and some who were studying part-time in FE. Of the non-participant sample, 16 said that they intended to go to university; about the same number explicitly rejected the idea, and the remainder, while expressing some interest, said they were unlikely to enter HE.

A further 17 focus group discussions were conducted with a total of 85 first year undergraduates from a range of courses at an inner-city, post-1992 university (51 women and 34 men). Approximately 30 per cent could be identified as 'white British', 20 per cent as Asian, 20 per cent as black and 27 per cent were from other (mainly white European) backgrounds.

All the groups in FE colleges and the university were conducted by Louise Archer, a white, middle-class woman. External researchers (in most cases women) were employed to conduct groups with members of the general public.[3] The two Bangladeshi groups were recruited and facilitated by Simon Pratt, a white male colleague. It has been argued that the researcher has an important and influential role within group discussions and interviews. He or she will both guide and bias discussions and the researcher's 'race'/gender will interact with the 'race'/gender of respondents within the research context, although this does not occur in predictable or homogenized patterns (see Phoenix 1994). Our decision to use only white (and predominantly female) researchers as facilitators was based more upon pragmatic than theoretical issues, although it is recognized that it has numerous theoretical consequences for the data. As an additional point of background information to the reader, it was noted that respondents generally perceived LA to be a student, and, on learning that she had been to university, engaged in considerable probing of 'what it is like'. We suggest that FE respondents may have been more inclined to talk about universities positively because of the interviewer's background. Interviewer 'race' and gender may also have worked to suppress the expression of some discourses; for example, when suggesting that universities may be racist, some black respondents apologized to the interviewer for their views, or would only utter them very quietly. Conversely, in two groups comprising only white participants, shared interviewer race may have facilitated the expression of racist points of view.

We now turn to consider the argument that working-class young people lack information about HE, drawing on the focus group data.

Do working-class groups lack information?

There is considerable evidence that many young people, particularly those from working-class backgrounds, feel that they do not have sufficient information about higher education (for example Connor and Dewson 2001; Howieson and Semple 1996; Keen and Higgins 1990; Thomas 2001). Connor and Dewson's (2001) survey of potential applicants and current students from lower social class groups identified gaps in their knowledge of costs and funding, and of potential economic benefits – the very areas that Dearing identified as necessary for making a rational decision about the value of higher education. When even current students feel that their knowledge of higher education is inadequate, it is unsurprising that those who are not on courses that may lead directly to university entry know less. An illustration of young people's lack of knowledge emerged in Grundy's (2001) report of focus groups with Year 10 pupils from socio-economic groups IV and V. He found that a small minority (8 per cent) believed that the *only* purpose of entering post-compulsory education was to retake GCSE examinations. They believed that if they passed their GCSEs in Year 11 they would not need to continue in education.

Data from our non-participant focus groups illustrate lack of knowledge of various aspects of higher education. In one group, respondents mentioned different qualifications, and Alison (18, FE student) asked, 'What's the difference between those courses? I don't know what is the difference between doing HND and doing a degree'. Foundation degrees, designed to widen participation, may add to such confusion (see Chapter 7).

However, it is not just the detail that confuses people, but knowledge that may seem basic. For example, Laura (30, white female bank worker) claimed that at school 'it was never explained to me fully what it [university] entailed or the difference between college and university and what you would get at the end'. Her comment highlights the linguistic complexity of post-compulsory education. Further education (usually sub-degree level) takes place in colleges, and higher education (usually degree and postgraduate level) in universities. The renaming of polytechnics as universities was designed in part to reduce the confusion arising from different institutions awarding degrees. However, not all degree-awarding institutions are universities; some are colleges of higher education. And at the most prestigious universities, Oxford, Cambridge, Durham and London, students are attached to colleges. It is unsurprising then that Laura was confused – but this illustrates that at every level, information about higher education is not straightforward.

Various arguments have been put forward to explain why working-class young people are less well-informed about higher education than those from middle-class families. Three are discussed here: that working-class young people know fewer people who have experienced higher education; that schools and colleges supply less information to those from working-class backgrounds; and that the information needed by working-class potential applicants is in itself more complex than that needed by their middle-class counterparts.

Having family members and friends who have experienced (or are currently in) higher education is a form of cultural capital that many working-class young people may lack – though Reay (1998) reminds us that there are intra-class, as well as inter-class differences in this respect. Connor and Dewson (2001) found that, of current students from groups IIIm, IV and V, only one in ten had a parent who had a degree. In contrast, four out of ten of those from groups I, II and IIIn had parents who had been to university, and the proportion would be still higher in social class group I with their long history of participation. As a result, going to university is viewed as a natural and expected activity for many middle-class young people (Allatt 1996). Many of their parents have some knowledge of the system (however outdated) and an understanding of how to access relevant information. They generally strongly support their offspring in their university applications.

In contrast, many young working-class people report that their parents will support them whatever they choose to do (Connor and Dewson 2001; Reay 1998), and will not 'push' them in any particular direction. This has been termed as a working-class discourse of 'child as expert' (Reay and Ball 1998). Moreover, the working-class parent who has not been to university knows less and is less able to advise their children (Pugsley 1998; Reay 1998). This scenario is also found in the focus group data: Chantelle (17, mixed-race female FE student) argued:

> You've got nobody to turn to except for friends ... I can just imagine what I would do when I reached a university level, because when I'm pressured and I don't understand something, who can I turn to? I can't turn to a bigger sister ... I've just got to rely on what the teachers tell me. My Mum can't help me because she hasn't been through it.

Another student in the same group recognized her relative advantage:

My brother is an engineer, my sister is an accountant, you know you've got all that in the background, so it's easier for me to, I can always phone my sister and say 'oh my God I'm like really stressed' and she can talk me through it.

(Loretta, 18, black African female FE student)

The Education and Employment Select Committee (House of Commons 2001b) proposed that, following a US model, those with no family back-grounds of HE should be identified as 'first-generation' students on their UCAS forms, though it is not clear whether this was simply for statistical purposes, or whether the intention was to offer positive discrimination to such candidates.

Having friends who are in HE or who are applying to enter is obviously also helpful, and again, this is more likely to be the case for middle-class pupils, though is becoming more common among working-class groups. But within this class-related difference, there are also age and gender distinctions. Reay (1998) found that while girls shared this sort of information, among working-class boys, choice of higher education was not a topic of conversation. In the same way mature people contemplating returning to study may feel very isolated and lack information.

A second reason why working-class young people may lack information is that there is evidence that schools and FE colleges supply less information to working-class pupils. Roberts and Allen (1997) found that students in FE colleges (more likely to be working-class) were less well-informed than those in schools. They concluded that this happened partly because, in FE colleges, higher education entry is not the main focus of careers support, and partly because many colleges are on several sites, and the information about higher education may only be provided on one of these. Similarly Connor and Dewson (2001) found that those in FE colleges and comprehensive schools reported being less satisfied with the information they had received than those in private and grammar schools. However, there is also evidence that within FE colleges information and advice are targeted, and that those on Access and A-level courses are told more about higher education (for example Beckett 2001). Connor and Dewson note the positive comments made by students about the support, encouragement and confidence-boosting offered by some FE tutors to those applying to higher education. But the support given varies between institutions and between courses: they report that at one college the BTEC students received much less information than the access group. The issue of concern here is that those on courses at lower levels are often told very little about the pathways that could eventually lead them to higher education, and so they may not consider working towards that destination (see Chapter 7).

The extent to which information is provided to different groups obviously reflects the expectations that staff have of pupils. In a selective private school it is assumed that virtually all the pupils will go to 'good' universities, and accordingly information and advice is disseminated to all (Reay 1998). In a comprehensive school or FE college this is not the case; staff target particular groups or pupils. But as a result, some pupils from working-class and/or ethnic-minority families have been found to receive less help and advice relating to higher education applications than do their middle-class peers; as one of Reay's interviewees put it, 'the school gives the posh pupils all the help' (1998: 522). Some schools may have a 'poverty of aspirations' (Trotman 1998) for their working-class pupils, which operates in terms of advice given and options made available to pupils (Pugsley 1998). Our data suggest that judgements made by teaching staff in colleges and schools about the likely routes of pupils may not conform to the trajectories that the pupils themselves aspire to. Here Loretta (18, black African FE student) tells her story – a story that was echoed in different forms by many others:

> On the university places, I was told not to apply, because, you know, I just wouldn't get the grade and whatever I needed, and the teacher turned round and said to me, 'Well I think £14.50 [the application fee] is a lot', and I said, 'Do you know what? When I go to university, whatever I make, I'm sure it will cover that £14.50, so I'll just spend it ahead.' I'm really cheeky when I want to be. So basically they sent the application forms, and all the teachers were sitting there rubbing their hands, saying, 'She's not going to get any interviews.' So I get three back ... and they all came with C grades, and I passed the mock exams. So I went back to my teacher and I said, 'I'm sorry you gave me bad advice', this was yesterday. And she goes, 'When?' And I said, 'About two months ago when you said I shouldn't put £14.50 because it was a lot of money', and I said 'I've got three acceptances and they all want C and Bs.' 'Oh, what did you get in your mock exam then?' 'The Cs and Bs that they really wanted.' So she was like, 'oh well, sorry', sort of thing.

Loretta, and some of the other African-Caribbean young women, were perhaps unusual in that they refused to accept the advice they were given, and persisted in their chosen pathways. This was not true for all the women. Janet (black Caribbean part-time secretary) told rather a different story:

> When it came on to like, the third years, and you had to choose your subjects, and what I wanted to do, I was told there was no point in doing it. ... Looking back on it now, because I was a woman I think, and there were many times you know I'd go down to see them because you wanted

advice, and they weren't giving any advice I wanted. And I wasn't sure myself, you know, I accepted what they said ... and I never got the opportunity to do what I wanted to do.

This story is perhaps rather more typical of the non-participants in our focus groups, many of whom felt that they had been 'pushed' or 'tricked' into particular educational pathways, and that they were not clear about where these could lead them, or whether this was where they wanted to go.

There is no easy solution here. It would obviously be inappropriate to tell everyone about all the possible routes; this would constitute a massive information overload. Young people report that they already have too much information; they would like it to be more specifically tailored to their particular needs (Connor and Dewson 2001). The question is, how can teachers and those offering guidance ensure that they identify the needs appropriately? At present it appears that some teachers make rather negative constructions of working-class young people's potential, and as a result, fail to supply them with adequate information and/or encouragement in relation to higher education.

A third reason why working-class young people may not have adequate information about higher education is that the information they need is in itself more complex than that needed by their middle-class counterparts. Increased flexibility, introduced with the aim of attracting students from under-represented groups, has created an almost overwhelming variety of offerings and opportunities (Williams 1999). New subject areas have been introduced including a considerable expansion of applied and vocationally-oriented provision, while complex modularized course structures require students to exercise greater choice (Jary and Thomas 1999). These changes have taken place particularly in those universities that traditionally cater for students from working-class groups. As a result the range of choices facing the working-class applicant is often very much greater than that facing the middle-class applicant to a pre-1992 university.

This complexity relates not only to the courses available, but also to entrance routes. Here, again, the complexity is greater for most working-class potential entrants than it is for the majority of those from the middle classes. The middle-class applicant is more likely to have A levels, universally recognized by universities and a relatively straightforward currency. In contrast, working-class entrants are more likely to have vocational or Access qualifications, which are not accepted by all universities or for all courses and, in themselves, present a bewildering range of qualifications and levels. Accreditation of prior (experiential) learning is also more widely used in post-1992 universities. Connor and Dewson (2001) noted that potential applicants taking vocational or Access courses could not find information about these routes in university prospectuses, despite their bulk. Entry routes are discussed in Chapter 7.

Similarly, middle-class applicants are likely to find the financial arrangements more straightforward than working-class applicants. The former will pay fees and take out loans, whereas the latter, who are more likely to enter as mature students, may also be eligible for and seek extra sources of funding such as hardship grants, childcare bursaries, funds from charities, etc. Many studies have identified that working-class potential applicants lack information about the financial arrangements for higher education study (for example Connor *et al.* 1999; Furlong and Biggart 1999; Hutchings and Archer 2001). Financial issues are the focus of Chapter 8.

In the early 1990s, Keen and Higgins (1990, 1992) showed that young people and adults had very limited knowledge of higher education. Williams comments that if that research were to be repeated today, when the information involved is so much more complex, 'it might yield even more unsettling findings, maybe even among [HE] staff themselves, let alone those seeking guidance' (1999: 20).

This section has discussed the way in which lack of family experience, differential distribution of information by schools, and greater complexity of information for working-class potential applicants may result in many young people feeling that they have a limited understanding of the options available. This introduces a considerable degree of chance into decision-making; Reay (1998) poignantly describes a girl applying to university who only found out the difference between old and new universities as a result of a chance conversation with a customer in her family takeaway business.

Can information be trusted? 'Hot' and 'cold' knowledge

This section focuses on the way that information is selected and received, and shows how some information sources may not be trusted.

Ball and Vincent (1998), investigating the sources that parents relied on in their choice of secondary schools, distinguish between 'hot' knowledge (acquired through the 'grapevine') and 'cold' knowledge (official or formal knowledge). They found that while most parents made some use of 'grapevine' knowledge, some were suspicious or doubtful about it and sought out official or 'cold' knowledge with which to replace, or at least supplement it. This group were mainly middle-class parents. Other parents used 'grapevine' knowledge unquestioningly, seeing it as a way of making choices 'grounded in the opinions of other parents like oneself' (1998: 392). Working-class parents tended to fall into this category.

In exactly the same way, information available to young people about post-16 educational choices can be identified as 'hot' or 'cold' knowledge. We found that the working-class young people we interviewed tended to rely more heavily on 'hot' knowledge and, partly as a result of this, they sometimes ended up with limited and confused information and misinformation. This echoes Connor and Dewson's finding that 'much information had been gleaned by potential students on an informal and *ad hoc* basis, and there was a degree of misinformation' (2001: 108–9).

The ways that young people perceive and act upon 'cold' and 'hot' knowledge are considered in turn.

'Cold' knowledge

Cold knowledge is provided by official sources that do not have a personal interest in the recipient of the information, such as university authorities or the government. Among the non-participants the 'most cold', or official, sources of information were hardly mentioned. Only one woman talked about published league tables, which rank higher education institutions in relation to factors such as inspection scores, research, etc. But having seen them, she intended to act on them:

> When we were looking at the league tables – I applied to Luton – there are about ninety-six and Luton came about ninety-fourth. And I thought, well I'm not going to the ninety-fourth university.
>
> (Loretta, 18, black Caribbean female FE student)

Prospectuses were more widely used. However, they were not necessarily considered to be helpful because they gave insufficient detail on the particular topic that interested the reader:

> It doesn't really tell you about the structure of how you learn things like all the different modules and that.
>
> (Martin, 18, white male HE student)

> Q: Did [the prospectus] give you enough information? Of the right sort?
> SIOBHAN: Well you know I don't think it did really. When I was reading the course contents it said, you can go into, kind of develop, mini-specialisms, and I thought, what can I do at the end of it? What will I be?
>
> (33, white female HE student)

But far more often 'cold' information was viewed with suspicion because the providers were perceived to be serving their own interests. This vested interest was often seen in financial terms. In this light, prospectuses may be seen as advertisements, rather than useful information. As one of the respondents commented: 'A place where it's not very good – they can make it look good in the prospectus' (Jem, 19, white female HE student).

Several focus groups brought up the idea that college funding depends on numbers recruited; consequently any approach from colleges was suspect.

MAJID: Do you know what they want to do yeah? They went to our school, yeah, they offered all of our students, the A-level students, a place yeah, so like a guaranteed place.

EVE: Yeah well more people equals more money.

(FE students)

In the same way, many young people expressed distrust and suspicion of suggestions from careers staff, teachers or lecturers. For example, Hussein argued that when teachers suggest to pupils that there is no point in entering them for particular exams, their real motive is to save money on the exam fees. Such suspicions made it hard for some students to accept that *any* of the advice they were given really had their best interests at heart. Those advised to study a particular subject suspected that the motivation was the teacher's prestige:

> I was going to stay on at six form. So I said, yes I'll think about [art], and the art teacher will say, yeah do it, but the maths teacher will say don't do it, do maths, cos he's doing that, the maths.

(Neville, 17, black male British FE student)

They also suggested that teachers may want to 'do down' particular students (on grounds of race or class) and, as a result, would make over-pessimistic predictions for their grades, as in Loretta's account of her university application.

Careers advisers were generally referred to in negative terms. In one construction, they were seen as serving the agenda of the government rather than the interests of the individual pupil:

> Nine times out of ten, whenever anybody went and said 'I want to do this,' they said, 'No, no, no, you don't want to do that, you want to do this.' So people just ended up, they never went or never paid any attention to what they were saying because it seemed to be that they were trying to push them into what they thought the country needed as such you know, like they were still having apprentice plumbers or something, and the guys wanted to be electricians. 'No you should be a plumber really' ... . I don't think I know one person that has got any help from a careers officer to be honest.

(Jodie, 27, white female unemployed hairdresser)

Jodie also criticized the selection of visiting speakers (as did the young people in Howieson and Semple's research, 1996). While the occupations represented could be seen as an attempt to raise pupils' aspirations, this was constructed as reflecting the advisers' negative view of their working-class lives:

I think the careers advice at school is very stereotyped. ... It would always be – there would be one nurse, one police officer, there would be one lawyer, one doctor, one this – but they were all really high powered. There wouldn't be your road sweeper or your café owner ... it would always be your hotel management, you know, it would always be the hierarchy of all them top-notch jobs where you would have to be like a silver spoon in your mouth before you could even get a look in, let alone trying to train for one. So I mean the underclass, what I call the underclass, I'm not degrading anybody in their job at all, but on those sorts of jobs, they never got a mention ... We don't do that, it's common.

(Jodie)

An alternative construction saw careers staff not as serving any particular agenda, but simply doing their jobs, and thus not personally involved. According to members of the African-Caribbean women's focus group: 'They just did what they had to', 'they're not there to help you' and they're 'just doing their jobs'. Thus they were criticized for simply taking up the pupil's initial (and tentative) idea, without helping them to explore other possibilities. This conforms with the views of young people studied by Kidd and Wardman (1999); they reported while the careers advisers were friendly, the interviews did not help with decision-making because the full range of options was not explored, and stated aims were not challenged.

Careers officers were also criticized for simply asking questions, rather than offering information or advice:

She just sat there and she listened. It was more like going to a shrink, 'just sit down and talk' kind of thing, and it didn't really help me at all. And from then I just had to suss it out myself.

(Chantelle, 17, mixed-race female FE student)

These suspicious and negative constructions of the advice received at school are echoed in some studies (for example Howieson and Semple 1996; Kidd and Wardman 1999) but conflict with others. For example, White *et al.* (1996) reported that pupils acknowledge that careers advisors and teachers have played a major role (more influential than family and friends) in decisions about which course to do after leaving school.

Distrust of teachers and career advisers can also lead to a sense of isolation, epitomized by Drew's remarks in a focus group. The interviewer was trying to find out who members of the group had consulted in relation to their decisions about post-compulsory education. Drew (21, black Caribbean shop assistant) replied: 'Who else was there to speak to anyway? I don't know, you gotta speak to yourself. Can't rely on no one else'. And he added, 'They're trying to get at who helped us and no one helped us.'

'Hot' knowledge

Ball and Vincent describe 'hot' knowledge as 'grapevine' knowledge from friends, neighbours and relatives. They argue:

> Significantly, the grapevine is seen as *more* reliable than other 'official' sources of information … . The comparisons between grapevine knowledge and official information … counterpose formal, public, abstract knowledge with personal, social knowledge. There is a degree of scepticism about the former and a general preference for and sense of greater usefulness about the latter.
>
> (Ball and Vincent 1998: 380)

'Hot' knowledge is 'socially embedded in networks and localities and is unevenly distributed across and used differently by social-class groups' (Ball and Vincent 1998: 377). Connor and Dewson (2001) found that lower social class potential entrants saw people as the most useful source of information, rather than printed information such as prospectuses and brochures. They were more likely to take on what they were told by those they liked and respected, or who had experience of higher education. Kidd and Wardman similarly reported that 'for many it seemed that career education and guidance had little impact. Parents, teachers, friends and the judgements of the young people themselves appeared to be more influential than guidance practitioners on choice of destination' (1999: 259). This was echoed in our own national survey: parents and family were rated as more influential than careers officers and teachers (see Chapter 4).

Some of those in the focus groups claimed that word of mouth was sometimes the only available source of information: 'That's the only time you ever actually realize well there's something going on, by word of mouth' (Chantelle, 17, mixed-race female FE student).

As was suggested earlier, family members in higher education are a key source of 'hot' knowledge: 'personal recommendation is perceived to be far more trustworthy than apparently "objective' data"' (Ball and Vincent 1998: 380). Their contribution involves not simply fact but also emotions. Benazir (18, Bangladeshi female HE student) explained how hearing about her sister's experience had helped her decide what to do:

> When you know that your brother or sister has already gone through things and you see them doing well, I suppose that inspires you as well. … My sister actually did computer science here as well, and she was

saying that even though the facilities aren't great, people actually enjoy the course.

However, it is not essential that the family member enjoyed their course; it was also seen as useful to know that success could be achieved despite some negative experiences:

> My mum, she's got a degree in social science. And I saw like the pressure and the stress, and she was a miserable cow. But it come out all right, and I think I could adapt to that because to see how she's come out of it.
>
> (Michelle, 16, black Caribbean female FE student)

Information from friends was equally valued: in finding out about his current course, Andrew claimed: 'I found out more from a friend than what I did from the careers'. An essential aspect of this was the relationship between the two people. The information-giver was liked and trusted:

> There was a friend of mine who was a lecturer and he said you know, you've just got to do it, you've got to go there this year, cos I was umming and ahing about it … He said, 'Oh you'll love it, have a ball.' OK I'll do it. And I really, you know, it was somebody that I really sort of admire.
>
> (Mike, 35, white male HE student)

Hot knowledge, however, does not necessarily come from family and friends; it also comes from 'people like me' who are perceived as having no personal interest, and no axe to grind. Thus information overheard at a bus stop is acted upon:

> I just heard some girls saying Tower Hamlets College … I just heard Tower Hamlets and I went to the operator and got the number and the prospectus and I came here.
>
> (Carmelle, 16, black Caribbean female FE student)

And as Ball and Vincent stress, some 'hot' knowledge takes the form of rumour or gossip passed on from one person to another, illustrated in this extract from a discussion among black and Asian students in an FE college:

> EVE: Yeah apparently we've all been heard, … we younger generation have heard that that Oxford is for those people that are like –
> MAJID: 'A's.
> EVE: White! E-yewell people! White! Like boffs people! [*laughter*]
> MAJID: Yeah, there was a guy, yeah, who had three 'A's, he had, so he

applied for Oxford, yeah, so he went there then you know when he got there the interviewer asked him, 'So what's your father's, er, profession?', whatever. He said 'Mr ...' – the name of it yeah, then he said 'Oh is he Mr? I was expecting like a doctor, or a what er, engineer', like you know the certain, the um what do you call them? The doctor and the Mr er, what do you call them names?

EVE: Title! Title?

Q: Title.

MAJID: Yeah he said his father's name was Mr. That's why they said they wouldn't allow him, the professor, that's why –

ZAIDA: I think that's horrible!

EVE: That's not right, though, is it? That's what I've heard, from what I've heard you've got to be, you've got to be a country bumpkin to get into them places, those type of places.

CARMELLE: It's cultural. That's not fair!

EVE: Yeah. And another thing, and, like we've always had the impression that it was just like for white people, like, white people.

Eve then referred to a 'cold' source, the prospectus, to support her assertion: 'And like when you see it up there, like actually see the prospectus, it's like white people, white people'.

Through 'hot' knowledge, gossip, rumour and urban myths, then, young people build up a construction of 'what people like us' do. This process is not confined to working-class young people; middle-class people construct cultural discourses in exactly the same way. These are equally based on 'hot' knowledge, though the constructed middle-class identity involves being people who also consult 'cold' sources of information. But our concern here is to show how working-class cultural discourses may lead some young people to reject the possibility of higher education, and others to embrace it. These discourses are examined in the section below, and are taken up in subsequent chapters.

Cultural discourses of higher education and students

This section focuses on the ways that some working-class young people construct going to university and being a student, and the ways in which they position students as Other, and themselves as 'people who could not be students' (see also Hutchings and Archer 2001). First the discourses of two very different young people are discussed.

Lucy, a white woman aged 20, worked as a hairdresser. In a rather large focus group composed of white women not in education, it was some time before she made any contribution to the discussion. Eventually she spoke about her experience of visiting a university:

> Well I had a friend that was in Cardiff University and I went for the weekend for a laugh and he took me round and I was just, oh my God, it was just the hugest thing you've ever seen in your life, and I thought, why would little old me want to go to somewhere like that? You know, it just swallowed me up, it was huge.

She contrasts the large, and implicitly powerful and daunting, university with a construction of herself as small, homely and ordinary, thus making entering higher education out of the question (despite the fact that she had a friend who was there). But having presented herself as a rather timid person, she later described students:

> I used to think [students were] people who were afraid to hit the big wide world to be honest. They were safe in the arms of being educated because they've got nothing else going for them in the big wide world, and they can't cope with it all, to be honest.

She joined in the discussion in her group that identified students as people with money who treat higher education as a time for recreation. This discourse was exclusively used by the white respondents:

> Q: What type of people do you think go to university?
> TINA: I think snobs, trendies.
> LUCY: Trendies, yes.
> KIM: But with money. Hippified people who smoke pot in the toilets and just get stoned every night and drink and –

Lucy explained that she had investigated the possibilities of doing various courses, but that she had been deterred, first by the manner of the person answering her phone call, and second, by the cost:

> I phoned a secretarial place and they were just so rude and I thought, 'I wouldn't even give you my money.' And that put me off. And I've got a friend that is helping out in the university and she was telling me some courses and the prices and I just thought, I can't afford it … . Some of the computer courses I was really interested in doing, you're looking at a grand. And I'm not being funny, but I haven't got that kind of money and how can I possibly go? I mean it would be lovely to have the qualification at the end of it, but I mean a grand, that's like a lot of money you know.

Like most of the young people with whom we talked, she did not know what qualifications were needed to go to university but believed that her own qualifications were insufficient: 'All I've got is a GCSE and a GNVQ. I ain't going to university.' Finally, she made it clear that she believed that university tutors would not offer the support she needed:

> LUCY: They're not going to help, like at school.
> KIM: Yes, it's not as though you're going to get as much help as what you needed, they're not there for you if you're doing a course like that.

Thus Lucy constructs the information that she has about university and students in ways that make going to university impossible for her. Her qualifications were not adequate, people would not help her (either in her enquiries or in studying), students were in every way different from herself, the buildings were dauntingly large, and the cost of study was prohibitive.

The second case study of the use of 'cultural discourse' focuses on Eve, a black African 18-year-old in a focus group with other members of her GCSE group at FE college. Like Lucy, Eve had visited a university and was pleasantly impressed, comparing it with her construction of inner-city universities:

> I see the surroundings, it looks so nice. It really does and like I know you can't always judge a book by the cover, but it's just the surroundings! It's like, ... it didn't even look like a uni! It was like a wow! And like you got the grass out there and you've got your place there and where you get your lectures over there and that little thing in the middle. It's so posh and that. I liked it.

But Eve constructs the university, and herself in relationship to it, very differently from Lucy. Having said that 'school was brilliant' and she enjoyed it, she than explains:

> But I just couldn't stay in there any longer cos I need a new environment, make a new life, I want a new start, yeah. It's good. This sounds like one of those documentaries.

She enlarges on this theme later:

> I want to go to university way outside London. Just get away from this place. ... Always, I dunno, for me, always if you want to go up a step in life, always start afresh. ... Cos always, you're always building yourself up.

Despite her comments that she enjoyed schools, she positions the teachers as racist in their low expectations:

> We'd all be talking and things and just discuss what we wanted to do and then the teachers would always turn round and say, 'Well ... you know you won't get the grades', you know what I mean? 'You're not going to make it' and things like that. And they wouldn't say it blatantly, they'd have, like you know, use their long words to make it sound –

But her reaction to this is one of resistance: indeed, having pointed out that Oxford is for white people, she comments: 'I would want to get there just to prove a point.' Like many of the black African respondents, she says that her family are strongly supportive of her efforts in education:

> All mothers' dreams are to see their son or daughter graduate, that's it! ... That's their goal in life as a parent ... I've never thought about you know, leaving school and saying, 'Oh I'll get a job'. My mum would shoot my head off! 'Job! I'll give you job!' It's always education, education.

She claims that to get to university you need four A-level passes, C to A star. But unlike many others she does not suggest that this is out of the question. The only thing putting her off university, she explains, is the money:

> Cos my brother went university ... and it's like he had some fat like loans and the money – he's always seeing like noughts like on figures ... he used to come back and say, 'Oh yeah, I've only got five thousand to pay', and it's like it's just too expensive, university.

In many ways Eve is characteristic of the black African women in this study, and it is hardly surprising to find that this group are now well-represented in higher education. The information she draws on is similar in many respects to the information Lucy used, but Eve's discourse is based in her family's attitude to education and resistance to racism.

Obviously these two individuals illustrate only two of the various cultural discourses that emerged in this study. One of the most common themes across all the groups was that students have to engage in hard, boring activity for long hours, and that this pressure leads to stress (Hutchings and Archer 2001). This conforms with Ozga and Sukhnandan's (1997) finding that, while conventional (young A-level) applicants anticipate minimal academic demands and an exciting social life, non-conventional applicants emphasize the workload:

> Up to boring lectures, like some of them you have to sleep through and then make up the notes afterwards, and then loads of essays, you're

sitting behind a computer all the time … And then at the end of it writing a really long long essay for everybody to see your dissertation projects and all that kind of stuff. That just drives you insane.

(Chantelle, 17, mixed-race female FE student)

[Education]'s boring. No one sits in here telling us that … it's going to be thrilling, it's going to be a buzz, it's going to be like a drug where you're going to want more and more and more. I don't get that impression at all.

(Jodie, 27, white female unemployed hairdresser)

Very few of the non-participants identified any enjoyment in university life; only a tiny minority suggested that they would gain satisfaction from either studying or social life. This runs counter to the findings of our national survey, where 'enjoyment of studying' was an incentive in deciding to go to university (Chapter 4), and may reflect the context of joint construction through the group discussion; to openly admit to enjoying studying may not be 'cool'. Some students were characterized as 'boffins' or 'bods':

There's a general stereotype isn't there? The Tefal man with a big head. Someone who needs glasses.

(Steve, 24, white male builder)

This construction was contrasted with a more desirable picture of youth:

When I see it in the media I can see pure books. People is walking with their books on their arm all the time, looking all sad and cold and that. They should just like just relax, be like cool! Put some shades on, maybe a little cap, cut the hair cut here and there …

(Patrick, 18, black Caribbean male FE student)

Thus students who enjoy study were seen as socially inadequate in terms of working-class and black male youth culture. Both this discourse, and the one used by Lucy which identified students as people who drink and cannot face the real world, tend to rule university out of consideration.

A third widely used construction saw students as 'people with high ambitions [who] want to do something with their life' (Jackson, 16, black FE student), or 'just people trying hard for their future, yeah for their kids' future' (Aziz, 16, Asian FE student). Such students aim to 'better themselves' by achieving economic success and a more affluent lifestyle and, in effect, becoming middle class. This notion of extrinsic rewards far outweighed notions of intrinsic satisfactions of studying, or of acquiring useful knowledge or transferable skills:

> I would have thought that's what the general thinking is for going to university, not just to, as Hercule Poirot said, to make the grey cells expand … It's money, it's not brain power is it?
>
> (Steve, 24, white builder)

This discourse opens up the possibility of participation for the working classes, and accords some value to higher education, a theme taken up in Chapter 6.

Discussion and implications for practice

This chapter has shown that many working-class young people do lack information, and that the information that they have is constructed in ways that relate to their cultural background and gendered identities. As a result some may rule out higher education. In the context of career choice, Hodkinson (1998) draws attention to the value of Bourdieu's notion of habitus, a socially grounded portfolio of dispositions to life which have their origins in a person's cultural background.

> Decisions made through the dispositions in habitus are partly intuitive, partly discursive, partly rational and, above all, they are pragmatic, making use of information, advice and opportunities that are perceived to be available and relevant at the time. … They are centred upon the person's standpoint – the social, cultural and geographical position from which they view the world.
>
> (Hodkinson 1998: 159–60)

As Hodkinson points out, this standpoint involves particular power relations. 'Choices are locked within the cultures in which young people have lived their lives and their, often unequal, interactions, negotiations and sometimes struggles with educational providers' (ibid.: 151). The distrust of official sources that we have described relates to the inequality of the power relationship.

What, then, can those involved in trying to raise aspirations and widen participation in higher education do? Responses that simply involve more effective provision of information may be of limited value? The information needs to be provided in a way that makes it 'hot' knowledge, that is trusted and valued. Many widening participation initiatives already do this, through their emphasis on personal contact with higher education students and staff (for example Heathfield and Wakeford 1993). Connor and Dewson (2001) conclude that colleges and schools could use past students' progress and achievements in higher education more effectively, and that mentors (who may be current students) should be more widely used among those who do not have friends or family with higher education experience. Many initiatives also emphasize the need to work with younger children, including those in primary schools, in order to ensure that higher education features in their 'landscape of choice' (for example Clark *et al.* 2001).

None of the young people in our study mentioned having been involved in such initiatives. However, many of the students we talked with spoke very positively of the opportunities that they had had for contact with higher education staff. For example, one commented that she had been offered places at two universities, but chose the one that had interviewed her. Open days were also see as an incentive:

> Yes I thought [the prospectus] was all right but I thought the Open Day was better. … You have really got to come and feel the atmosphere if you like it, and that's when I came up and visited and I liked it because they organized it really well and I got a tour around the Halls and that and got to chat to people about the courses which I thought was good like.
>
> (Jem, 19, white female HE student)

Such positive experiences were contrasted with stories of 'awful universities' where you were 'just left to wander around like a great huge building' (Stella, 18, white HE student). Some non-participants felt that an Open Day would be insufficient; they wanted a longer opportunity to try out higher education:

> STEVE: Maybe they should do, like, I don't know, a tester thing, a couple of weeks to see what you're all about.
>
> DEREK: But I mean, six weeks, if you're going for something that's going to last three years, it's about right to see if you're suited. I mean two weeks would be like nothing.
>
> (White men in construction industry)

While 'hot' knowledge was preferred, the analysis in this chapter also has implications for 'cold' information such as prospectuses. The students in focus groups were clear that they would have liked more emphasis to be placed on the course itself and on the employment possibilities on graduation. Many of them felt that the emphasis on social life and the bar was a dangerous distraction and temptation, which might lead them to become the idle, drinking students that they rejected.

The young people in the 'non-participant' focus groups identified a need for more information, and suggested ways of providing it. Their suggestions included wider advertising: 'It may be something that's never crossed your mind until you see it advertised and you thought, God I really fancy that, that looks really interesting' (Laura, 30, white bank worker). They also wanted opportunities and invitations to visit universities and colleges in an informal way, 'to go in and have a wander round and chat to people who teach at the college, chat to people who have actually been to college' (Jodie, 27, white unemployed hairdresser). They also devised the idea of the High Street education shop where 'it's not so frightening to go in and ask'; many universities have set up such shops.

Thus the suggestions made by non-participating young people generally involved personal contact. Many widening participation initiatives are based on such approaches. There was no support for greater provision of information through publications or via the Internet; the respondents preferred to acquire information in a context where they could develop some relationship of trust with the information provider, and to have first-hand opportunities to experience what higher education is like.

Notes

1 It was not possible to assign individuals to specific social-class groups. Respondents filled in a form indicating their own and their parents' employment. However, more detail would be needed to allocate to a class. Some parents were unemployed, and their class category is therefore ambiguous, although the range of parental and personal occupations fall within the lower socio-economic groups. It can also be noted that it is often quite hard to assign social class to young people in their 20s – while they may no longer be classified according to their parental class (for example by UCAS), their initial positions in the labour market may also be unstable and liable to frequent change.
2 Respondents used a range of labels to classify their ethnicity, and in this chapter we use these self-descriptions to identify speakers (this accounts for the lack of strict continuity of description, whereby speakers from similar backgrounds may label themselves differently, for instance as 'black British' or 'black Caribbean').
3 Researchers from the Office for National Statistics (ONS) were commissioned to assist with the four non-FE discussion groups. Both of the external researchers were assigned to the project by the ONS.

Chapter 6

The 'value' of higher education

Louise Archer

This chapter introduces questions concerning the 'value' of higher education and discusses whether participation is, as respondents put it, 'worth it' for working-class groups. As we have written elsewhere (Archer and Hutchings 2000), the value of participation in HE can be conceptualized in terms of an equation comprising risks, costs and benefits, but it will be argued that risks, costs and benefits of participation are not equal for all social groups. The balance between the potential benefits as weighed against the risks and costs of participation are differently structured across social class ('race' and gender), with the result being that working-class students face greater risks of failure and more uncertain rewards.

This chapter begins by examining some different views regarding the value of participating in higher education for working-class groups. State perspectives and educational institutional discourses are introduced and outlined. These official discourses are then compared with the views of working-class respondents, as collected during focus group discussions.

It is suggested that the value of higher education, as perceived by actual and potential participants, is cross-cut by three general themes: the hierarchy of universities; issues around retention; and graduate employment/employability. These themes emerged within discussion groups with both working-class participants and non-participants, and were raised in relation to numerous issues, as discussed within subsequent chapters, impacting for example upon knowledge and information about HE (Chapter 5), access routes into universities (Chapter 7), student funding (Chapter 8) and social identity concerns in relation to participation (Chapter 9). This chapter discusses the importance of these three themes within respondents' views about the value of HE participation and their assessments of the risks, costs and benefits of participation. The chapter concludes by suggesting that working-class groups occupy structurally 'riskier' social locations than middle-class groups, and this may translate into working-class perceptions of higher education participation as entailing higher costs and uncertain rewards. Consequently, respondents framed the value of participation in higher education in ambiguous terms.

Why study? Dominant and 'official' views on the value of higher education

Government justifications for widening participation in HE are primarily framed in terms of economic motivations and, to a slightly lesser extent, social justifications. In the Dearing Report (1997), the value of widening participation in higher education is identified through a combination of economic and social benefits at national, community and individual levels:

> Higher education is fundamental to the social, economic and cultural health of the nation. It will contribute not only through the intellectual development of students and by equipping them for work, but also by adding to the world's store of knowledge and understanding, fostering culture for its own sake, and promoting the values that characterize higher education: respect for evidence; respect for individuals and their views; and the search for truth. Equally, part of its task will be to accept a duty of care for the wellbeing of our democratic civilization, based on respect for the individual and respect by the individual for the conventions and laws which provide the basis of a civilized society.
>
> (Dearing 1997: para. 8)

Economic motivations are, however, accorded primary importance within the report, encapsulated within conceptualizations of an increasingly crucial relationship between HE and the economy ('There is growing interdependence between students, institutions, the economy, employers and the state.' ibid., para. 9). Government perspectives have also predicted that the relationship between higher education and the labour force will be amplified by the new technological advances, with universities being accorded considerable responsibility for producing a pool of graduates trained in relevant information technology to sustain the new economy:

> The new economic order will place an increasing premium on knowledge which, in turn, makes national economies more dependent on higher education's development of people with high level skills, knowledge and understanding, and on its contribution to research.
>
> (ibid.)

Juxtaposed with these imperatives, the Dearing Report also stresses that, in order to widen participation, higher education needs to demonstrate that it represents a 'good investment' for individuals as well as society.

The national economic benefits of widening participation have thus been represented in terms of producing a highly qualified work force that will enable the nation-state to be a globally competitive economy. Within such a perspective, national prosperity is understood to follow from the maintenance of a workforce comprising highly and appropriately qualified employees. Thus, it has been argued, the country's economy can improve and benefit from widening participation initiatives that will increase the pool of highly qualified university graduates. These economic arguments for the expansion of HE have been echoed elsewhere. As detailed in the House of Commons Select Committee for Education and Employment Report 6 (2001a), Sir Christopher Ball argued that higher education plays a central role in ensuring the maintenance of a globally competitive workforce (he also suggests that participation results in a range of social and personal benefits for those who participate). Similarly, Soskice (1993) has argued that HE needs to expand in order to meet the national skills shortage.

Since the Dearing Report, espousal of this economic imperative has only increased, as evidenced by David Blunkett's (then Secretary of State for Education and Employment) speech, 'Modernizing higher education – facing the global challenge' given at the University of Greenwich on 15 February 2000. In his address, he underlined the government's belief that 'higher education is now at the heart of the productive capacity of the new economy and the prosperity of our democracy'.

Official rhetoric has also presented widened university participation as economically beneficial for the working-class groups, communities and individuals themselves, because it is assumed to result in increased personal earning potential and improved local and regional economic conditions. Personal satisfaction and fulfilment are also assumed to benefit individuals who have developed their capabilities and potential through HE participation.

However, a number of challenges have been made to the economic rationale for expansion. For example, Keep and Mayhew (1996) have suggested that there is little evidence to support the claim that economic benefits will automatically follow expansion. Citing evidence from the CBI (1994), Hogarth et al. (1997) also detail arguments made during the enquiry that 'the lack of a clear labour market rationale for further expansion appeared to be echoed by industry, or, at least, expansion per se did not appear to be considered a priority by employers' (p. ix). John Field additionally suggests that there is only a very weak economic case for expanding mature student entry to HE (mature students constitute one of the government's key target areas for expansion in order to meet the 50 per cent participation target). He argues instead that widening mature student participation has a very strong social justice justification, and should be framed as such.

The Dearing Report does also construct the value of widening participation in social and social justice terms. Enabling working-class, and other disadvantaged groups, to access higher education is understood within the report as forming part of the process of working towards greater equality of opportunity and tackling social inequalities within society. However, critics have suggested that such government rhetoric around social justice contains undercurrents of social control, evidenced by the government's stated aim of using HE expansion to play a major role in shaping society and social relations. For example, official discourse suggests that increased levels of participation in education can help alleviate various social problems, such as reducing crime, disaffection and low literacy (Mudie 1998). This 'civilizing' function of HE participation is evident in the government's espousal of the important role of HE for shaping a democratic, civilized and inclusive society (DES 1978).

The motivations for widening participation that are cited by higher education institutions (HEIs), however, reflect a range of conflicting interests. As highlighted in a number of sources (for example House of Commons 2001a; Squirrell 1999; Hogarth *et al.* 1997) there are differing views and commitments to widening participation across the sector. While institutions are encouraged by financial incentives to widen participation, the expansion of HE has been accompanied by fierce debates and concerns over whether this diversification will affect the 'quality' of higher education. Generally speaking, widened participation has been embraced (and largely undertaken) by the 'new', post-1992 sector, where institutions, such as the London Metropolitan University, have mission statements espousing 'higher education for personal development and social change'. Older, pre-1992 and 'elite' institutions have tended to recruit fewer students from under-represented groups and have attempted to resist diversification through the defence of 'quality'.

In comparison, those working in the field of adult and community education have drawn primarily on social justice concerns to argue for widening participation (for example Woodrow and Crosier 1996). Many working within these areas have tended to draw on academic/activist traditions which have theorized the value of education as a means of achieving social transformation and the empowerment of disadvantaged groups, illustrated for example by bel hooks' notions of 'teaching to transgress' (1994) and Paolo Freire's (1972) vision of education as the practice of freedom. These more radical and emancipatory perspectives have not, however, tended to be reflected within mainstream and official discourses.

Why study? Views of working-class participants and non-participants

Relatively little is known about the views of working-class groups and whether they share or contest dominant views about the value of participation in higher education for working-class students.

Metcalf (1997: 11) suggests that young people from more affluent backgrounds are more likely to view participation in economic terms, as 'vital for securing better job prospects', whereas those from less affluent backgrounds regard higher education as irrelevant to their future employment. However, a number of other studies have found a broader range of classed views on the value of HE. For example, Connor *et al.* (1999) conducted a large national survey of HE applicants and found that among the most important reasons for studying given by respondents were: 'to study a subject that really interests me', 'to have a professional career', 'to improve my job prospects' and 'to gain entrance to a well-paid career'. They also found that there were differences by gender and ethnicity within these views. Girls were more likely to focus on subject interests while boys cited more financial and employment reasons. Minority ethnic students gave more importance to career outcomes than white respondents.

Squirrell (1999: 12) examined inner-city young people's views and found that most of the respondents who were intending to apply to university thought that 'HE was about getting qualifications which would lead to better jobs or into the type of job they wanted to do'. However, she also found that a minority of respondents resisted the notion that there is any value in HE participation, regarding it as irrelevant to the (mainly manual) jobs and careers that they wanted to pursue. For these young working-class people, university was only for 'eggheads and wealthy people' (ibid.: 11).

The data from our own study suggest that working-class respondents were broadly divided in their views on the value of participation in higher education, although the most commonly cited motivations to study were framed in terms of improving personal and familial economic situations and gaining social status and prestige. Generally speaking, men were more likely to cite personal economic motivations for going to university, whereas women were more likely to cite a combination of personal, social or family motivations, for example to become a 'better' person, to benefit their families (see Chapter 9). Minority ethnic respondents were most likely to cite social motivations for participation, such as making their family proud and/ or gaining community respect and status. However, it is important to note that these views were not restricted to these social groups, nor were they necessarily shared by all respondents within a particular social location.

The instrumental and economic value of higher education

Echoing, to some extent, dominant government rhetoric, many working-class participants and non-participants seemed to value higher education in primarily economic and instrumental terms. As we have written elsewhere (Archer and Hutchings 2000), reasons for undertaking a degree were largely framed within personal economic terms: to earn more money and to avoid 'crap' (hard, dirty or dangerous) jobs. Graduate jobs were envisaged as well paid, of higher professional status and offering 'perks'. Being a graduate was also positively associated with offering increased personal flexibility, choice and freedom in the job market. However, respondents' views differed from dominant discourses in several important ways. Higher education was valued not only in personal economic terms but within a family economic context. Several respondents also strongly resisted the national economic value of widening participation as distinctly not in their own, working-class, interests. There was also considerable resistance (particularly among non-participants) to the idea that economic rewards from graduate jobs relate to higher levels of skills, or the idea that higher education results in personal fulfilment through development of skills/potential. Rather, several groups of respondents recognized that HE operates as a system of privilege that can deliver economic rewards but does not necessarily entail intrinsic personal value or fulfilment.

Perhaps the most popular view of the value of higher education was thus as a means of getting 'more money and better jobs'. Graduate jobs were understood to be better paid and with more pleasant working conditions on account of being 'higher status' and/or professional. For example, many respondents conceptualized graduate jobs as office jobs, that are physically easier to do and are often equally, if not better paid. As one young man put it:

> I'm fed up with breaking my back for £7.50 an hour when I see some other person sittin' at a computer.
>
> (Arthur, 19, white English decorator)

Several minority ethnic group young men also talked about the benefits of graduate jobs as not being 'dirty' forms of work. For example, Kelvin, a black young man in FE talked about wanting a job 'that won't get my hands dirty [where I] don't have to lift nothing'. These comments echo Lloyd's (1999) findings from his research with young men from minority ethnic groups. In addition to 'better pay' (Derek, 29, white Irish man), graduate jobs were associated with 'perks', such as company cars (Darius, 19, black young man). Graduate jobs were also talked about as enabling social mobility, being associated with the notion of a 'career' (upward job mobility) and 'choice'. A higher education was perceived as offering the chance 'not to be stuck' (Steve, 24, white man) in particular jobs, providing routes to 'move on' (Carmelle, 16, black Caribbean woman).

In short, the value of higher education was widely regarded by men and women participants and non-participants as offering the possibility to escape from the daily 'struggle' (Simon, 18, white young man). The link to increased earnings and improved working conditions, was summed up by Melanie as to 'get a good life, ... a good job, good money and a career, have a wonderful life' (Melanie, 17, white young woman). But in addition to supporting the government's notion of personal economic benefits to HE participation, many respondents talked about the value of HE participation as a means 'to earn more to support my family' (such as Alison, 18, mixed-race female). There is some evidence to suggest however that the extent to which these expectations of higher earning potential are borne out may vary according to the social class, gender and ethnicity of the graduate (Audas and Dolton 1999).

However, respondents did not appear to share government understandings with regard to the means by which HE facilitates these graduate careers. The Dearing Report refers to 'highly qualified' graduates who have 'realized their potential' and developed particular knowledge and skills. In comparison, non-participants in particular constructed degrees merely as a form of 'paperwork' that enables a 'foot in the door' or a 'head start' in the job market (Sanjeeva, 17, Pakistani young man; and Hussein, 16, Turkish young man). Some, such as Derek, suggested that the value of participation lies in the ability to make 'contacts' at university who will later open job opportunities in particular fields. A number of non-participants explicitly resisted the idea that higher education offers any particular skills or training (issues of curriculum are discussed further in Chapter 7), arguing that graduates are less employable because they lack 'common sense'.

An important difference emerged however between respondents' views and government rhetoric in respect of the value of widening participation in HE to the national economy. It was widely recognized by participants and non-participants that the government wishes to increase participation among under-represented groups. This goal was understood to be primarily motivated by concerns to boost the national economy, but many respondents argued that these 'money-making schemes' (to encourage participation, or, their own words, to put 'bums on seats') were not in their own individual or working-class people's interests. Only a few African-Caribbean women supported government views, suggesting that widened participation should be encouraged because 'it's the country's investment. If they invest in education it will then be good' (Joan, age not given, black Caribbean woman).

The social value of higher education

As suggested at the beginning of this chapter, dominant discourses around widening participation have drawn on 'social' and 'social justice' arguments to emphasize the value of higher education. Respondents in our study also voiced numerous social reasons supporting the value of HE participation, but only African and Caribbean women drew on social justice arguments. The social value of participation was mainly framed in terms of improved family and community social status (developed further below).

A number of non-participant working-class women, who suggested that they hoped at some point to apply to university, suggested that participation has a valuable social prestige and esteem function, offering the chance to no longer be 'looked down on'. As one young woman suggested, a degree 'talks'. The source of this social gaze varied between black and white women. For Loretta, a degree would give social standing within the Nigerian community:

> Every Nigerian is qualified in something ... it's just for the shut-up factor you know.
>
> (Loretta, 18, black African young woman)

In comparison, Tina viewed a degree as able to improve her status more generally within the workplace and wider society:

> I think you're looked down on nowadays though if you haven't got higher education ... Our boss, he says I can tell you never went to a posh school or a school that had money.
>
> (Tina, 24, white woman)

For many minority ethnic group respondents, HE participation was strongly valued within their families. Participation was regarded as a way 'to make my mum more than happy' (Winston, 17, black Caribbean young man), because 'all mothers' dreams are to see their sons or daughter graduate' (Eve, 18, black African young woman).

A few HE students, but particularly women respondents, talked about their motivation to participate in order 'to be a role model' to younger family members. In comparison, some non-participating black women argued that participation is important in order to engage with inequalities by proving racist teachers wrong in their lower assumptions and aspirations for black young women. As we discuss further in Chapter 9, these discourses reiterate Mirza's (1992) findings from her research with young black women, as many of our young black women respondents were also negotiating, what Mirza calls, 'backdoor' routes through the education system.

The value of higher education for personal development and class mobility

Few, if any, respondents valued participation as a way to develop 'high quality skills', but a sizeable number valued participation as a means of changing social class and becoming socially mobile. Notions of mobility were associated with leaving disparaged, deficit class identities and achieving an idealized 'middle-class' lifestyle. However, as will be developed later in the book, these were not unproblematic discourses.

Thus, higher education was valued as a means of 'bettering myself', becoming a 'different (better) person' and accessing a middle-class lifestyle with its different values, norms and activities. As Janet said:

> It's that opportunity innit to actually live, I shouldn't say a middle-class

life cos I'm putting myself in a class, but to have – to be able to … think towards that car … I'd like to buy a house … send my daughter to a different school.

(Janet, 22, black HE student)

The value of degree was not understood simply in terms of quantifiable skills or knowledge, but was internalized as entailing a qualitative change. As Violet put it, 'you know the difference from somebody with a degree, not just the paper but the way the person behaves in everything' (Violet, 38, black HE student). The motivation for trying to achieve this change was framed in terms of escaping from deficit working-class identities ('I just didn't want to do that anymore, I just didn't want to be that person,' Grace, 26, black HE student) towards a 'normalized', 'whole' (middle-class) identity ('I want to be trained to be a rounded, complete woman' Violet, 38, black HE student). However, these values were not uniformly accepted, and were resisted by non-participants and participant women alike. For example, Billie (a mixed-race student) was adamant that she would not change as a result of being a student ('I hope it wouldn't change me') and Amy (a white student) was also clear that she wanted to stay the same type of person.

As the above examples suggest, these constructions were mostly used by women, particularly mature, black women students. However, it was also evident in George's (a non-participant young man) valuing of participation:

When you finish, if you pass … get some money together, do an MSc course … pass it, get head-hunted, get a job, get job security, get a car, get a wife and kids, get a nice village, get pets – possibly gerbils, especially dogs, a family favourite. Er, in-laws, the whole hack!

(George, 16, mixed-race Nigerian and white male, basic skills FE course)

As Beck (1992: 4) argues, engagement with education requires 'the individual's expectation of upward mobility', and 'these expectations remain effective even where upward mobility through education is an illusion, since education is little more than a protection against downward mobility'.

Other reasons

A few respondents suggested that an additional reason to study would be for personal interest, to study a subject they enjoyed. This compares with middle-class students, who are far more likely to cite personal subject interest as a reason for studying (see Connor *et al.* 1997). Several Asian young men in FE also suggested that HE participation might provide valuable social and life skills such as increasing their independence through living away from home. Respondents identified a number of other positive, but less important, benefits of participation, such as the stereotype of university life as characterized by sex, drinking and parties (see Chapter 5), but these factors were talked about as outweighed by the 'real' costs and risks of participation for working-class students.

As will be introduced in the sections below, respondents gave far more reasons as to why participation in higher education may *not* be worthwhile for under-represented groups. These centred around the kind of participation open to working-class students (mediated by the hierarchy of universitites), the threat or risk of non-completion (retention issues) and the types of jobs open or available to working-class graduates (graduate employability). These themes cross-cut perceptions of the value of HE participation in terms of entry routes, knowledge, finance and identity, which are addressed in separate chapters. Whether respondents viewed the risks of participation as too great, or whether like Hussein they wanted to 'go for it', was largely determined by the social, economic and cultural capital available to them.

The hierarchy of universities

As was found for respondents in Roberts and Allen's (1997) survey, we found that all our respondents (both non-participants and participants) were aware of some sort of hierarchy between higher education institutions. As noted in Hutchings and Archer (2001), this hierarchy was seen as simultaneously facilitating access and widening participation while increasing the risks of participation for working-class students, because only lower status institutions were perceived as accessible. Thus respondents were generally aware that while access has been widened, the elite institutions remain mostly closed for working-class groups and this would reduce the value of their degrees in the graduate labour market.

Almost all respondents, whether participants or non-participants, thought there were differences between higher education institutions. The majority conceptualized these differences in terms of status and quality. The best institutions were unanimously named as Oxford and Cambridge, but 'good' and 'better' universities were also constructed as campus universities, outside London, with grass and pleasant surroundings. The best universities were often talked about as maintaining strict access criteria, not only in academic terms but socially, for example, only admitting students with titled, professional parents. A few minority ethnic non-participants also suggested that this stratification is amplified by 'race', demonstrated, for example, by prospectuses that contain photographs of white students ('And like when you see it up there like actually see the prospectus it's like white people, white people' (Eve, 20, black African female, FE student). In comparison, respondents described the 'worst' institutions as the 'sad', 'concrete' inner-city universities, without trees and catering for 'working-class' and minority ethnic student populations (see also Reay *et al.* 2001).

Respondents were thus generally aware that widening participation for working-class groups generally refers to a restricted form of access to lower status institutions, leaving entry to elite institutions as closed to working-class groups, as it has largely always been. As Giddens (1973) suggests, wealthy middle-class groups dominate particular elite routes to ensure the reproduction of privilege within an expanded higher education system:

> What influences elite recruitment is not that the aspirant recruit possesses a degree in physics or in engineering, but that the degree is conferred at Oxford or at Harvard [...] ownership of wealth and property continues to play a fundamental part in facilitating access to the sort of educational process which influences entry to elite positions
> (Giddens 1973: 263–4)

These realizations, of the status differences between institutions, were not without consequence. For some, like Neil, the psychic costs of recognizing or 'owning' his disadvantage can be read in his following extract:

> I came here because I did an access course and the college I went to had links, whatever that means, with the university. And I passed the access course. I only filled in one institution and one course code on my UCAS form and I got in. Because anyone can get into [university name], it's an inner city polytechnic for God's sake! Like you don't have to be academically elite to get into [University] because that is why I'm here. Because I live locally and I am stupid basically.
> (Neil, 31, white male HE student)

Neil's comments can be understood by drawing on work by Reay *et al.* (2001), who cite Bourdieu's (1984: 471) assertion that a psychic sense of one's place leads one to exclude oneself from places from which one is excluded, such that the expectations that people develop are grounded within notions of what is acceptable for 'people like us' (Bourdieu 1990: 64–5). As Reay *et al.* also point out, working-class students' sense of place may carry negative psychic consequences because they are bound up with feelings of deficit. Thus Neil's 'choice' of university does not equate with the 'real' choices exercized by Reay *et al.*'s middle-class students, but both reflects, and further contributes to reproducing, his position of disadvantage.

For others, the perceived lower quality of the higher education accessible to them was a major disincentive, which led them to question whether participation would be worthwhile. The lower standard of the accessible institutions was perceived to hinder the individual's potential success and the quality of the degree they might attain: this was perceived as being both because you 'could be in with some right thickos' (as one non-participant woman said) and because a degree from a lower status institution would carry less value in the workplace. The continued dominance of particular (elite) institutions by white people can also work to render particular institutions unthinkable choices for minority ethnic applicants. Indeed, as Modood (1993) indicates, in Britain the majority of black students are concentrated within a small number of post-1992 universities. Thus despite the expansion of HE, universities are still strongly stratified and minority ethnic students remain largely excluded from more prestigious routes. Reay *et al.* (2001) found that respondents associated the best universities with 'whiteness' and 'middle class-ness', whereas universities with large proportions of black and working-class students were not recognized as good institutions.

Many respondents recognized that employers were also aware of the hierarchy of universities, as publicized through league tables, and argued that going to a lower ranking institution would compromise the value of a degree. As Loretta said,

> I thought well I'm not going to the 94th university ... fair enough I [would have] studied hard for that degree but they [employers] would just assume that my quality of education was different from somebody who went to a higher universities.
>
> (Loretta, 18, black African female)

Some respondents had a very clear picture of how they thought the hierarchy of universities would prejudice their later chances of getting a job:

> The way I think they do it is they take all the application forms and they put them into piles so its like Oxford, OK that goes in one pile, they might see North London, that goes in one pile ... and then they start off ... OK let's look at this Oxford lady first ... and I think that's why a lot of people even though with university degrees, they have to wait so long before they can finally get a proper job.
>
> (Chantelle, 17, mixed-race Caribbean/white female)

As Giddens suggests, 'in a modern society, the educational system, or the domination of certain key areas or levels of education by a particular class, is thus a central (and typical) mode of class exploitation' (Giddens 1973: 131), to which we would emphasize the psychic aspect of this domination.

Retention

Issues of retention have steadily become a key concern within government and institutional discourses. As the House of Commons Education and Employment Select Committee report on student retention suggests,

'Increasing non-completion rates could undermine success in opening higher education to a broader spectrum of the population, put off potential students, and cause institutional instability' (House of Commons 2001a: v). But increasingly, as the report details, universities and government concerns with failure have focused primarily upon the financial costs of non-completion to the state and HE sector. Thus concerns have been raised that, in addition to an emphasis upon increasing access, widening participation strategies must also take account of how to retain 'non-traditional' students, who appear to be at greater risk of non-completion (for example Hogarth *et al.* 1997; House of Commons 2001a; Smith and Naylor 2001). Consequently, non-completion/non-continuation rates have been built into funding council (HEFCE) performance indicators for HEIs in England (see also Chapter 10).

Few studies have examined students' reasons for non-completion, but the evidence that does exist points to numerous factors. Yorke *et al.* (1997) surveyed 1,478 English undergraduates via postal questionnaires and found eight main factors effecting retention among full-time and sandwich students: wrong choice of subject/study area; unsatisfactory experience of study programme; inability to cope with demands of programme; financial problems; dissatisfaction with institutional facilities; dissatisfaction with institution location; relationship problems; and health problems. Of these, they suggested that subject choice, study programmes and workload, and financial issues were the most frequently cited. However, an in-depth development of this study (Ozga and Sukhnandan 1997) found that different reasons emerged between younger and mature students' reasons for non-completion. Younger students appeared to drop-out because of a lack of preparation for, commitment to, or compatibility with their degree study. On the other hand, mature students were more likely to leave because of external circumstances (such as home and/or job demands). Working-class students were much more likely to cite financial reasons for non-completion. Pre-1992 university students were more likely to leave because of poor choice of course than post-1992 university students. Clearing students were found to cite dissatisfaction with the institution more often within their reasons for leaving.

These findings suggest that young and mature working-class students (who often come through clearing and may be less prepared due to no family history of HE participation) may (though not necessarily) be at greater risk of non-completion (see also Chapter 10). In our study, while most respondents acknowledged the potential for financial, situational and personal factors to hinder success, only a few mentioned the risk of a potential mismatch between expectations and experience.

All respondents in our study did, however, feel themselves to be facing a very high risk of non-completion. It was widely recognized that failure to complete was the single largest risk, and a very real threat, to working-class participation.

Yes, but it's all good going to uni but if – it's after the three years you've gotta pass ... I know people who are supposed to have passed all their exams and they don't pass – and that's what bothers me.

(Drew, 21, black Caribbean male)

This fear was based on a combination of factors, including: experiences of prior educational failure, racism, time and financial constraints (see Chapter 8), qualifications routes (Chapter 7) family and social demands and responsibilities, and personal feelings of deficit in relation to institutional cultures.

The majority of respondents in this study talked about failure in terms of passing assessments, and constructed educational failure as a very real risk, supported by personal anecdotes and urban myths (stories concerning unknown others, that respondents had heard). Most respondents had already experienced some form of prior educational failure and/or low levels of attainment within compulsory education, and perhaps unsurprisingly, extended these prior experiences to predict their own failure within higher education. Thus, as Diane Reay (2001) has written, working-class students may be painfully aware that within dominant educational discourses working-class identities are not traditionally associated with academic success.

Most respondents positioned themselves as at a greater risk of failing because they were 'non-traditional' learners. For example, Laura (white, 30, Scottish female) positioned herself as more at risk of failure as a mature student ('Just because I had a good level of learning a long time ago, doesn't necessarily mean I would be on that same level now'). Younger students in FE also stressed that having vocational qualifications (rather than A levels) would disadvantage them, both because it was claimed that universities prefer A levels ('You're going to be labelled ... You won't be able to be the top': Michelle, 16, black Caribbean female), and because vocational qualifications do not prepare students adequately ('he's really struggling cos the course didn't prepare him for university,' Theresa, 20, white Italian female), see also Chapter 7.

Several minority ethnic respondents raised the issue of racism as potentially effecting their chances of success and the quality of the degree they might attain. They suggested that institutional racisms may mean that the quality of their work is judged differently from other students, and that institutional cultures (see below) would effect the types of institution accessible to them. Conversely, a small number of white non-participant women voiced racist discourses and suggested that the ethnic balance of accessible institutions might disadvantage their own learning and progress (see also Archer, Hutchings and Leathwood 2001).

Issues around money and responsibilities were also heavily implicated in the potential for failure to complete degree courses, by participants and non-participants alike. Respondents suggested that poorer students are more likely to fail because they will be preoccupied with their financial situation, spending more time 'thinking about paying back loans' (Mushtak, 16, Bangladeshi male) and fearing the consequences for failure to complete a course. Indeed, it has been argued that recent changes in HE, such as the introduction of fees and the replacement of student grants with student loans will reinforce inequalities of access, acting as 'a further source of exclusion for working-class students' (Reay 1998: 520). Financial concerns were amplified with family responsibilities, such as childcare, that demanded students to juggle time, resources and paid employment. Lone parents suggested that they were particularly at risk of not completing degrees on account of their intense, competing responsibilities.

Although there is very little consideration of the impact of institutional cultures within dominant, official discourses around widening participation, it has been suggested by many academics that working-class students are disadvantaged by dominant institutional cultures that position them as Other (Tett 2000; Lynch and O'Neill 1994). Indeed in our own study, respondents positioned themselves as able to take advantage of the benefits of HE participation, but they did not convey any sense of ownership (Archer and Hutchings 2000). Institutional academic cultures have been defined as dominant discourses of knowledge, communication and practices within HEIs (Ballard and Clanchy 1988; Bartholomae 1985; Lea and Street 1998; Marton 1997). Many of the students' responses in this study point to the possible negative consequences that dominant institutional cultures may have upon the retention of working-class and Other students. As two black women students said:

> I'm just coming from an access course it's about I mean more higher, higher level. It's like I'm just trying to look in, learning how to break down – but some of the terms I don't know … . Because when he's giving the lecture and he's like talking, talking talking, saying those words and things. I said, my God, I don't know what you're saying! I'm lost …

> I think that's another culture shock in a sense, the language. It is a different language from being at college, from being at school, it is a totally different language.

It has thus been suggested that there is a need to

> examine ways of changing the culture of many higher education institutions and departments and to make the eligibility to participate of some under-represented groups more explicit, while also recognizing that admissions criteria should reflect as accurately as possible the skills, knowledge and experience essential for participation in particular courses
>
> (Hogarth *et al.* 1997: 11)

In opposition to the preoccupation with the economic costs of non-completion within official discourses, respondents constructed the consequences of non-completion in more than just financial terms. Failure to complete and attain a degree was talked about as resulting in a combination of economic, social and personal failure. Among minority ethnic respondents in particular, emphasis was placed on the family and social consequences of failure (see Archer and Hutchings 2000).

Graduate employment and employability

As already mentioned, respondents constructed the value of higher education closely, though not exclusively, in terms of enhanced employment prospects and possibilities in the labour market after graduation. But respondents perceived that the employment value of a degree was mediated by the risks around working-class graduate employability. Thus, although there was considerable consensus as to the social and economic possibilities offered by a degree, it was widely argued across all the discussion groups that there are considerable risks attached to post-graduation employment. In particular, a popular risk discourse was that the graduate job market is overcrowded (largely as a result of the expansion of HE and many more people having degrees). The jobs aspired to may not be available on graduation. Widening participation was thus widely regarded as potentially dangerous, creating an overcrowded graduate market. This was closely linked to the hierarchy of universities, through which working-class students risked being the first to get squeezed out in a competitive graduate job market. Respondents were also worried that in such a workplace, the value of a working-class student's degree would be lower and would potentially put them at risk of being overqualified.

Respondents thus suggested that the two-tier system of higher education prevents real social mobility across class boundaries for working-class students. As long as working-class students remain disadvantaged through their concentration within less prestigious institutions (Paterson 1997; Reid 1989; Robertson and Hillman 1997), then they will remain disadvantaged in an overcrowded job market. These fears have also been echoed in recent research findings, showing that graduates who stay living at home to study (as many working-class students do) are far less likely to get well-paid jobs as compared to students who left home to study (Audas and Dolton 1999).

Many respondents suggested that as a graduate you may run the risk of being overqualified and therefore not employed at all, or (for mature students), the job you get on qualifying may be no better than the job you had before you went to university. Younger respondents also suggested that it might be possible to achieve the same degree of social mobility by working one's way up within a job, rather than studying for a degree.

The problems of being overqualified in an overcrowded job market were talked about as wasting time, money and effort, with the additional danger that one may become depressed and forced to do 'dirty' jobs:

> I know a lot – loads of people like got law degrees and they're working in these places ... like Boots and Sainsbury's doing manual. It's dirty yeah, that's why I'm saying there's too many people doing law nowadays ... especially after ... degree yeah they can't find a job that's when the real depression start.
>
> (Aziz, 16, Pakistani male)

Thus the social mobility aspirations accorded by a degree rendered certain manual work illegitimate.

Several of the young people, who conceptualized the value of a degree in solely economic and instrumental terms, argued that the value of a degree would be seriously questioned if it did not increase their ability to find a suitable graduate-level job. An over-crowded graduate job market would suggest that it might not be worthwhile to spend years studying only to end up 'over-qualified':

> All this money innit is really not worth it because at the end of the day you could get your degree and all that and you can't get a job you're sweeping the streets with your degree! So what's the point?
>
> (Carmelle, 17, black Caribbean female)

> I know a man, he was my Mum's partner, he had a BA and PhD in front of his name, letters and everything, and he was a tiler and that was all he did. He didn't use them at all.
>
> (Tim, 19, white male)

The 'overcrowded' discourse was largely (although not exclusively) voiced by respondents who did not want to go to university. This discourse drew upon a notion of a finite pool of graduate jobs, with the risk that 'too many' people going to university would result in unemployment:

> It's getting overcrowded, there's too many people going to university and how many jobs are there for those people? There's none, there's hardly any, especially nowadays, hardly any.
>
> (Liam, 22, white male)

A few men, who did not plan to go to university, also argued that leaving the job market (or current employment) to go to university carried a greater risk of future unemployment, or could be detrimental to their career due to the time delay and loss of earnings.

I feel it would be more beneficial to me if I sort of leave now and sort of get on with my career and whatever then if I sort of stay on at uni for three years or whatever. Cos I feel I'd be further down the line and be doing what I want to do.

(Alex, 18, white male)

Summary: risky positions, risky choices

As outlined in Chapter 1, Beck (1992) proposed that risk is a central characteristic of modern society and is implicated in the reproduction of social (class) inequalities. We suggest that working-class groups occupy structurally riskier positions, which translates into making higher education a riskier, and unequal, 'choice'. This theme is taken up, developed and expanded in the following chapters. It will be argued that working-class respondents perceived participation as being highly costly (with regard to time, money, personal relationships and identity) with little certainty of academic, social and/or economic success at the end of it. Risks were counterbalanced by views regarding the potential long-term economic, social personal gains that might be possible as a result of participation, although for working-class students university remained more of a gamble, with higher stakes, than for middle-class students.

Chapter 7

Entry routes to higher education

Pathways, qualifications and social class

Carole Leathwood and Merryn Hutchings

Introduction

This chapter examines entry routes to higher education, discussing the different routes that are available and the range of qualifications that students may take which potentially offer the possibility of university study.

Entry to higher education in the UK is largely dependent upon prior educational achievement, with potential students expected to possess the necessary entry qualifications at an appropriate level. One reason why fewer working-class than middle-class young people go to university is that working-class students continue to do less well educationally than their middle-class peers, although there are considerable differences in relation to ethnicity and gender. 'One of the depressing findings is the relative performance of the disadvantaged has remained similar even when the absolute performance of such groups has improved' (Mortimore and Whitty 1997: 9), and social class remains a powerful predictor of educational achievement in the UK (Bynner *et al.* 1998). Indeed, Coffield shows how the gap between high and low performers is actually widening, hence increasing inequalities based on social class (Coffield 1999).

A number of reasons have been put forward for this differential achievement, including poverty, family expectations, classed (and raced/gendered) assumptions about ability, cultural capital and parental involvement in schooling, and of course the cultures and practices of educational institutions themselves (Connolly and Neill 2001; Epstein *et al.* 1998; Foster 1998; Gillborn 1995; Reay 1999). It is not simply a case, however, of working-class young people doing less well than their middle-class peers in the same examinations. As will be seen, working-class and middle-class young people tend to take different educational routes and qualifications. Those routes more likely to be taken by working-class students are widely considered to be of lower status, and are less likely to lead to entry to prestigious universities, than the routes and qualifications taken by those from middle-class backgrounds.

This chapter begins with an overview of the different educational pathways and qualifications in England, with a particular focus on the academic/

vocational divide. The status and respect awarded to different curricula and qualifications, and the benefits they potentially confer, will be explored. The routes and achievements of working-class students will be discussed, with specific reference to the accounts of the experiences of the working-class young people in our own study. Attention will be drawn to the ways in which social divisions and inequalities are reflected and reproduced through educational institutions, curricula and qualifications.

A divided system

The educational system in England has always been one characterized by divisions between institutions, curricula and qualifications (see Chapters 2 and 3). A primary divide is that between the private (public) and state systems; the former are the preserve of the upper and upper-middle classes and retain privileged access to universities and the professions for their students. Private schools tend to be characterized by their highly academic curricula, and they are not bound by the requirements of the National Curriculum. Such schools traditionally reflected the dominance of aristocratic and anti-industrial values in the UK in the nineteenth century, which included the assumption that 'science and engineering were not suitable subjects for study by gentlemen' (Pratt 2000: 16). The academic/vocational divide in England therefore has a long history, one that is imbued with social class. This history is also gendered, with girls and women thought to be unsuited to an academic curriculum, both because of their presumed destinies as wives and mothers, and because of 'an apparently genuine fear that the workings of the female mind were in conflict with the workings of the female body' (Weiner 1994: 36). As such, in the early part of the twentieth century, a more practical education was recommended for girls (ibid.)

Within the state schooling system too, the division between academic and vocational institutions, curricula and qualifications has been clearly evident. As noted in Chapter 2, the tripartite system of state secondary schooling, established as a result of the 1944 Education Act, was designed in part to open up educational opportunities for all children, but enshrined separate, and differentially valued, educational pathways. Tests of 'ability' at age 11 (the '11-plus' examination) were used to allocate children to the most appropriate secondary school. In practice, however, it continued to ensure that it was mainly the children of the middle classes (with few exceptions) who were able to access the more prestigious grammar schools with their academic curricula and preparation for university study. From 1950 grammar-school children took GCE (General Certificate of Education) O levels at age 16 followed by A levels at age 18; the latter provided entrance to English universities from the 1950s (Wolf 1997). Other children were either steered into the technical schools (to become future technicians), or into secondary modern schools that catered for those young people who were not thought to be capable of more academic study. Such schools were overwhelmingly populated by working-class children. The main examinations offered at age 16 were the CSEs (Certificate of Secondary Education), which were not introduced until the 1960s. They were widely regarded as the poor relation of O levels, and led to very few opportunities for further academic study and thus of acquiring the qualifications necessary to enter higher education.

Considerable criticisms of the 'wastage' of working-class ability, which had been articulated throughout the early part of the twentieth century (see for example Tawney 1931) and also following the introduction of the tripartite system in the 1950s and 1960s (in, for example, the Crowther and Robbins Reports), led to the creation of comprehensive secondary schools. These were intended to provide a range of opportunities for all children of secondary school age within the same school. While the comprehensive system succeeded in opening up opportunities for many working-class children to take the more prestigious academic examinations (McPherson and Willms 1997), and thus to bridge the academic/vocational divide, the government's voluntaristic approach to their introduction meant that in many areas, grammar schools remained to 'cream off' the students with the highest 'ability' levels and a two- (or more) tier system remained. Streaming within schools by ability levels also ensured that some children remained within the lowest stream with few opportunities to obtain the qualifications deemed necessary to progress.

A major problem remained the division between GCE O levels and CSEs, with the latter being regarded as of lesser worth. In the mid 1980s, O levels and CSEs were replaced by a common GCSE, thus in principle moving away from the class divide in qualifications taken at age 16 and enabling the vast majority of children to sit for the same examinations. What has happened, however, is that only an A–C grade at GCSE is regarded as an acceptable pass and equivalent to the old O level, and examination boards offer different levels of examination paper. Students who are considered by their teachers to be unlikely to be able to achieve in the higher level papers are therefore only entered for the lower ones, some of which have a maximum possible achievement level of grade D. Some of our respondents had experienced this.

Of those who leave school at age 16, the vast majority are working-class young people. For 16–18-year-olds who remain in full-time education, the divisions of the school and examination systems are replicated by a division between those who attend school sixth forms or sixth-form colleges and those who go to further education (FE) colleges. The former are more likely to be middle-class and taking A levels (widely regarded as the 'gold standard'), with the latter more likely to be working-class students studying the less prestigious vocational qualifications. FE colleges, the technical colleges not selected for advancement as polytechnics (see Chapter 3), have long been the poor relation of the English education system, lacking the prestige (and levels of funding) of many schools and universities. Up until the 1970s, they catered predominantly for part-time craft and technical study for working-class men, although they subsequently began to offer vocational and pre-vocational courses for 16–19-year-olds, and in many cases GCSE retakes and A levels. Wymer (1994: 89) argues that despite their history in offering educational opportunities to those without qualifications, equality of opportunity continued to be damaged by the separation 'between education and training, sixth forms and colleges' and between the academic and the vocational.

Vocational education and training

It is worth paying some attention to the complexity of the vocational education and training system in England. Students who leave school at age 16, often with few or no qualifications, face a bewildering array of courses at their local FE college. The range of examining bodies, course types and levels has long been far from straightforward. Some courses offered no nationally acceptable certification, and others, qualifications from awarding bodies such as City and Guilds and BTEC. BTEC National qualifications were designed to provide another entry route to higher education.

Various government attempts have been made to bring some coherence to this system, although competition between awarding bodies has ensured that it remains complex (Raggatt and Williams 1999). The UK government commissioned a review of vocational qualifications in 1985. This led to the setting up of the National Council for Vocational Qualifications (NCVQ) and the development of National Vocational Qualifications (NVQs), which are primarily work-based qualifications of vocational practice. These have also been subject to criticism both from employers and educationalists and, although provision is made for NVQs at 5 levels (with level 4 being degree equivalent and level 5 being postgraduate/professional), the vast majority of qualifications awarded have been at levels 1 and 2, with only 3.6 per cent of those awarded in 1997 being at levels 4 or 5 (Raggatt and Williams 1999). The widely held assumptions that vocational qualifications are of a lower level than academic ones is thus reinforced.

Further developments in vocational qualifications came about with the establishment of GNVQs as part of a three-track qualifications framework alongside A levels and NVQs (DES 1991). GNVQs, introduced in 1992, aimed to offer a broad vocational curriculum which would prepare students for work in specific occupational fields, for entry to higher level vocational courses such as the HND (Higher National Diploma), or for entry to degree programmes. Yet again they have been subject to criticism for their competence-based approach (Howieson et al. 1997). Although they became the predominant vocational qualifications for students aged

16–19, other vocational qualifications such as BTEC continued to exist, and the range of courses became more complex. Plans to develop level 4 and 5 GNVQs were shelved, and more recently the introduction of foundation degrees, vocational courses at sub-degree level, has been heralded as the basis for further expansion of participation in higher education (DFEE 2000). However, many of the institutions offering these courses are FE ones. Melville and McLeod note that 'there are over 17,000 different qualifications available within further education colleges spanning general and higher education through to job-related training', and that less than half of these are for academic and vocational courses within the national framework (2000: 32).

The academic/vocational divide in English education does not, of course, stop at sixth forms and FE colleges. The binary system of higher education, discussed in Chapter 3, maintains this division in higher education. Despite unification, the old elite institutions have retained their highly academic reputation, with the new, post-1992 universities being widely regarded as more practical, vocational, and of lower status, something that is discussed further in Chapter 6.

The value of vocational qualifications

Different pathways, curricula and qualifications accrue differential value and benefits. As has been seen, the English aristocracy, whose values continue to influence private schools and indeed the wider society, rejected technical and engineering studies as unsuitable for gentlemen. Middle-class resistance to vocational education, with the exception of that leading to elite professions such as medicine and law, remains. The warnings implicit in phrases such as 'getting one's hands dirty', or 'being too near to the coal face' are reflective of the lack of the respect associated with manual occupations amongst the upper/middle classes, and vocational education has long been seen as the preserve of the (male) working classes. Indeed, research on consumer pressures in relation to the upper secondary age group shows how the creation of quasi-markets in schooling has enabled some middle-class parents to exert their influence in favour of a highly academic curriculum, thereby deterring schools from the provision of high quality vocational education (Davies and Adnett 1999). A traditional academic curriculum, enshrined in A levels, remains the only one of value for some.

Resistance to vocational education, or to some forms of vocational education, has come from a number of different directions, including academics on the left of the political spectrum, New Right traditionalists and aspects of the media. Ainley (1994) noted the anti-vocationalism of academics in sociology and English who were keen to construct their subjects as 'properly' academic in a context where the more abstract the subject (such as traditional philosophy or theoretical physics), the higher the prestige in traditional academia. Attacks from the New Right on new vocational subjects have added to the resistance of some academics to vocational routes to higher education. At the same time, there has been sustained criticism of the form of vocationalism inspired by economic rationalism, whereby education is reduced to the performance of narrowly defined competencies (Esland 1996), and, as already noted, GNVQs have been subjected to such criticism. Zera and Jupp, both with experience as principals of FE colleges, are also very critical of GNVQ. They note that student numbers on GNVQ courses at levels 1 and 2 (that is, up to GCSE-equivalent level) are going down, 'perhaps because these pseudo-vocational courses are poorly constructed, repetitive in content, boring and frequently use culturally biased tests for accreditation' (Zera and Jupp 2000: 134).

Vocational qualifications themselves are not undifferentiated in the value and status they accrue, and several feminist academics have further contributed to their critique. Skeggs notes how the 'major role' of caring courses in an FE college 'involves enabling working-class women to know their place, winning consent for the social placement of them as unpaid domestic labourers, willing to sustain both their own families and provide Community Care if necessary' (Skeggs 1997: 52). Blackmore (1997) demonstrates how educational policies in Australia, aimed at providing a more highly skilled workforce and embodied in a 'discourse of vocationalism', were often presented as improving opportunities for the working classes, yet ignored the ways in which skills and the labour market are gendered. Similarly, Kenway and Willis (1995) discuss the key competences developed to bring together general and vocational education in post-compulsory education in Australia, and argue they are masculinist in both conceptions of the workplace and the notions of competence they utilize.

Although vocational education could be constructed very differently (see, for example, Ainley 1994, for the ideals of a polytechnic education), given the widespread critique it is not surprising that many of the young people we interviewed also articulated negative views of vocational courses:

> BTECs and GNVQs aren't really recognized like. Well my parents don't really recognize it.
>
> (Sofia, 18, white Italian female FE student)

> When I told my Mum 'I'm not doing A levels I'm doing a BTEC', they just laughed at me. ... They thought BTEC's a cartoon character or something! That's the truth! Do you know what I mean? My Mum and Dad and my uncles don't recognize BTEC as a qualification.
>
> (Abdul, 20, Asian male FE student)

Abdul's comments could be interpreted as indicative of his and/or his family's negative views of BTEC qualifications and/or as an indication of their lack of knowledge of such qualifications, something that is compounded by the range of different vocational options and the lack of prestige they attract.

As Zera and Jupp note:

> Only the most exclusive sacred cows (A levels and degrees) are understood at all, while the huge collection of arcane acronyms that label the majority of qualifications are an inaccessible mystery to most people.
>
> (Zera and Jupp 2000: 133)

They go on to argue that lack of knowledge and understanding of vocational qualifications leads to people assuming that they are not worth much. Smith (1997), in research conducted in five FE colleges in 1995–6, found that GNVQ students perceived A-level students as more 'academic' and 'theoretical', indicating the ways in which courses and qualifications contribute to identity construction, and the potentially negative implications of this for those on GNVQ and other relatively low status courses. Avis (1991) has also shown how courses and curricula can reinforce and reconstruct classed identities for students.

A unified curriculum?

The lack of prestige of vocational qualifications has prompted a number of attempts to bring about some unity between the academic and vocational curricula, with Howieson et al. (1997) identifying educational, economic and social arguments in the case for unification. The perceived weakness of vocational education in the UK (Raggatt and Williams 1999), and the desire to link education more firmly to the needs of the economy (Hatcher 1998b), can be seen as key elements of government policy. Despite a government sponsored report which recommended that A levels be broadened (Higginson 1988), early attempts at reform failed to make any changes to these 'gold standard' qualifications as a result of the resistance of the Conservative government of the time, led by Margaret Thatcher. Such resistance reinforced the status differences between the academic and the vocational (Davies et al. 1997). However, in an attempt to broaden the post-16 curriculum, AS levels, equivalent to half an A level, were introduced. Persistent calls have been made for a unified curriculum (for example, see Spours and Young 1988) including proposals for a British Baccalaureate and, in 1991, the Labour Party proposed an 'Advanced Certificate of Education and Training' which would include an amended A-level curriculum along with vocational units. Ongoing problems with A levels (such as a 30 per cent drop-out rate), GNVQs (OFSTED 1996), and NVQs into the mid-1990s (Howieson et al. 1997), set the scene for further post-16 curriculum reform.

The result was Curriculum 2000. This initiative was designed to enable students to take a combination of academic, vocational and key skills units, while studying a wider range of subjects. A-level and AS units are still available as part of this package, and Advanced level GNVQs have become Vocational A levels (AVCEs). As Williams notes, the renaming of vocational qualifications to include 'A level' is a device to symbolize enhanced standards (Williams 1997). While there has been some support for the principles of the new curriculum, a number of difficulties associated with student workload, the lack of value placed on the key skills qualifications and problems with Vocational A levels have been identifed (QCA 2001). In addition, plans were announced to introduce Vocational GCSEs from September 2002, to replace foundation, intermediate and part 1 GNVQs as a new vocational alternative for 14–16-year-olds. A number of concerns about these have been expressed (FEFC 2001). Of course one of the dangers is that more working-class young people and more of those from specific minority ethnic groups will be steered into the vocational route at age 14.

Discussions of a unified curriculum from 14–19 are however still on the agenda, along with a renewed interest in various forms of baccalaureate (Woodward 2001). The latest government proposals at the time of writing are encapsulated in a new Education Green Paper: *14–19: Extending Opportunities, Raising Standards* (DfES 2002). This provides a framework for a new 14–19 curriculum containing a common core from the National Curriculum, and different, flexible, academic and vocational pathways. They are intended to have parity of esteem, and to that end the word 'vocational' is being dropped: 'We also believe choice and parity of esteem would be better served by no longer attaching labels to signal that GCSEs are general or vocational, and instead simply naming them all GCSEs' (DfES 2002: 30). Whether this will tempt high-achieving students into the vocational routes remains to be seen. A new over-arching qualification, a 'matriculation diploma', is also proposed which will recognize achievement in the core units (in maths, English and science) and in both general and vocational pathways. This is to be offered at three levels:

- Intermediate, reflecting the usual level of entry for employment
- Advanced, for entry to higher education
- Higher, 'rewarding greater achievement at advanced level and reflecting a common entry level for high ranking universities' (DfES 2002:40).

Parity of esteem for higher education institutions is obviously not envisaged.

Entry routes for mature students

The entry routes to higher education discussed above, namely A levels and their vocational 'equivalents' of BTEC and GNVQ, have predominantly been used by 18-year-olds to enter university. In addition, alternative entry routes have been established for mature students. Access courses, offered mainly in FE colleges, were specifically designed for mature students without standard qualifications, and they were officially recognized for entry to higher education in 1987 (Williams 1997). They have had a great deal of influence in widening participation in higher education for mature students, though there have been criticisms that they have been 'colonized' by the middle classes (Davies 1995; Wakeford 1993). Some universities also accept adults with appropriate work and other experience under special entry arrangements, and some attempts have been made by some universities to accredit prior experience and learning (APEL), although progress has been slow and there remains considerable resistance to this approach within HE (Peters 2001). The extent to which universities welcome mature students is discussed later in this chapter.

The next section will examine working-class achievements more closely, drawing on data from our own study that highlight working-class young people's concerns and understandings of entry routes to HE.

Working-class routes and achievements

The institutions which pupils/students attend both reflect and construct inequalities. As has already been seen, working-class students are more likely to attend state schools rather than private and, even within the state sector, they are more likely to be in schools in poorer neighbourhoods with fewer resources than the schools of their middle-class peers. Post-16, working-class and minority ethnic students who do stay on are more likely to be in further education colleges than sixth-form colleges, and those in FE colleges achieve both lower level and fewer qualifications than those in sixth-form colleges, who in turn do less well than those in selective and/or independent schools – in A levels, GCSEs and GNVQs (DfES 2001). One explanation for this is likely to be the lower achievements at GCSE level for those who go to further education colleges, with students with five or more A–C passes at GCSE more likely to be in schools and sixth form centres (Melville and Macleod 2000). Research also indicates, however, that 'A-level students in school sixth forms and sixth-form colleges had a significantly lower risk of being unsuccessful than students in FE colleges, even after taking into account total points score[1] in Year 11 GCSEs and other relevant factors' (Payne 2001). One factor is likely to be the historic resourcing differences in post-16 institutions, with students in further education colleges attracting a lower unit of funding than those in sixth-form colleges.

Classed, raced and gendered assumptions about students' ability and potential were identified by many of our respondents as key issues in determining the routes they should take:

> I went to the careers advisor and they're trying to put you down saying
> 'Oh you won't get the grades'. How can they tell you that?
>
> (Carmelle, 16, black Caribbean female FE student)

> But most of the teachers are very stereotypical, so it was like 'You could
> go into that', so they brand you.
>
> (Joan, 33, black Caribbean female secretarial temp)

Some described how they had not been allowed to sit particular exams, and a number expressed their and, in some cases, their parents' resentment at being advised to study for vocational rather than academic qualifications. As Trotman (1998) and Pugsley (1998) found, some respondents also said that their teachers had advised them against HE entry. One example is Loretta's account of her application to university (see Chapter 5). Many of the black African and Caribbean women expressed a confidence in their own abilities and a determination to resist what they saw as prejudicial advice from teachers and careers officers. Loretta explains:

> They wanted me to do a GNVQ or a BTEC, which I don't like that style
> of learning, so I just decided to redo my GCSEs ... So she said to me 'I
> don't think you should continue with this path, you know your GCSEs
> and on to A-level path, I think really you should go on to a BTEC'. And I
> said 'Do you know that I won't join your course, but I will join a course
> and when I pass it I will show you my slip' and when I did pass I went
> and showed her my slip, just to be cheeky.
>
> (Loretta, 18, black African female FE student and sales assistant)

> They gave me a choice, they said 'Well look you can do GNVQ Science
> or you do AS levels' and I said 'No, I refuse' ... and I put my foot down.
> ... 'I can prove to you that I can do better than this', and so they allowed
> me to stay on.
>
> (Leeza, 18, mixed-race female FE student and sales assistant)

Some respondents, however, had clearly been discouraged by their teachers' and careers officers' advice, which could be seen to have contributed to their own self-identities as 'stupid' and not capable of academic study. Recent research (Goddard 2001) also suggests that students from further education colleges are at an additional disadvantage as their teachers tend to give predicted grades which underestimate their subsequent achievement, in contrast to teachers in private schools who overestimate their students' grades. As predicted grades are used by universities in their selection processes, such predictions are important.

It comes as no surprise that entry routes to HE are differentiated by class and ethnicity:

The profile of applicants entering through different qualification routes varies, for example, Access and GNVQ applicants tend to be mature, from social classes IIIM, IV and V and of Black and Asian ethnic origin, whereas applicants with A-level qualifications tend to be under 21 years old, from social classes I, II and IIIN and white.

(UCAS 1999: 8)

The extent of the variation in entry routes by ethnicity is evident from UCAS data for applicants to full-time higher education, which show that in 1999:

* 27 per cent of black applicants had A levels, and 14 per cent had GNVQs
* 49 per cent of Asian applicants had A levels, and 18 per cent had GNVQs
* 61 per cent of white applicants had A levels, and only 7 per cent had GNVQs[2] (UCAS 2000).

It was evident that some of our respondents and their parents were very aware that A levels were the predominant and favoured route to HE entry, and African-Caribbean women in particular were prepared to challenge attempts to divert them into other routes. For many others, however, the qualifications needed to enter university remained as much a mystery as university itself. Hutchings and Archer (2001) have discussed the qualifications that respondents thought were needed to get on to a degree course:

Quite a lot. Ones higher than I have.

(Aimee, 21, white female childminder)

You have to have your GCSEs. You can't just go to a college course with nothing ... I suppose a couple of GCSEs but they have to be a certain grade and above.

(Kim, 18, white female secretary)

Eight GCSEs.

(Reka, 17, Asian female FE student)

You need probably A levels – I think it doesn't matter if you get Es in them.

(Aziz, 16, Asian male FE student)

A levels – you need excellent grades or you're not going nowhere.

(Patrick, 18, black Caribbean male FE student)

High level GNVQs and Youth Entry.

(Aziz, 16, Asian male FE student)

> BTEC, City and Guilds.
>
>   (Sanjeeva, 17, Asian male FE student)

> Higher than Einstein.
>
>   (Laura, 30, white female bank worker)

The suggestions of the qualifications needed were generally significantly higher than the qualifications the speaker had achieved or was working towards. Laura's reply makes it quite clear that such qualifications are utterly out of reach (Hutchings and Archer 2001).

Some of those who said that they hoped to go to university had acquired more information, though even for this group it was often rather vague:

> What I've been told is if I pass this course then I go to GNVQs Advanced in IT. Then that's a two year course. If I pass ... then I can go and do a degree in computers at university.
>
>   (Amjed, 17, Asian male FE student)

> Well you need points innit? There's this points ... about ten in the unit innit? Ten points like Bs or As or something. C is six and D is er ... .
>
>   (Majid, 16, Asian male FE student)

Others, even some young people on BTEC courses that could lead straight to university, did not consider such information important:

> NEVILLE: We just got into college ...
> WINSTON: So we've still got another two more years
> NEVILLE: There's no like sense even knowing about it. It's irrelevant.
>
>   (Black Caribbean male FE students on a
>   BTEC National programme)

The experiences of these respondents contrast sharply with the planned and knowledgeable experiences of many middle-class young people (Ball *et al.* 2000a; Reay *et al.* 2001), where going to university is more likely to be assumed and taken for granted.

Even when working-class students have the same qualifications as those from the middle classes, fewer apply to university (Hatcher 1998a; Metcalf 1997). Some of the reasons for this, in particular the financial, social and identity risks associated with participation in HE for many working-class people, are discussed in other chapters. The final sections of this chapter will consider the implications of the different academic and vocational routes for entry to university, staying the course, and progression to the job market.

Entering and studying in higher education

There was concern amongst a number of our respondents that vocational qualifications were likely to be seen as of lower value by universities and less likely to lead to university entry:

> at the end of the day ... they're looking for A-level students. GNVQ, the whole lot of it, they're all glamorized. Yes, they want A levels they want As and Bs, and if you haven't got it, you might get in, ... but you're going to be labelled ... you won't be able to be the top.
>
> (Michelle, black Caribbean female FE student)

One respondent who had successfully entered higher education also said:

> I was very surprised that I was accepted here because I applied to six universities and the other five categorically said no, not a chance, not even an offer. Cos I've got Advanced GNVQ plus GCSEs and that's not usually enough to get into any university.
>
> (Ewan, 21, white HE student)

Similar concerns were expressed by a few students about applying to university from an Access course:

> There is a limited choice being an Access student ... cos many of the other colleges just want A levels.
>
> (Birgit, 56, white HE student)

Research has also supported these respondents' concerns. Paczuska (1996) discovered that universities favoured A-level students because A levels were assumed to provide more appropriate skills for academic study, with vocational qualifications being seen as second best. A recent report on mature students by the DfES (Davies *et al.* 2002) also suggests that there was a great deal of variation between universities and departments within universities in the extent to which they encouraged or discouraged mature applicants. Some argue that universities are right to be so selective. Smithers insists that 'A levels, GNVQs and NVQs have their origin in qualifications designed to take young people in different directions – to degrees, to supervisory and technician posts, and to the shopfloor' (Smithers 2000: 67). He argues that:

> If those with at least five good GCSEs predominantly take one type of award (A level) and those who do not, another (GNVQ or NVQ), it makes little sense to try to treat these awards as equivalent. Universities know this and will, where they have a choice, admit on good A-levels. Where they do not, they tend to ply the rhetoric of access.
>
> (Smithers 2000: 67)

His use of language in referring to 'the rhetoric of access' suggests that he is less than sympathetic to widening participation initiatives, and it is indicative of the 'discourse of derision' (Ball 1990; Kenway 1987) that academic traditionalists have long adopted in relation to any attempts to widen participation in HE (Thompson 1997). What he apparently ignores, apart from the inequalities in the school system and the class issues in educational routes and achievements, is the possibility that students can improve on their previous attainments. Lack of success in GCSEs does not necessarily mean that students lack the potential to do well academically, as indicated by the many mature students who go on to achieve good degrees despite a poor academic record at school.

University acceptance is not, however, simply based on possession of the preferred qualifications. Modood and Shiner argue that many pre-1992 universities are less likely to accept applicants from ethnic minority and lower socio-economic groups, even when their qualifications are the same as those of middle-class applicants (Modood and Shiner 1994).

A further concern about the viability of vocational qualifications as an entry route to university related to their perceived accessibility, which could be seen to contribute to their lack of prestige. Some young people expressed concern that the numbers of people taking these qualifications would lead to them becoming devalued. One respondent criticized GNVQ Leisure and Tourism:

> So like at the end of the day you're going to have how many odd people with this qualification and ... At the end of the day, it's rubbish.
>
> (Michelle, 16, black Caribbean female FE student)

The implication here is that a GNVQ (especially in Leisure and Tourism), is not worth very much because of the numbers of people who take this course. In terms of qualifications, scarcity is seen to confer status, and attempts to widen participation have generated a moral panic about educational standards. As Williams notes, 'the essence of excellence in higher education, unlike compulsory education, lies therefore in the inability of the vast majority of the population to achieve its standards' (Williams 1997: 32). Yet more and more people have managed to achieve once scarce qualifications. In the early to mid 1960s, A levels were taken by only 6 per cent of population, but they are now taken by over a third of the age group (Wolf 1997). Although there are annual concerns in the UK media about whether the rise in the numbers of students doing well in GCSEs and A levels is indicative of a fall in standards (as opposed to changes in teaching practice or the hard work of students) there is no real evidence that A levels are losing their 'gold standard' status. Wolf shows similar patterns in achievement in France, with increases in the numbers taking the baccalaureate and entering university, and similar increases in

Germany and Australia. She argues that there is a 'tyranny of numbers' whereby the more people that carry on in education, the greater the pressure on others to do the same, and the more employers look for those with even higher qualifications.

There was also some concern amongst some respondents as to whether non-traditional entry routes would provide adequate preparation for university level study. When one group of FE students on a vocational programme were asked what advice they would give other young people, they strongly recommended A levels, arguing that 'you learn more in A levels', 'they are harder', 'more intense'. One recounted:

> My friend did travel and tourism [GNVQ] and he found it crap as well and now he's at uni he's really struggling cos the course didn't prepare him for university. So I don't think this course prepares you for uni cos it's so relaxed and the work's just, well I don't think the work's difficult at all.
>
> (Theresa, 20, white female FE student)

There were isolated voices in support of vocational qualifications. Chantelle felt that the 'practical side' of GNVQ was important, and that 'a lot of universities look for that'. Another respondent who was at university acknowledged the negative reputation of vocational courses, but argued that her course had constituted a more useful preparation for university than an A-level programme would have done:

> And like coming here from my college course, cos I did a BTEC, it was just like this. It was really independent and everyone, even now, kind of frowns on BTECs rather than A levels and kind of says 'Oh you get a really easy time, you don't have to do exams'. But we'd have just so much work, a lot of practical work, and you really were going off and doing it yourself, so I think … it is much more independent and it's kind of not quite so shocking.
>
> (Stella, 18, white female HE student)

There is a strong correlation between average A-level points and the percentage of students who either achieve an award or transfer to another institution (National Audit Office 2002b). It has also been found that those individuals who withdraw have significantly lower entry qualifications than those who go on to graduate. This has implications for the curriculum, levels of support, resourcing and academic cultures of those higher education institutions accepting considerable numbers with vocational qualifications. Robertson predicted that if higher education didn't change, GNVQ students would be regarded as 'second class entrants' (1995: 297).

Entering the graduate labour market

As was seen in Chapter 6, a number of the young people in this study questioned the value of the degrees that might be open to them, i.e. those from the less prestigious post-1992 universities. Their fears are not unfounded.

Many employers continue to target their graduate recruitment activities at the old, elite universities. The Association of Graduate Recruiters reports that traditional notions of the reputation of a university and the calibre of its graduates continued to be influential, with employers favouring institutions that have high entry requirements. Indeed 29.5 per cent of employers stated that they currently used A-level point scores in their graduate recruitment (Association of Graduate Recruiters 1999), indicating that the 'gold-standard' reputation of A levels is still important even when the applicants have a degree. Data from the first destination survey of UK graduates show that those students with most A-level points are most likely to be in employment six months after graduation. Of students with 25–30 points, 94.9 per cent are in employment, whereas the corresponding figures for GNVQ and Access qualifications are 90.5 per cent and 87.3 per cent respectively (HEFCE 2001a). Even three-and-a-half years after graduation, pre-entry qualifications still impact on earnings, even after controlling for degree class and subject studied (Elias *et al.* 1999). Fletcher (2001), in a review on the economic returns of different qualifications, concludes that vocational qualifications produce lower returns than academic ones at an equivalent level, and that this remains when individual ability differences are controlled for.

Respondents' concerns about the increasing number of people able to access higher level qualifications also have some resonance. Coffield (1999) notes that as more students get degrees, the value decreases, so there becomes a greater emphasis on the university attended and the class of degree, thereby keeping the 'hierarchy of prestige' intact. Hirsch also noted that:

> The ... excess of apparently qualified candidates induces an intensification of job screening that has the effect of lengthening the obstacle course of education and favouring those best able to sustain a longer or more costly race. These are the well off and the well connected.
>
> (Hirsch 1977: 50 cited by Brown 1997: 741)

It is not surprising, then, that for the majority of the non-participant respondents in our research, the risks of university study were high.

Conclusions

Despite some successes, repeated government attempts to ameliorate class-based inequalities in education over the last century have not managed to seriously challenge these inequalities. In this chapter we have argued that the academic/vocational divide in educational institutions, curricula and qualifications has been key to the reaffirmation of middle-class privilege in education and employment.

Government policy in this arena has been motivated by a complex mixture of human capital concerns to produce a suitably skilled workforce, and social justice concerns to promote inclusion. As Hatcher (1998b: 490) has shown, however, 'the reality is that the human capital Bac C argument does not entail a radical equalizing upwards of the future workforce but a stratified and differentiated school population which roughly corresponds to the stratified hierarchy of the future labour market'. At the same time, Levitas has argued that the Labour government's concerns with social inclusion are less about attempts to reduce class inequalities than to disguise them (Levitas 1998).

The extent to which the most recent attempts to reduce the divisions between academic and vocational institutions, curricula and qualifications are successful in reducing social class differences in achievement and opportunities to progress, remain to be seen. To some extent the academic/vocational divide in institutions has changed as Curriculum 2000 applies to both sixth form and FE colleges, although in practice there are still very distinct patterns of study in the different institutions. In 1997, Williams concluded that none of the alternative qualifications 'has the discursive power of A levels. They remain the gold standard, the normal method of entry, the signifier of both individual and institutional worth, the predictor of quality output' (Williams 1997: 60) and, as yet, there seems little evidence to challenge this.

Wolf (1997) argues that one implication of educational and economic changes is that new hierarchies and divisions emerge. She notes how in France, people value the general (academic) baccalaureate over the technical one, although they are both meant to have the same status. The Bac C which has a maths specialism has the highest prestige as it is regarded as the hardest. Wolf concludes that this is inevitable as societies have elite positions, and some qualifications will always be identified as the hardest and worthiest. Hatcher points out that the French baccalaureate is also differentiated by class, with working-class young people far less likely to get a Bac C than their middle-class peers (Hatcher 1998a). He examines the case of Sweden to conclude that class inequalities in education are entrenched.

It remains to be seen whether new plans for the 14–19 curriculum in the government's recent Green Paper (DFES 2002) will be successful in reducing the class-based inequalities of the academic–vocational divide.

Notes

1 'Points score' refers to the system of awarding points for each A-level pass, with more points awarded for higher grade passes. Universities use point scores in their selection processes.
2 The remaining applicants in each ethnic category held a range of other qualifications including Scottish Highers, Access and foundation courses, etc., or had no disclosed qualification.

Chapter 8

Financial barriers to participation

Merryn Hutchings

The financial cost to the student of higher education is often spoken of as the greatest barrier to increasing working-class participation (for example Lynch and O'Riordan 1998; Woodrow 1999). Whereas schools and universities can devise widening participation strategies that address some aspects of the barriers relating to information and qualifications, the barrier of cost is entirely dependent on central government policy. At the time of writing a review of student support arrangements is ongoing. Announcing this review, Estelle Morris, Secretary of State for Education and Skills, was quoted as saying:

> I recognize that for many lower income families the fear of debt is a real worry and could act as a bar to higher education. I want to make sure that our future reform tackles this problem. Our aim is to get more children from less privileged backgrounds into higher education and we hope to achieve this by changing the combination of family, student and state contributions.
>
> (DfES 2001)

Ironically, these aims are little different from those the government set out in 1998 when it argued that the changes to student funding at that time recognized 'the need to widen access particularly for students from lower income groups' (DfEE 1998b: 52). Yet, as this chapter will show, there is overwhelming evidence that the 1998 changes to funding have had the most negative effects on students from lower social class groups. These students have the largest, and most rapidly rising, debts, and are most likely to undertake term-time employment (with possible negative effects on their academic work). They have to cope with a very complex system that does not enable them to plan their income and expenditure, or to make an economic assessment of the costs and long-term economic benefits of higher education in the way that Dearing suggested.

This chapter will review the effects of changes in funding policies since 1990, and will discuss the ways that these are constructed by non-participants and by those at university. It will consider how financial factors feature in decision-making, and how working-class respondents perceive the current system to be unjust.

Changes to student support 1990–2002

As outlined in Chapters 2 and 3, between 1962 and the late 1980s there was little change made to the arrangements for financial support of full-time undergraduate students. Tuition was paid by the state, and living costs were funded by means-tested maintenance grants and, where necessary, social security benefits (Callender 2001). But as numbers in higher education increased, the costs to the state escalated. The Conservative government argued that, as the students were the ones to benefit from higher education, they themselves should contribute more substantially to the costs. This reflects the Thatcherite ideology of individualism and of freedom from state intervention (ibid.). The government claimed that the financial burden on parents and taxpayers should be reduced because 'many ... taxpayers do not share the advantages that students have once they graduate' (DES 1988). From 1990, the level of maintenance grants was frozen and a loan was offered to all full-time students. The ratio of the loan to the grant element increased between 1990 and 1998. Repayments started once the graduate was earning 85 per cent of national average earnings, and loans normally had to be repaid within five years (Payne and Callender 1997).

As Chapter 3 explains, the Dearing Report (1997), in its wide-ranging review of higher education, considered student funding arrangements. It recommended charging tuition fees on a flat rate, while retaining a system of means-tested maintenance grants for those most in need. But the new Labour government rejected these recommendations and published different proposals; these were included in the 1998 Teaching and Higher Education Act. Tuition fees were introduced, as Dearing had suggested, but the level of contribution was means-tested. Maintenance grants were replaced entirely by loans.

Those entering full-time higher education in autumn 1998 had to contribute towards their tuition fees (set initially at a maximum of £1,000). Maintenance grants, albeit at a reduced rate, were still available to this cohort. For those entering in autumn 1999, student loans entirely replaced grants. The loans now included a component (a quarter) that was dependent on means-testing. Arrangements for repayment changed; the threshold income above which repayment had to be made was lowered to £10,000, and the level of repayment varied with income.

David Blunkett, then Secretary of State for Education and Employment, claimed that these funding arrangements were 'designed to address the crisis' inherited by the Labour government, and that the Act 'modernizes student support in higher education in a way which is fair to individual students and their families' (DfEE 1998a). The main justification for the changes was that 'those who benefit from higher education should share the costs' (DfEE 1998b). This policy signals a continuation of the Conservative government's policies and of the move to shift the burden from tax-payer and parent to student. Despite some early criticism of these changes, both government and CVCP stated that the new arrangements would benefit students from low-income families:

> In terms of widening access to higher education, the new funding scheme benefits students from the poorer backgrounds in two key ways. The state will pay their tuition fees in full; and they will have access to larger subsidised loans for living costs.
>
> (CVCP 1999: 3)

It is hard to understand how CVCP could construct these as benefits: students had for many years had their tuition fees paid in full, and subsidized loans, however large, are less financially beneficial than maintenance grants.

What, then, have been the effects of these changes on students from low-income backgrounds? Claire Callender, who has studied student finance extensively through the Student Income and Expenditure Surveys in 1995–6 and 1998–9 (Callender and Kempson 1996; Callender and Kemp 2000), is absolutely clear that the reforms have 'their most negative effects on the most disadvantaged students' (2001: 5).

She argues that student funding in the past largely benefited the middle classes, in that they were the main people to enter higher education. The new arrangements can then be seen as progressive in that the public subsidy to those who are better off is reduced. However, she points out that despite the increased numbers in higher education, the proportion from lower social class groups has hardly increased (see Chapters 3 and 4). As a result the proportion of funding going to the middle classes remains high, even though more of the costs have been shifted from the government to the student. Crucially, the effect of the Labour government's policy is that 'the financial burden is far greater for low-income students than for high-income students' (Callender 2001: 9). Thus she argues that the policies are regressive, in that the least well-off students benefit the least.

Callender sets out a model that she uses to support her argument. This assumes that the cost of a student loan to the government is around 30–50 per cent of the actual loan. This is because the interest paid by the government on their borrowings to fund student loans is greater than the interest paid by students, and because there is a time lag as students defer payments. Thus the amount going from the state to a student in a high-income family has fallen only slightly, as the parental contribution towards tuition fees balances the subsidy provided through the loan system. But for the student from a low-income family, the subsidy offered through the loan system is substantially less than that previously offered by a maintenance grant. As a result, Callender claims, the amount of state subsidy to a student from a high-income family has fallen between 1989 and 2001 by around 2.5 per cent. But for a student from a low-income family, the subsidy has fallen by about 35 per cent.

Another way of looking at this is to say that the main difference in support received by a student from a high-income background and a student from a low-income background now amounts to only £1,075 a year: the current level of the tuition fees. Those from low-income backgrounds can take out larger loans – but these have to be repaid. Depending on their circumstances, they may also have access to a range of statutory and discretionary grants and loans; these are discussed below.

As the effects of the 1998 changes have become more apparent, they have been increasingly condemned by a wide range of bodies. Following devolution, the Scottish Parliament set up an Independent Committee of Inquiry into Student Finance led by Cubie (1999), as a result of which tuition fees have been abolished and a different and more generous support system has been introduced. In Wales an Independent Investigation Group on Student Hardship and Funding in Wales (Rees 2001) has rejected Westminster's policies. Connor and Dewson, of the Institute for Employment Studies, in a report commissioned by the DfEE on issues affecting decisions about participation by lower social class groups, argue that finance is not 'the single prohibitive factor' (2001: viii), but concluded that there 'seems to be a need to improve the level of support available or reduce costs, as there are widely seen to be financial disincentives to going on to HE study' (2001: 75). The Institute for Public Policy Research condemns the current system as 'socially regressive … complex, confusing and bureaucratic' (Brown and Piatt 2001: 15). The recent *Social Class and Participation in HE* report commissioned by Universities UK (Woodrow *et al.*) concludes that the changes to student support since 1997 'are widely held to have been regressive and a disincentive to participation' (Woodrow *et al.* 2002: 4). The National Audit Office report on *Widening Participation in Higher Education in England* comments that 'final removal of the means-tested grant is likely to have widened the gap between the social classes' (2002a: 13).

The ongoing changes to the system suggest that the government is aware that current arrangements provide insufficient support for those from the poorest backgrounds. Each year new measures have been introduced for those students most in need. Thus for those entering higher education in autumn 2000, the Access Bursary became available. This was a non-repayable mean-tested bursary of up to £1,000 for those students over 25 years old at the start of their course, paid through higher education institutions (HEIs). Students already had to make applications relating to financial support to the LEA and the Student Loans Company; now for some a third application was necessary, to the HEI. Other changes included the introduction of a statutory School Meals Grant, a particularly welcome measure for lone parents who lost their income support entitlement on starting higher education. Changes were also made to the regulations relating to discretionary Hardship Funds (again provided through the HEI). For those students starting in 2001, there have been further changes. The Access Bursary is replaced by a statutory Childcare Grant, and Opportunity Bursaries are now available for a limited number of young students from disadvantaged backgrounds. In announcing these David Blunkett claimed that they would 'give able young people from backgrounds without a history of participation in universities or colleges the extra financial incentives and confidence they need to embark on a higher education course' (DfES 2000). Implicitly, then, he acknowledged that the existing support system did not provide sufficient incentive.

The announcement in October 2001 of a review of student support created the impression that further, and more dramatic, changes would be brought in for the 2002–3 academic year. However, it is now clear that the review is taking longer than anticipated and that the implementation of any changes is likely to be delayed to 2003–4 (*THES* 2002a).

The discussion so far has focused on full-time student support. Since the 1998 measures were introduced, there have been indications that a higher proportion of mature students have chosen to study part-time (Davies *et al.* 2002). The financial issues for part-time students are rather different. They have always had to pay tuition fees, though like full-time students they pay an agreed figure rather than the real cost of the course. Since 1998, some limited measures have been introduced to provide greater financial assistance for part-time students. These include small loans (£500 per year) for new and existing low-income students, and help with tuition fees for those who lose their jobs after the course has started, or who are on social security benefits or a low income.

The effects of the changes

The current student support system has given rise to a wide range of concerns. Students have faced increasing levels of debt, and as a result some have suffered hardship. Increasing numbers of students are engaged in term-time employment. Financial difficulties have been implicated in levels of student non-completion. For prospective students, these concerns may be a disincentive to application. In addition they are faced with a system that is daunting in its complexity and opacity. Inability to understand what support is available and how it is accessed, or to predict future income, has been identified as a major problem. Each of these issues will be addressed in turn.

Student debt

The level of student debt has been rising since student loans were introduced, and the last few years have shown a very marked increase. The full effect of the abolition of maintenance grants will only become apparent in the levels of debt of those graduating in summer 2002. The MORI Unite survey (*THES* 2002b) shows that in 2001 the average debt of third-year students was about £7,000, and that those from lower social class backgrounds had larger debts.

The current funding arrangements mean that those who are poor before going to university are most likely to end up owing the most, because they are entitled to borrow a larger sum, and will probably need to do so. Thus those who take out their full student loan will inevitably end up with much higher debts than those found by MORI. A three-year course for a student living away from home would produce debts of £11,200, and studying in London, of £13,805 (2002–3 rates). Many students also arrange overdrafts and bank or personal loans; thus debts over £15,000 may be common.

These sums represent a year's income for many families, and it is hardly surprising that they are a disincentive for potential applicants. Knowles (2000) in a survey of Year 12 school pupils from lower socio-economic groups, found that 57 per cent said that they were less likely to apply to university in the light of the new funding arrangements. The majority believed that their choice of course or of higher education institution was now constrained. The young people we spoke with were generally very concerned at the prospect of long-term debt; they spoke of the risks of being credit blacklisted, or of having their household goods taken. In particular the older respondents tended to rule out taking out a loan, as did many of those who had entered full-time employment:

> Actually getting myself in debt to go and do it, I just wouldn't do it now because I know what it's like to have money and pay this and pay that, whereas when I was at school it was different.
>
> (Kim, 18, white female secretary)

Connor and Dewson (2001) surveyed non-HE entrants from lower social class groups (those who were qualified to enter higher education at age 18 or 19 but chose not to do so). They asked them how likely they were to get into debt for different reasons. About 80 per cent said that it was very likely or quite likely that they would get into debt to buy a house, and the same proportion said they would do so to pay for education. But this leaves around 20 per cent who were not prepared to contemplate such debts. Moreover, half the sample said that the possibility of being in debt was a factor in their decision not to enter higher education.

Even among those who do enter higher education, a number of studies have found that a significant minority of students from the lower social class groups choose not to take out loans. Callender and Kemp (2000) found that about 28 per cent of students in the 1998–9 Income and Expenditure Survey had not taken out loans, but it has to be remembered that this group still had access to reduced maintenance grants. Of those students who had not taken out loans, 56 per cent said that this was because they were unwilling to get into debt – and this debt aversion was most common among those students from the poorest backgrounds, and particularly women. Once students had taken out any sort of loan, they were more liable to borrow from other sources (for example, those who already had bank loans were more likely to take out student loans). Asian students were the least likely to take out any sort of loan, and when they did, they borrowed the smallest amounts (Callender and Kemp 2000). One explanation for this is that many Muslims hold that it is against their religious beliefs to incur interest-bearing debts. Connor and Dewson (2001), conducting their survey in 2000, found 81 per cent of students from classes IIIm, IV and V had taken out loans and a further 9 per cent intended to do so. Thus 10 per cent had no loans and did not intend to take them out.

Those students who are unwilling to get into debt have employed a variety of strategies: living at home to save money (Callender 2001; Connor *et al.* 1999; Farr 2001); enrolling for shorter courses (Connor *et al.* 1999; Knowles 2000; Forsyth and Furlong 2000); and taking on long hours of employment (Barke *et al.* 2000; Connor and Dewson 2001).

A specific concern is the low level of salary triggering Student Loan repayment (£10,000). The National Audit Office (2000b) found that young people thought this was so low that a person earning at that level would be in difficulty even without loan repayments.

Fewer part-time students accumulate debts, but certain groups are more likely to do so; among lone parents 76 per cent have debts, and among those from social classes IV and V, 70 per cent are in debt (Callender and Kemp 2000). This was because they generally earned less than those from the higher social classes did, and they were less likely to receive help towards their tuition fees from their employers. Their debts were more likely to be in the form of overdrafts or borrowing from friends or parents rather than bank loans, because it is less easy for those from lower-income backgrounds to obtain credit.

Student hardship

Reports of student drinking and partying are commonplace, and some spend huge amounts on alcohol (Morgan *et al.* 2001). This can distract attention from the reality of financial hardship experienced by some students.

The extent to which those from the lower social class groups are seeking other sources of income may be some indication of hardship or potential hardship. Callender (2001) found that between the Student Income and Expenditure Surveys carried out in 1995–6 and 1998–9, the income from charitable trusts of students from social class V had increased by 205 per cent, from Access Funds by 300 per cent, and from their savings by 160 per cent. Those from social classes IV and V and lone parents expressed the highest level of concern about money; over 76 per cent of each group felt that financial difficulties had adversely affected academic performance.

Many students have not realized the extent of study-related costs. The National Audit Office (2002b) found that students had not expected to spend as much on books and printing. The students they spoke to claimed that university libraries did not have enough copies of books, and the demand that course-work assignments should be word-processed added to students' costs. Students in our focus groups were similarly taken aback by the amount they had to pay:

> MARGO: I paid £70 for three books yesterday ...
> LEROY: If you look at the module, the module handbook, you have to buy that too. £5.50 for one. To me it is not fair. To me if the teacher give it to us as a handbook [it should be] free.
> MARGO: And the copy machine is 10p each whereas there is a place next door where I live, it is a photocopier and you pay 4p, and I thought it would be cheaper for students.
>
> (Mature HE students)

For those who live away from home, student accommodation is a considerable expense. The press has repeatedly drawn attention to the proportion of the student loan that is eaten up by hall fees with headlines such as 'Loan – rent = misery' (*THES* 2000: iv); 'Student rents soaring' (*Guardian* 2001: 9). The point repeatedly made is that rents for student accommodation are now so high (particularly in London) that after paying the rent, there is very little money left over from the student loan to pay other expenses.

For lone parents the loss of benefits is a particular issue. Those we spoke with had not expected to lose their benefits, and identified items such as prescription charges as an unwelcome additional expense. The government has introduced a variety of funds to address these problems since Siobhan spoke to us:

> The other thing is as well with the loan ... [that] would be what I was getting on income support, but now I have to pay full rent, I've got to pay for an au pair and I have to pay school meals and I got free milk when I was unemployed so, I've got those four extra things out of the same money. And the rent is £73 a week ... I was really excited, even kind of up to yesterday when I just got the bills, bills, bills in the door and then kind of the council saying I'm not entitled to any housing benefit which I found out today. I just thought oh what's the point? I might as well go and work for Tescos, sod the degree.
>
> (Siobhan, 33, white female HE student and lone parent)

Student term-time employment

Many students from the lower social class groups are engaged in term-time employment. It is difficult to give an overall figure for the proportion involved, since surveys carried out in different universities obviously reflect both the social class composition of the students and local employment opportunities. Most surveys suggest that over 40 per cent of full-time students have jobs in term-time (for example NUS 1999: 41.6 per cent; Callender and Kemp 2000: 46 per cent). The recent MORI Unite Student Living Survey (*THES* 2002b) reports a sharp rise in term-time employment, from 30 per cent of all students in 2000 to 43 per cent in 2001.

The average number of hours worked per week has been found to be about around 11 or 12 hours (Barke *et al.* 2000; Callender and Kemp 2000). However, some individuals work very much longer hours; Barke *et al.* found that 6 per cent of those in employment worked more than 25 hours a week, and Sawyer and Carroll (2000) found that a fifth of those who had term-time jobs worked over 21 hours a week. The variation between universities is evident in recent findings presented by Pokorny and Pokorny (2001). In their survey of around 300 students on a business studies module at the University of North London, they found that almost 60 per cent had term-time jobs, and they worked for an average of 16.6 hours a week.

It has repeatedly been found that those from poorer backgrounds are the most likely to be in term-time employment (for example Barke *et al.* 2000; Callender and Kemp 2000; Humphrey 2001). The trend for students from lower social class groups to have jobs appears to be increasing. Callender (2001) found that between 1995–6 and 1998–9, students from the lowest social class group (V) had become far more dependent on income from paid work (up by 33 per cent), whereas for those in social class I income from work increased by only 2 per cent.

While some students work to achieve a better social life or a desired standard of living, the NUS found that the main reason was to meet living costs. Barke *et al.* found that 43 per cent of those working did so 'simply to enable me to stay at university' (2000: 17). There is a link between work and debt aversion; Barke *et al.* found that 49 per cent were working because they did not want to borrow or to borrow more. Of those in employment, 20 per cent had not taken out a loan and did not intend to do so; they preferred to work their way through university.

Those in employment have been found to be less involved in university life (Humphrey 2001), and to say that they lack study time and are tired. Some miss lectures and course work deadlines (NUS 1995, 1999). A significant proportion of student workers believe that their work is detrimental to their studies; McKechnie *et al.* (1998, quoted by James 2001) found that working over ten hours a week was significantly related to a perceived negative impact on academic performance. Humphrey (2001) reports that at the

University of Newcastle those in term-time jobs were awarded marks on average 3 per cent below those of 'non-working' students, and that this was not dependent on subject or previous schooling. While this may sound a small difference, Humphrey points out that it could result in 35 per cent of those who have term-time jobs achieving degrees of a lower classification. Barke *et al.* (2000) at the University of Northumbria found a variation by subject, with those in the business school achieving marks 4.5 per cent below non-working students.

There are of course some benefits to those students who are unemployed. Employers welcome graduates with work experience, and jobs related to the degree course may be very beneficial (Barke *et al.* 2000). However, most students are employed in sectors unrelated to their courses (generally in shops, hotels and pubs), and they work excessively long and often anti-social hours for low pay (NUS 1995, 1999).

In our focus groups, both students and non-participants were aware that the need to earn money added to the risk involved in entering higher education:

> I don't see why we should have to work. I really don't cos at the end of the day if we fail our degree where are we gonna work after that? We've come to university to get a degree, we're full-time students and we are working, let's say twenty hours a week, we're going to end up failing some of our tests and stuff like that, what's going to happen to us then?
>
> (Brett, 23, white HE student)

In Germany and Sweden, regulations have recently been introduced to protect student performance by ensuring that they do not take on excessive hours of employment (National Audit Office 2002b). But in both these countries, students receive maintenance grants and do not contribute to tuition costs. Thus the need to work is much less. The Select Committee Report on Student Retention (House of Commons 2001a) recommended that higher education institutions should provide guidance to their students that they should not work in paid employment for more than 12 hours a week. It acknowledges that this strategy to improve retention may not work if students are working to fund their living costs, and that an improvement is needed to financial support for the less well off.

Student non-completion

Financial hardship is one of the factors cited in studies of student withdrawal (for example Ozga and Sukhnandan 1997; Yorke *et al.* 1997) (see Chapter 6). Callender and Kemp (2001) found that a higher percentage of those in social classes IV and V had contemplated withdrawing for financial reasons. Even though the students in focus groups were only in their first term, several of them were already talking about the way in which financial pressures combined to make life extremely difficult. Withdrawal was already seen as a possibility:

> You get penalized from every angle ... You have to pay for prescriptions and I don't get free school meals. I have to pay for the children's meals ... I work for Iceland 4 days a week. And that's from the crack of dawn until I'm ready to go to university, and then I go and pick up my daughter and take her back and then the following morning, up again and do the same thing, and it's so tiring. It's just so tiring, and no-one appreciates that you are *trying*, you know what I mean. They don't think you are trying but you *are* and I swear to God, it is so hard ... My main aim is not to drop out, I don't want to but if it happens, it happens.
> (Janet, 22, black Caribbean HE student and lone mother)

The complexity of the system

The Dearing Report recommended that the student support system should be 'easy to understand, administratively efficient and cost-effective' (Dearing 1997: para. 20.2). However, one of the major concerns about the current system is its complexity. Woodrow *et al.* characterize it as 'user-unfriendly' (2002: 4), and claim that the various different sources of support 'present a confusing picture to potential students' (2002: 167).

> One of the difficulties is the number of agencies that a student may have to deal with. A lone parent ... might have to deal with up to seven agencies: the local education authority, the Student Loans Company; the higher education institution; the Benefits Agency; the Inland Revenue; and the Prescriptions Pricing Authority.
> (Fidler 2001)

This complexity makes it impossible for a prospective student to calculate what their income will be, which is surely necessary if they are to make an informed decision. It is a particular problem that some sources of funding can only be accessed after enrolment and are discretionary; the uncertainty arising from this impacts most on those with dependants.

The ongoing changes to the system add to the complexity that students have to cope with. The majority of the newly created funds are specifically targeted at the less well off, so working-class students have to deal with more complex information than middle-class students (see Chapter 5). The extra funding is very welcome, but with so many different sources available, it is very difficult for those who are considering higher education as a future prospect to know what they may be entitled to receive. Figure 8.1 sets out the sources available at the time of writing.

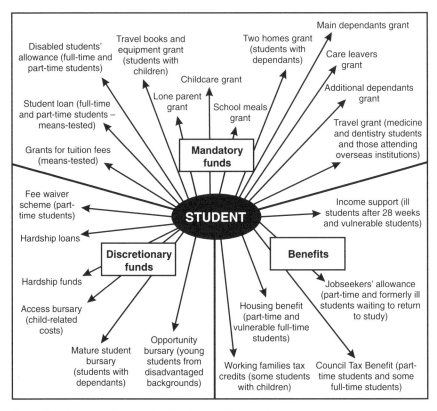

Figure 8.1 Sources of public funding from which students may seek support

Source: National Audit Office 2002a: 30

Moreover, the frequency of the changes made to the funds available poses a further problem. There is a time lag in the process through which such information becomes common taken-for-granted knowledge among potential applicants. This partly results from their tendency to prefer 'hot' knowledge (see Chapter 5). Thus rather than looking at the DfES website, they will rely on what their friends tell them. The focus groups we carried out with non-participants took place in 1998–9. For these people, then, there was no prospect of grants. The interviews with participants were held in 1999–2000, the first year in which students entering did not have grants. Yet we found that these facts were not widely known. As we have written elsewhere (Hutchings and Archer 2001), a substantial minority of the non-participants believed that university students are still eligible for grants. Among this number were some who were already applying to go to university:

SIMON: I say, if you can't get funding for a grant like from your local authority then how do you go about it?
ABDUL: It's decisions like that that make me want to leave education.

(FE students applying to HE)

Most of the non-participant respondents knew that fees had to be paid, though estimates of the amount varied wildly. But not one mentioned the fact that the fees are means-tested, and it was likely that most of them would not in fact have had to pay. While the cost of going to university was assumed to be high, there was considerable vagueness and some misinformation about how much money would be needed (reflecting the findings of Connor *et al.* 1999; House of Commons Select Committee 2001b).

Like the non-participants, many of those entering higher education in 1999 claimed that when they first applied to university, they had been unaware that they would not receive any form of student grant:

I found out like, I mean I knew I had to pay like, um, fees and stuff, but right at the end of it they go, 'You know you don't have no grants.' And like, 'Excuse me?' Cos I went there and I go, 'What about the student grants?' 'We don't have grants love, you have loans now.' And I'm like, 'Forget it then.' I mean I've applied anyway, if I need it I'll take it, but I'm gonna try and avoid it.

(Janita, 19, Asian female HE student)

Some students had not realized they would have to pay fees for the specific course they were entering. For example, BEd students had heard that fees were not paid for teacher training, and had not realized that this applied only to the PGCE. Others had received conflicting information about the level of fees that they would have to pay:

I mean with me I'm paying my university fees myself, so I mean it came as a big shock to me cos we thought it would only be £1,000 a year that we would have to pay, but it's like when we got in it was like £2,100 every year that we would have to pay. So that came as a bit of a surprise.

(Kiran, 18, Asian female HE student)

This particular confusion appears to have arisen from the distinction between £1,050, the maximum home fees then charged to those whose income had been assessed, and the full rate of home fees chargeable to those who have not been assessed. What Kiran needed to do was to have her family income assessed; the fees would then be automatically capped at £1,050.

A particular issue for many respondents was that, as a result of applying to university late, they did not know, in the early weeks of the autumn term, what their financial situation would be. Meanwhile they had no money:

> I think the loan system is terrible because I have been here three weeks now and I still haven't got my loan or heard any word. I have no support from my parents, so I have no money at all … I have no one else to turn to give me money … At the same time I am not even sure if I am entitled to it [a loan]. They don't even send you out that much information to say you can get a loan.
>
> (Ian, 19, white male HE student)

This is a particular issue for post-1992 universities which traditionally rely heavily on late applications, and where a high proportion of students come from lower income homes.

The complexity lies not only in the student finance system itself but also in the process for accessing it:

> But even the leaflets don't really help to make things particularly, you know, clear. I don't know it just seems like an over-complicated process.
>
> (Amy, 19, white female HE student)

> The booklet was like reading something in video manual language.
>
> (Stella, 18, white female HE student)

The government is currently engaged in a programme of modernization which should simplify the system of administration and make it more customer-focused. This can only be good news. The application forms have already been improved and can be filled in online, and it is no longer necessary to make a separate application to the Student Loans Company.

The current student-funding regime has, then, created a variety of problems. It has had a particularly negative impact on working-class students and has deterred potential applicants. Before turning to possible ways forward, the role of financial factors in potential students' decisions about higher education is considered.

Financial decision-making

Chapter 5 discussed the view that with adequate information, the decision about whether to enter higher education involved weighing the costs against the potential benefits. The Dearing Report argued that:

> The economic benefits to individuals from participating in higher education … are probably the most significant factor affecting demand. They are substantial and consist of

- employment rates which are, on average, above those for people who were qualified to enter higher education but did not do so
- pay levels which are, on average, above those for people who were qualified to enter higher education but did not do so.

(Dearing 1997: para. 6.16)

The 'private rate of return' of investment in higher education can be calculated by setting pay and employment benefits against the costs incurred (including opportunity costs). Dearing suggested that the rate of return is between 11 per cent and 14 per cent.

> These private rates of return, were they to be well known by potential students and reasonably certain to continue, would be likely to stimulate high levels of demand for higher education.
>
> (ibid.: para. 6.23)

However, Dearing also identified specific factors that could lower the private rate of return: an increase in numbers achieving higher education qualifications, and an increase in costs, such as the introduction of tuition fees. Both these factors, together with debt payments, have now reduced the rate of return from the figures quoted above.

Moreover, the rates of return from higher education are not the same for all students. Graduates from social classes IV and V earn on average 7 per cent less than graduates from social classes I and II (Elias *et al.* 1999). There are also different returns from different courses. Those that have the highest returns (such as medicine and law) attract very few students from the lower social class groups, partly because the courses themselves are long and therefore more expensive (Brown and Piatt 2001). Different returns are also associated with different higher education institutions. Many employers prefer to take on candidates from the older institutions (ibid.) and those who entered higher education with A levels (see Chapter 7). Thus the economic benefits of higher education are not the same for all graduates, and they are least for the groups for whom participation is the most costly and debt levels on graduation the highest. As a result, the rate of return available would perhaps not be an incentive if it were 'well known by potential students'.

We have seen that in the focus groups, many young people saw the spectre of debt as a deterrent. However, some students were quite clear that they were investing in their futures and that the investment is worth while – though they did not appear to have any real knowledge of either the level of debt or of potential earnings:

DEBORAH: I'll be quite heavily in debt I think by the time I finish, cos I've applied for every loan possible, but I see it as like an investment into my future, and I'm gonna hopefully get a better job at the end of all this and do something that I like, so I'll probably pay it off most of my life, but I don't care. I really do not care at all.

GRACE: No, because you might as well take what you can get and you know, it, it is an investment, you're right ... Because you can earn loads of money, you know.

(First-year HE students)

It is clear from Deborah's comment that potential job satisfaction is also an incentive. Chapter 6 has shown that while the most popular discourse of the value of higher education was that it was seen as offering a route to better jobs and more money, this was not the only discourse of value. Some students, and particularly the women students, talked of becoming a different person and accessing a middle-class lifestyle (see Chapter 9).

Another problem with the notion that prospective students will be motivated by the private rate of return is that, as Chapter 5 showed, those from the lower social class groups tend to trust 'hot' knowledge rather than official information. Thus figures showing gains in average income have much less effect than knowing an individual who has increased their income as a result of gaining a degree – or conversely, someone who has not done so. Chapter 6 showed that many of our respondents gave examples of individuals who had not achieved 'graduate' well paid jobs. These individual cases may outweigh any statistic of average benefit. Thus the Dearing Report's notion that the economic benefits can be rationally weighed against the costs, and that greater knowledge of the private rates of return would result in more people entering higher education, is perhaps over-simplistic.

Social justice?

This chapter has described the current financial arrangements and how these were understood by, and impacted on, working-class higher education students and non-participants. Respondents' discussion around student finances also offered an insight into the ways that these working-class young people feel they are being excluded from society.

A deep sense of injustice was apparent in many of their comments. The removal of student grants was seen as at odds with goals of increasing numbers in higher education and of equality of opportunity. One young man argued that the government should fund higher education students 'because they want more to go there ... they want more ethnic people in jobs but they're making it harder' (Patrick, 18, black male FE student). Particular groups were considered to be more heavily disadvantaged; these included mature students who had worked and 'know what it's like to have money' (Kim, 18, white female secretary); single mothers; and those living on benefits. It was strongly argued that students should be financially supported by the government because this was a potential route out of their current poverty:

> I can't understand why they charge … because going to school, it's free … you can't get a job if you haven't got the higher education and yet you have to pay for it. If you can't pay for it, you can't have the higher education, therefore you don't get jobs. So it's Catch 22 there.
> (Jodie, 27, white female unemployed hairdresser and lone mother)

The changes in the system of finance were widely perceived to be unfair and ill-conceived:

> I was so angry. I was fuming. What is the point of actually taking the time out and studying and at the end of it you are in debt! … And it's so unfair because I pay taxes, my mother's paid taxes, my granddad paid taxes and the taxes that they paid should help anyone go to college of university cos that should be a free, free education for everyone. I don't think it's fair that they are making us pay. Honestly, I just don't think it's fair. There is so much money, look at the amount of money they are putting in to the Millennium, of all things, and this is to bring up the up-and-coming generation that could be running this country in ten, twenty years, and we are going to come out in debt, it's just so unfair.
> (Janet, 22, black Caribbean HE student and lone mother)

Students pointed out that when they graduated they would be paying higher taxes, which would contribute to society: 'at the end of the day, the more you earn the more tax you going to pay, and the more you going to contribute to the society' (Ruth, 34, black female HE student).

And above all, they wanted their voices to be heard by those in positions of power:

> VIOLET: You, ah [to Q] you, put in that survey, or whatever, something to go up to the head Mr Blair … They said in that handbook, the student handbook that no-one should be exempt from full-time education because of money. And people want to return to study and a major part of it is money [*all agree*] and every time they're being turned down because of money.
> PAULA: You get penalized in this system.
> VIOLET: Yeah. So you put it in there. Let them know how we *feel* about it. Because a lot of people reach university, enrol and have to go back home because of *money*.
> (Black Caribbean mature female HE students)

The future

By the time this book is published, the current funding review will have put forward recommendations. A great many voices have offered strong advice about what these should be, and it is clearly impossible for the government to satisfy them all.

The House of Commons Select Committee for Education and Employment report on student retention calls for government to 'tackle the consequences of student poverty for retention by improving access to financial support for less well-off students, raising very substantially the income threshold at which graduates have to begin repayment and addressing concerns about debt escalation' (2001a: para. 109). But the Committee's report on access (House of Commons 2001b) makes limited recommendations on student finance. Quinn (2001) criticizes it for its 'failure to engage with the thorny topic of student finance' (2001: 6). It does suggest that the current arrangements should be closely monitored, but Quinn argues that this ignores the existing evidence that the current arrangements are not compatible with a widening participation agenda.

Connor and Dewson (2001), reporting to the DfEE, argue that more needs to be done to support potential students from low-income families, and emphasize the need for 'more relevant and timely information on student finance' (2001: viii). Woodrow *et al.*, in the *Social Class and Participation in HE* report, recommend that the funding system should not discriminate against the very groups whom the government has claimed it wishes to attract into higher education. For them this would involve 'a change in the system of fees and loans to one in which the gradient of means-testing is steeper (and in which the poorest can receive non-repayable grants)' (2002: 4). They suggest doing this through a combination of a mean-tested loan and a means-tested grant. They also argue for 'a radical simplification of the avenues through which other student support is channelled' (2002: 4). It is important to ensure that when potential students are making decisions about whether to apply to enter higher education, the 'full possibilities inherent in the student support system are made fully available' to them (Woodrow *et al.* 2002: 6). Brown and Piatt (2001) of the Institute for Public Policy Research also argue for a system that can offer greater clarity to prospective students.

Other suggestions put to the government include the introduction of market-rate rather than subsidized loans (Brown and Piatt 2001). The National Audit Office (2002a) suggest that sources of financial support should be streamlined so that prospective students have more certainty about what they will receive. They also urge a review of financial support for part-time students.

The system initially under consideration, a reintroduction of maintenance grants for some or all students and a graduate tax, met with varying responses. There was widespread public support for the return of means-tested grants; 73 per cent of people in a MORI poll conducted in March and April 2001 thought that they should be reintroduced, and 63 per cent believed that the current system of fees and loans deters people from going to university (*THES* 2001). The benefits of a graduate tax were listed in the press: there is no up-front payment for going to university; the cost is borne by the graduate rather than the parents or the tax-payer; the payment eventually made relates to the income of the graduate. Thus a graduate tax redistributes money from the affluent to the poor (*Independent* 2001). However, this idea apparently proved very unpopular in focus groups (*Guardian* 2002).

But the difficulty for the government is that it has multiple, and often conflicting, agendas. It needs to balance its budget (and this chapter, in focusing on student experience and perspectives, has ignored issues of funding educational institutions, and the consequences for the budget of such a large increase in numbers in higher education). It claims that it is working towards greater social justice. It has set itself a target of raising participation in higher education to 50 per cent by 2010, and it has to report on progress toward this in 2002. However, this target could be achieved without widening participation amongst the lower social class groups. And for the government, getting re-elected and retaining the support of the swing voters often seem to take precedence over the social justice agenda. While this is the case, we are unlikely to have a system of student funding that genuinely promotes participation and retention of those from poorer backgrounds.

Note

1 For full details of the assumptions and calculation in this model, see Callender 2001: 15.

Chapter 9

Identities, inequalities and higher education

Louise Archer and Carole Leathwood

As suggested at the beginning of the book in Chapter 1, critical sociologists and feminist researchers have highlighted the importance of recognizing how multiple identities and inequalities of 'race', ethnicity, social class and gender (among others) affect the ways in which people construct, experience and negotiate different educational opportunities and routes. Issues of identity are central to the differential ways in which middle-class and working-class people (are able to) negotiate educational systems. For example, notions of identity impact upon the educational routes that working-class people may perceive to be accessible, worthwhile and desirable, and identity assumptions on the behalf of middle-class professionals may underpin the forms of advice and guidance made available to particular working-class groups. This chapter discusses how various identity issues are evident within working-class non-participants' and participants' negotiations around higher education. Analysis teases out the often subtle, yet important, ways in which respondents frame their resistance, or desire, to participate in relation to class, gender and ethnic identities. The role of identity issues in relation to retention of working-class students is also drawn out.

Identities and inequalities of social class, 'race' and gender structure the resources and capital (cultural, economic and social) available to working-class groups which, in turn, mediates their potential, and likelihood, of their participation in higher education. However, this does not mean that working-class identities should be conceptualized in deficit terms, nor as passive products of structural inequalities. As we have detailed elsewhere (Archer, Hutchings and Leathwood 2001) identities are actively, and continually, constituted, asserted and reconstituted in relation to multiple structures and networks of social divisions. There is no singular 'working-class identity' or 'view' of higher education, and data from our study reveal a multitude of ways through which working-class individuals actively resist, or embrace, higher education as a possibility. The focus upon 'identity' within this chapter will also underline not only themes of rationality and pragmatism, but also the strong emotional forces at work within working-class HE negotiations and choices. These three motivating identity themes are embedded within tacit/common-sense notions of 'what is appropriate for people like me' which, as Ball *et al.* (2000a) suggest, are specifically gendered, classed and racialized. Data presented within this chapter will show how some respondents' views about higher education participation can be read as sites of resistance within which they enact and contest particular racialized gender relations. Many of the very 'rational' reasons for non-participation given by respondents were clearly grounded within discourses of identity and emotion, yet it is also worth noting that discourses of identity and emotion are not always easy to tap into and may not be readily articulated. As Diane Reay and her colleagues found:

> while material constraints on choice were readily articulated by respondents, there were often only hints, and barely articulated suggestions of emotional constraints on choice.
>
> (Reay *et al.* 2001)

Such an analysis thus requires an in-depth, sensitive approach to the texts in question.

This chapter is organized into three main sections. The first part considers issues around higher education as changing (working-class) identity, and discusses how working-class respondents in general used this theme in their views on participation. The second and third parts of the chapter take up identity issues in greater depth, examining specific gendered and racialized themes emerging within the views of working-class men and women.

Higher education participation and 'changing identity'

> Identity is socially and culturally 'located' in time and space and inflected by rejection, displacement and desire. Post-16 'choices' are bound up with the expression and suppression of identities.
>
> (Ball *et al.* 2000a: 24)

As detailed in Chapter 6, dominant government discourses have framed working-class participation in higher education as a way of achieving 'change'; that is, for working-class participants to change themselves and the national and/or local population by becoming more educated, skilled, affluent, socially mobile, 'civilized' and (implicitly) middle class. These changes are assumed to be 'good' and worthwhile, and carry a further assumption that it is the working-class individual who must adapt and change, in order to fit into, and participate in, the (unchanged) HE institutional culture and wider system. Thus, working-class individuals' negotiations around participation may involve engagement with this ideal of identity and social class change. However, it is also important to note that respondents did not simply take up, or resist, dominant discourses around HE participation and class identity change, rather they engaged in complex, sometimes contradictory negotiations.

Many respondents discussed this theme of 'change', although opinions were broadly divided as to whether identity change was embraced, resisted or, in some cases, subverted and reconstructed. Relatively few respondents wholeheartedly embraced the notion of changing classed identity. Of these few there were, unsurprisingly, more students than non-participants who aspired to 'become middle class' through HE participation. This change was conceptualized in various ways, but was generally framed in terms of 'taste' (Bourdieu 1986). For example, Janet, a black woman student, talked about her boyfriend's fear that her working-class tastes, accent and behaviour would change when she became a student:

> Well my boyfriend keeps on telling this saying to me ... once I come into university I will start *acting* like a uni student, I will start *talking* like a uni student, I'll start reading the papers that they read, you know? [*laughs*] I'll start behaving properly like one. And will you be listening to radio stations and um watching different things on TV, that I don't watch now, you know? And I do find myself doing that.

As various feminists have written, social markers such as accent (Hey 1997), dress and appearance (Skeggs 1997), and preferences and lifestyles (Lawler 1999) form the sites of struggle over 'authentic' or 'pretentious' classed identities. Issues around 'change' and 'leaving' classed identities are explored further later in this chapter, but it is interesting to note here that such views were much rarer among non-participants, particularly among men. As detailed in Chapter 6, one young man (George) did aspire to university participation as a means of achieving an idealized vision of middle-class life, which he called 'the complete hack'.

In comparison, we found that resistance to identity change was reasonably widespread through participants and non-participants alike. Like the working-class adult Scottish students in Lyn Tett's (2000) study, who valued and were proud of their working-class identities and did not want to become middle class, a number of students in this research made it clear that they did not want to change their classed identities (for example Amy and Billie, reported in Chapter 6).

These students drew clear boundaries between themselves and the middle-class institution, positioning themselves as able to benefit from participation while not belonging to, or feeling ownership of, the institution. As Fela (a black male student) suggested, in order not to 'allow' university to change him, he intended to adopt the same strategy as his friends, whereby 'they go through university, uni doesn't go through them'.

Many students, and various non-participants, took up and subverted notions of 'changing identities' by constructing particular fractured spaces within higher education, (such as particular institutions, courses, modes of study) as 'working class', where people 'like us' can participate without damaging or changing valued working-class identities. For example, various non-participants suggested that they if they were to consider going to university, they would only consider part-time, evening and/or distance learning. Similarly, local, post-1992 universities were constructed as places offering a chance to 'belong', or at least, not to stand out (for example one black student, Fela, explained choosing a university with a large black-student population due to 'not wanting to be the only speck'). As we discuss elsewhere, these expectations of belonging were not always necessarily borne out in students' subsequent experiences (Read *et al.* 2003). Some black African and Caribbean women also constructed specific working-class identities within which HE participation is both a normalized educational route and a resource with which to engage with class, 'race' and gender inequalities (see later in this chapter). Thus in a range of ways, most respondents resisted the middle-class transformative ideal of higher education participation.

While these subversions highlight the agency and diversity within working-class negotiations of HE participation in relation to dominant assumptions around 'identity change', they also point to an important, yet neglected, issue of *who* does, or does not, change. The strategies employed by our respondents are pragmatic, yet leave the status quo largely unchallenged because institutional cultures remain unchanged. For example, working-class students may adopt individualized forms of resistance to the dominant academic culture by participating but 'not changing', yet such strategies do not redress the unequal balance of power nor the bias within these cultures. Furthermore, leaving the focus of responsibility for change within the individual working-class student (who has to choose particular lower prestige institutions in order to encounter fewer problems 'fitting in') may entail various negative psychic consequences. As we detailed in Chapter 6, Neil's recognition of himself as 'I live locally and I'm stupid' is only a short step away from Groucho Marx's well-known statement about 'not wanting to be a member of a club that would have me'. Indeed, Reay *et al.* (2001) have also noted such processes of disidentification among working-class and minority ethnic students, who are painfully aware that only lower status institutions are accessible to them. Thus structural inequalities and the hierarchy of universities are centrally implicated in the (re)production of emotional and identity costs of participation for working-class and Other students.

The majority of non-participants also resisted identity change, suggesting it was undesirable, and as we have written elsewhere, 'many respondents did not "buy into" the middle-class transformative ideal of HE, and instead embraced potential economic mobility but resisted social class identity change' (Archer and Hutchings 2000: 570). As the following part of the chapter will discuss, men and women used quite specific and different discourses to argue against participation in order to retain valued working-class masculine or feminine identities. Issues around (racialized) gendered identities were also important concerns in relation to retention.

Working-class men: masculinities and HE participation

The working-class men students in Tett's (2000) study prioritized class over gender identities in their accounts, but we found that the men respondents in our research (participants and non-participants) largely explained, and argued, their views on HE participation through (classed and racialized) discourses of (working-class) masculinity. As we have detailed in an earlier publication (Archer, Pratt and Phillips 2001), the form and type of masculine identities drawn on by the working-class men in our research varied considerably across 'race', but it is important to note that constructions were not voiced homogenously by *all* men from particular backgrounds.

Both students and non-participants talked about HE institutions as middle-class places, but whereas those men who argued against going constructed participation as incompatible with notions of working-class masculinity, male students suggested that they would 'cope' with participation by attempting to come out 'untouched' and unchanged by HE culture.

Men respondents voiced various reasons for not going to university. HE participation was overwhelmingly associated with negative, undesirable images of masculinity, encapsulated in stereotypes of students as socially inadequate men who enjoy study. These student masculinities were positioned as incompatible with, and derided in terms of, particular (working-class) masculine ideals demands of 'doing' working-class masculinity. Non-participant men, irrespective of any expressed interest in HE study, mostly conceptualized university students as middle-class men. For example, they suggested that 'It is always the rich people going into uni' and, more specifically, identifying typical students as rich, white middle-class men.

Non-participant men also reproduced a theme of there being a general incompatibility between 'educational' and 'hegemonic masculine' identities, referring back to their own school experiences. As Connell (1989) suggests, masculinity is organized around social power, and education provides a particularly salient arena for a 'contest for hegemony' between different groups of men. Some versions of masculinity are more powerful and dominant than others. It has been suggested (see for example Connell 1989; Edley and Wetherell 1995; Gough 1998) that hegemonic masculinity is organized around the discursive subordination of Others, particularly women and gay men. Thus Paechter (1998: 17) suggests that the construction of difference between 'male Subject and female Other' is a particularly powerful and consistent feature of masculinity. Education (as 'feminized') is resisted as 'not manly' – particularly because masculinity is defined through work (which is again juxtaposed with study).

The majority of non-participant men defined themselves through work (albeit different types of work), and many argued from this position that education was not useful or relevant to their lives, or suggested that it could even be potentially risky ('You can have all the education in the world but still can't find a job ... that's the risk I'm not willing to take, the dole', Drew, 21, black Caribbean shop assistant). Their transcripts clearly echoed 'the centrality of work in the lives of men' (Morgan 1992: 76) and exemplified how, in contemporary British society, the achievement of manhood for working-class men may be closely linked with the achievement of secure and skilled work, both as a source of income and of social status. Consequently 'not working' (for example through unemployment or study) may represent a serious loss to masculine identity (see for example McClelland 1991; Tolson 1977). As we have written elsewhere (Archer, Pratt and Phillips 2001), notwithstanding the contradictory nature of paid employment (which can constitute a source of both fulfilment and restriction/oppression) and multiple contemporary changes in the nature of work and labour markets, the pervasiveness of this ideology of work-based masculinity among the young men in our study is striking.

Working-class men respondents in our study, like those in Tett's (2000), overwhelmingly justified HE participation in terms of instrumental discourses. But while many male respondents acknowledged the potential benefits of participation in terms of the ability to get better jobs and money, a large proportion of non-participant men also resisted this position by dissociating education and qualifications from money and work. These men argued that HE participation constitutes a relatively insecure route to (stable) employment due to its inherent riskiness. Thus, as one young man put it:

> I wouldn't ask for a degree I'd just ask for money ... That's what you're going to get at the end of the degree the money so you might as well ask for the money straightaway.
>
> (Shabid, 16, Pakistani FE student)

Among non-participant men, more immediate economic and employment demands were thus given precedence over the potential for long-term personal growth or betterment and they resisted the notion of there being any intrinsic merits to studying for a degree, stating simply that it is 'all about money':

> You have to realize that the current society that we live in comes down to the money, you go to university to get a better job ... you do your study, you make all the sacrifices all because you want to earn money.
>
> (Shimon, 22, Bangladeshi customer service worker)

From this perspective, taking several years to study for a degree was compared unfavourably to direct entry into paid work. These views were reinforced by non-participant men's perceptions of degree study as highly risky due to there being no certainty of secure employment at the end of it ('because you can have all the education in the world but still can't find a job': Neville, 17, black British FE student). Plenty of cautionary examples were cited to reinforce this view; for example Aziz warned 'my cousin got a degree – he's sitting at home for a year doing nothing with it' (Aziz, 16, Pakistani FE student).

The risks associated with HE participation were also presented as potentially interfering with the men's constructions of 'popular' working-class masculinities. These masculinities were invariably constructed as heterosexual and were performed through consumption of the symbols of material success (ownership of a car, house, fashionable clothes and so on):

> At the end of the day you can have the qualifications but you can't go and buy no car. You can't go and buy no house or whatever. No clothes if you've got no job to get no money. That's what it comes down to.
>
> (Drew, 21, black Caribbean shop assistant)

As detailed earlier, the actual experience of being a student was widely regarded as antithetical to such images of popular masculinity, being characterized by insecurity, an impoverished lifestyle and financial hardship and insecurity. Thus both participant and non-participant men talked about participation as potentially entailing numerous costs and risks to masculine identities.

HE participation was generally associated with middle-class masculinity, but non-participant men from different ethnic backgrounds also produced slightly different arguments that participation in HE was not for 'men like us'.[1] Some Bengali young men positioned Muslim masculinity as ideologically incompatible with HE participation in relation to the stereotype of students as drinkers and drug-takers. In contrast, white men often talked about students as immature middle-class men who could not fulfil the demands of a hegemonic masculinity. They negatively contrasted 'immature' middle-class students with their own valued characteristics of 'common sense', 'taking one's drink' and 'hard' manual working identities (claiming, with pride, their identities as 'chippies' and 'sparkies'). These (positive) manual work identities were directly contrasted with 'brain' (academic) work, which was derided:

> If you've got to be there swotting over a book, you can't be out grafting can you? And you can't have a social life, if you're like me and you've got to do so many other things.
>
> (Derek, 29, white Irish labourer)

Thus for many white non-participant men, it was argued that participation in further education would be 'unthinkable' (Cohen 1988) because a period of study would entail 'not working' and would be incompatible with the men's visions of themselves as defined through manual working identities.

Unlike their white peers, many black and Asian men specifically rejected manual identities, arguing that 'doing manual it's dirty' (Aziz, 16, Pakistani FE student), but this did not mean that they necessarily embraced the possibility of HE participation. For example, some African-Caribbean non-participant young men argued that their identities as 'cool' black men were not compatible with going to university, which was widely regarded as 'uncool'. Several black and Asian men defined their masculinity through themes of 'responsibility', which they argued precluded them from studying, in opposition to 'immature' male students. Among African-Caribbean men, this responsibility was conceptualized primarily in terms of the demands of maintaining the symbols of hegemonic success, namely a car, a home/territory ('my yard') and a (heterosexual) relationship. Among many non-participant Bengali young men, responsibilities were talked about in terms of familial and cultural commitments and their identities as 'breadwinners' and providers, in which they defined their identities and 'our culture' through the male 'breadwinner' role (see Archer, Pratt and Phillips 2001).

Participation in HE was thus framed as involving various potential costs to working-class male identities. It is noticeable that almost none of the young men in these groups spoke of university participation in terms of personal development and fulfilment.[2] There was a pronounced fixity to these discourses of masculinity, which closed off options in ways that were not evident among the women respondents. Apart from the (imagined) more immediate gains of money and steady work, the defence of non-participation in HE also served to enable the maintenance of hegemonic male identity (and its associated power) in a world of unpredictability and risk. Put simply, many non-participant men felt they had too much to lose through participation for it to be worth the risk.

As we have suggested elsewhere (Archer, Pratt and Phillips 2001; also see Archer 2001a), the non-participant men's powerful attachments to these discourses may relate to the way in which these identities allow the men to exercise various forms of local power in relation to other working-class men and women. In comparison, participation in higher education could 'interfere' with the maintenance of these powerful identities, for example by removing the men from spheres of (manual) work in which identities are produced and reducing their 'masculinity capital' within an arena where middle-class men exercise greater power/competency. It is possible that participating in HE could be particularly disruptive and undesirable for the men, because masculinity is never an 'achieved' identity, but is continually produced, requiring constant (re)affirmation and assertion.

As Gramsci (1971) argues, the hegemony of the dominant culture is never complete or absolute. It has to be continually reworked and defended against challenging alternatives.

> Manliness … is a contested territory, it is an ideological battlefield. And … if we look back in time, not only do we see that at certain points in history, one specific discourse of masculinity has dominated over all of the other alternatives … but we also find that the efforts to control the meaning of masculinity have played a central role in the struggle for power between various social groupings including classes, 'races', nations as well as men and women.
>
> (Edley and Wetherell 1995: 17)

Similarly, not all working-class men resisted education as unthinkable and unmanly.

Participating men, plus a few non-participant men, did argue in favour of HE participation, suggesting that it can be a way to achieve mobility, affluence and security for ambitious, hard-working, aspirant working-class men (see Hutchings and Archer 2001). Rather than wanting to become 'like middle-class men', men who argued in favour of participation generally framed their reasons in terms of achieving 'practical', not identity, changes to their lives.

But the men's personal views and motivations were not the only sources of discouragement. Students such as Fela and Neil also talked about how they had experienced discouragement from friends, colleagues and/or family. These attempts to dissuade the men from returning to study seemed to be voiced through negative views of both students and/or study. For example, Neil was strongly discouraged by his brother who referred to him as a '31-year-old loser' about to spend three years 'dossing around'. This lack of support from family and friends may have had particularly negative implications in terms of retention, as some of the students, such as Neil, reported feeling lonely and isolated at university. This loneliness was partly attributed to the university modular system which hindered the formation of friendship through regular contact between students, but was exacerbated by the competing demands of having to undertake paid employment and domestic responsibilities.

The data also point to a complex and contradictory process by which the non-participant young men negotiated HE participation, they were not simply 'pro-participation' or 'anti-participation' or 'resistant', and many non-participants did not clearly rule themselves out of ever participating. Rather, when questioned many non-participant men positioned themselves as potentially able to benefit from higher education, but suggested that they were constrained by their personal, social or economic factors and practicalities from doing so, and as a result, felt they could not participate. For many non-participant men, however, it was also clear that participation was more of a 'non-choice', one that had never entered into their spheres of everyday decision-making.[3] The men in this study did not appear to follow any clear linear routes in terms of participant or non-participant educational trajectories. Willis' (1977) work might suggest that most working-class boys follow from resistance at school to 'non-participation', but the process of 'dropping out' and/or 'returning' appeared to be far more complex.

The men differed in their views as to the desirable ways in which participation might change them for the better. Generally speaking, more Asian men (and one mixed-race white/Nigerian young man) argued that participation would enable them to achieve a middle-class job and lifestyle, which they suggested was a normative lifestyle to which they aspired. In contrast, some white men argued that participation would only be justified or beneficial if it did not entail class identity change, in other words, if you 'stay the same as you were before'.

Working-class women: femininities and HE participation

The majority of women talked positively about higher education as a potential route for 'bettering' oneself, whether or not they were planning to, or thought it likely that they might, participate. It is interesting to note that a number of the women in the study did not envisage themselves as continuing with, or returning to, education. This is particularly pertinent given the wider current educational context, which is replete with moral panics regarding the under-achievements of working-class boys, the 'feminization' of the education system, and claims that 'the future is female' (see Epstein *et al.* 1998 for a critique). A small number of non-participant women strongly resisted participation, citing it as an impossible and undesirable goal. These women argued that participation was impossible due to various barriers, but particularly, their lack of formal qualifications, financial factors and family responsibilities. University was also regarded as an undesirable option due to negative images of students and because of unpleasant associations between learning and earlier painful school experiences. Non-participant women also generally talked about degrees as less useful than 'common sense' in the labour market.

Like the men, many of the women respondents reported having negative experiences at school, but both women participants and non-participants were more likely to blame themselves for their educational failure(s). This psychic burden of blame reflects what Greed (1991) has termed the 'intellectual carnage' inflicted upon working-class girls by the education system. Within the women's accounts there were recollections of the differential channelling of girls and boys into particular subject areas and accounts were given of teacher's having low(er) expectations of the girls' abilities and future possibilities. These recollections are reflected by work which has documented and revealed the ways in which women's educational choices have been generally constrained through notions of 'acceptability', steering girls towards particular subjects (domestic science, languages) and careers (see Stone 1994). Issues around stereotyping and teachers' lower expectations of their female pupils appeared to be amplified in the case of black women respondents:

JOAN: But most of the teachers are very stereotypical, so it was like 'you could go into that', so they brand you, and it's only if you've got strong parents like shall we say 'no she's not doing that', and then they … whereas they're not listening to a student.

JANET: Can I just say something there, you say 'you've got to have strong parents' again, like no disrespect like my Mum, like she come from the West Indies and whatever, so she's not really clued up on how the system is over here, and she send you to school and you go and do your business …

MICHELLE: Yes exactly.

JANET: Things like 'do your homework', they don't sit down, and you know they don't have a clue, you know and it's all that, and that's what I'm saying respecting you, and your Mum pushing you, because I mean if my Mum had pushed me, I would have been far, I wouldn't be here.

RONNIE: I think as well we're the first generation.

JANET: That's what I'm saying, yes.

RONNIE: Your parents have been in this country so they know what it's like.

JANET: That's right.

RONNIE: Because with my parents they think the teachers are doing their job the teachers are right, 'yes, what do you mean she can't have said that'. They believe that the teachers are educating their children, and they're not. Yes but your Mum, she's probably wised up. Ours like literally just came over here and they said that they'd given them a damn good job, which they're not.

(Joan, 33, black Caribbean temporary administrator; Michelle, 16, black Caribbean FE student; Janet, age not known, black Caribbean part-time administrator; Ronnie, 30, black Caribbean unemployed)

As we have written elsewhere (Archer, Hutchings and Leathwood 2001), despite some generational differences, the majority of black women non-participants talked about having been 'held back' by teachers at school. However, unlike first-generation black women, second-generation women had been able to draw on parental support in order to resist being placed in lower ability streams and on lower-level examination papers. Many of the black women students also recounted their 'back-door' routes (Mirza 1992) into further and higher education (see also Archer 2001a).

Across the discussion groups, the women's engagement with, and negotiation of, educational routes and identities were grounded within classed and racialized discourses of femininity. These discourses of femininity (femininities) were also almost universally constructed within notions of 'compulsory heterosexuality' (Rich 1986), being linked to the over-riding importance of seeking/maintaining romantic love and relationships with boys/men (see also Tett 2000 who records this in the accounts of working-class women students).

For example, Elizabeth, a white young woman studying in an FE college, reported having enjoyed school and had achieved a BTEC National qualification which would provide an entry route to higher education. She stated, however, that she 'wouldn't go' to university because she is 'fed up' with education. She describes herself as a 'family person' and says 'I'm not being funny but like the people that go to university are gay'. She then retracts this but goes on to say 'But they seem to come back ... like I knew this girl ... a couple of girls I know and they come back and they look like grungers. Well they are now. It's not the way they went'.

Skeggs (1997) shows how the working-class young women in her study invest in and perform femininity as a way out of dominant pathologized and sexualized (vulgar, gross, tasteless) constructions of working-class women. Skeggs argues that 'for working-class women, the sexual has to be disavowed' (p. 110), but glamour and (heterosexual) desirability can provide recognition and 'the marks of middle-class respectability' (ibid.). Lesbian sexuality, along with the sexuality per se of black and white working-class women, have thus been constructed within dominant societal discourses as deviant, dangerous, perverse and 'other' to respectable femininity. Elizabeth's construction of herself as a 'family person' is one of safe and respectable heterosexual femininity, and a higher education that potentially challenges that identity (becoming gay or 'grungers'), presents too great a risk.

In general, though, women's more positive evaluation of the possibilities of higher education study stood out from the more ambivalent views of working-class men in the research. The main motivation cited by women respondents was framed in identity terms: HE participation was talked about as a means to 'better myself'.

Despite their rejection of higher education, a number of the non-participant women also wanted to 'better' themselves, but saw this potential for improvement in terms of financial security and employment rather than educational terms. For example a group of white young women hairdressing students stated that their ambitions were to have their own mobile hairdressing business or possibly a hairdressers' shop. For these young women, school had been 'dreadful', while hairdressing was something that they enjoyed and enabled them to avoid the perceived boredom of office work. It was also thought more likely to provide them with the possibilities for a secure future as, although computerization could threaten other areas of work, as Gemma, a trainee hairdresser put it, 'nobody's going to want robots to cut their hair'. These young women's future identities and aspirations are structured by classed and gendered occupational 'choices'. Their concern with a ensuring a secure future can be seen to reflect notions of responsible femininity (Skeggs 1997), although this did not prevent them from having aspirations to 'go on higher' (Claire, trainee hairdresser).

Many of the women students, however, had experience of unfulfilling work, and framed 'bettering' predominantly in terms of realizing 'wasted potential' and 'wanting more':

> I did an access course, and basically I was sitting in a job for like ten years doing customer service and you know, it's not the greatest [laughs] you know, answering phones to irate customers that haven't got their cars on time and stuff like that you know. And it's like um, I just didn't want to do that anymore. I just didn't want to be that person. I wanted to – I knew I had more to offer. I did er, I did a little mini um what they called, City and Guilds in media and I really enjoyed it. But then I thought I want to do something where I can write as well as, as well as do the practical side. Cos I think I could write critically. And like the access course, you know, I ended up getting all my credits and I just felt that I, that I was quite academically at home, you know. And you know when I started this course I felt, I felt good about it you know? I felt that I can achieve something.
>
> (Grace, 26, black woman, student)

Grace explicitly rejects her work identity of a customer services person: 'I just didn't want to be that person'. She knows she has more to offer, and bettering herself through a return to study provides personal fulfilment though her newly constructed identity as someone who 'can achieve something'. Green and Webb (1997) also identified 'untapped potential' and 'wasted potential' discourses in their study of alternative entrants to HE, with 'soul-destroying' work often providing the motivation to change for women.

Grace's desire to study, her pleasure at being 'quite academically at home', could also be interpreted as a symbolic escape from an embodied working-class 'feminine' identity associated with drudgery and demeaning work, to a middle-class and authentic femininity (Skeggs 1997) in which (some) autonomy and freedom from the bodily experiences of childbearing/rearing and domestic labour becomes a possibility. Grace felt that it was only because she did not have children that she had been able to return to study.

Getting a degree was seen to provide an escape from restricted life choices and open up new opportunities for a number of the women students in the study:

It gives you a bit more opportunities anyway when you got a degree, you're not sort of like stationed in one place. If you don't have a degree, I mean if you've just got GCSEs you're less likely to expand your horizons.

(Janita, 19, Pakistani)

To broaden your horizons, you've got more of a choice, whereas before I didn't have much of a choice, just got stuck in a rut with the same sort of job, so it's to broaden horizons.

(Deborah, 26, white)

Similarly, Shauna describes thinking about her future because the job she has (as a kitchen hand and waitress) is not what she wants to be doing: 'It is not enough – you can do more in life so get on with it'. Shauna also epitomizes many of the young black women in Mirza's research (Mirza 1992, 1995) who acknowledge the values of educational credentials and articulate a meritocratic belief system:

I think I will go for the degree as well because sometimes it is good when you prove that you are good in some things but then again you want some sort of paper or document that you have a qualification in something that you are applying for a job. Any job nowadays they want to see your qualification before they even say that you can go on. So I think a degree helps for you to get there and towards your life.

(Shauna, 23, black)

Shauna, like Grace, feels that she can do more, and this sense of a hidden and wasted potential, one that was rarely realized in school, underpins a number of the accounts, including that of Siobhan:

For me it's that I want to have educated myself. Like before in school, for me, I never put any effort into it ... and if you just see the kind of potential resting in your hands, you know, just that er and then if I sort of think about getting a job, a good job. I mean I don't want to get a degree and then go, end up working at Tescos anyway cos there's no field for me or whatever. You know, just things that I can't get now, like I live in a council flat and I want to get a house at some stage, I'd like to do things.

(Siobhan, 23, white Irish)

The desires of some working-class women to escape from their working-class lives, or what Sennett and Cobb refer to as 'the hidden injuries of class' (1977), are frequently pathologized and trivialized. While much widening participation discourse rests on the assumption that working-class people *ought* to want to better themselves through education, and *ought* to want to adopt middle-class lifestyles and identities, actual desires by working-class women to acquire the material and cultural markers of a middle-class identity 'are marked as apolitical, trivial, pretentious' (Lawler 2000: 125). Citing Steedman (1986) and Fox (1994), Lawler points out that 'what is withheld is constituted as *inherently* desirable and *inherently* normal' (stress in original), and she asks 'why are desires like this trivialized? Is it because they are represented as peculiarly "feminine" affectations? Is it because they stake a claim on an existence to which you have no "right"?' (ibid.).

Many women in this study reported meeting considerable family resistance to their participation, which was interpreted as trying to 'get above my station'. 'Escape' could be seen to present a challenge to working-class values and lifestyles, and so pose a threat to those 'left behind':

> Um yeah, sorry, where I'm from, I'm from Manchester, and the area is just very sort of working class. I had these dreams above my station you know, sort of to go to London and do a degree. It was all very sort of [acts indignation, disapproval] well like, what is this not good enough for you? So I've had to deal with a lot of my family, none of them into education at all, not even stepped onto the A level ladder, just gone you know straight from school and what not. And it's really been shunned, I've really been shunned for coming here actually. But I'm smoothing it over and hopefully I'll prove to them that it's not a bad thing me going away. I can go back and put something in maybe. Not that I want to go back there! [laughs] It's – it is really difficult to come down here. Especially when parents, they don't understand at all, you know, you sort of explain why you want to do it and they're like Yeah but you've got a job, you've got all these things, all these physical objects that you have, computers, a car, whatever. And they think it's great and you, you know, your mind wants something else. And that's very difficult to sort out.
>
> (Sally, 22, white woman student)

Sally articulated a theme that ran through several of the white women's accounts: that she knew 'her place' in society, and that a desire to move beyond that was somehow illegitimate. Like Hatton (1999: 214), who describes the guilt she experiences as 'a working-class girl gone wrong'. Sally expresses some guilt at leaving, guilt she can perhaps ameliorate by giving something back. She wants to smooth over the conflict with her family and to persuade them that her going away isn't 'a bad thing', indicating her desire to maintain family relationships and hold on to her identity as a 'good' (and still feminine) daughter. The contradictions between wanting to escape from, while at the same time preserve, working-class identities are apparent here (Lawler 1999).

Stephanie (a white woman student age 26) explained how her parents had compared her choice to enter higher education negatively with that of her cousin:

> When are you going to stop mucking around and get your act together?
> You are nearly 27 now and you still haven't got any money in the bank.
> They compare me to my cousins who haven't been to university or any-
> thing like that but they have got children and a mortgage and they are
> married or have a steady boyfriend and boring. My Mum compares me
> because I have a crappy little Fiat Uno and they have got a Mercedes and
> it is all materialistic and she doesn't understand that's not the way I am.

Sarah said that university always seemed like 'a far-away option' because no
one in her family had been. Eventually she 'made the jump' but received
strong discouragement from her entire family. Violet was similarly dissuaded
by friends and family who told her she would not be able to cope or understand anything. Violet wanted to study at university in order to 'be trained
to be a rounded, complete woman', thus illustrating the ways in which
'woman' and 'femininity' become established as middle-class signs, from
which working-class women are positioned as distant (Skeggs 1997). It is
only through training that Violet hopes to gain access to the category
'woman'.

For both Sarah and Violet, discouragement centred around their mother-
hood, which rendered being a student 'irresponsible' behaviour. Perhaps as a
response to these pressures, many student women voiced a more 'acceptable'
motivational discourse for participation in terms of 'doing it for my family'
(children and siblings, being a role model, etc.). Siobhan draws on her
identity as a mother to emphasize the importance of this for her:

> I don't want to end up working in Tescos or something like that. I want
> to have something better, as well as, with kids it makes a difference with
> kind of um, even though mummy has three kids she worked hard to
> get her degree. She maybe didn't do it straight after school well, not me,
> but ... [laughs].

> (Siobhan, 23, white Irish student)

This is an acceptable face of (authentic) femininity, as 'selfless', 'caring', a
mother doing the best for her children. Only a couple of young black women
voiced a more autonomous discourses of 'because I deserve it', 'because I'm
worth it' and 'doing it for myself'.

It is also worth noting that women students were more likely to report
feeling alienated by the academic culture within the university. As cited in
Chapter 6, some of the black women in particular recounted feeling 'lost' and
'left behind' by the academic language and procedures, to the extent that they
talked about only 'looking in', rather than fully 'belonging' to the institution
(Read et al. 2003). While we have discussed elsewhere the classed inequalities
underlying these feelings of deficit, it could be speculated that gender differences in relation to negotiation of academic culture may relate to dominant

constructions of the 'normal' student as male (white and middle class) (see Harding 1990; Leathwood 2001; Wolffensperger, 1993).[4] Thus, students from 'non-traditional' backgrounds are disadvantaged by institutional cultures that position them as 'Other' and such cultures may discourage a conception of oneself as a potential university student (Tett 1996).

Summary

We have argued that classed identities are complex and, therefore, the relationship between identity and HE participation is necessarily complex and multiple. As Reay (1997) suggests, it is important to move beyond treating class identities in binary terms, utilizing instead a theorization of class as process. While these multiple and shifting classed identities and inequalities may be difficult to 'pin down' theoretically, as Walkerdine *et al.* (2001) suggest, this does not mean that they are any less 'real' or important issues in people's lives. Indeed, many of the women's (and men's) interviews illustrate what Walkerdine *et al.* refer to as 'the immense physical, material and centrally psychic work that class mobility requires' (Walkerdine 2001: 48).

This chapter has presented various respondents' negotiations in relation to participation in higher education, all of which serve to contradict dominant views of educational choices as rational or neutral individual processes. Similarly to the work of Stephen Ball and colleagues, our accounts add to criticisms of 'the uni-dimensional, calculative, individualistic, consumer-rationalism which predominates in official texts' (Ball *et al.*, 2000a: 21). Instead, we have attempted to highlight how working-class participants and non-participants engage emotionally with negotiations around HE participation, which are grounded within gendered, racialized, classed and sexual identities. Thus issues of identity issues will not only impact upon propensity to participate but, as Reay *et al.* (2001) argue, they can render some 'choices' invisible/unthinkable and others 'automatic'.

Notes

1 It is important to note here that in so doing, we do not propose these discourses as 'essentialized' or representative of all men from any particular ethnic background.
2 In comparison many more of the young working-class women did see education as a means of bettering themselves and were willing to take the risks involved.
3 It is perhaps also worth noting that there was generally a lot of agreement within the groups on this point (only one group of black men expressed real contradictions of opinion about participation).
4 A contributory factor may also have been that some of the men respondents were less inclined to want to talk about their feelings and/or insecurities to a female interviewer.

Chapter 10

Widening participation in higher education

Implications for policy and practice

Louise Archer, Merryn Hutchings, Carole Leathwood and Alistair Ross

In this book we have introduced and discussed a range of theoretical and policy literature around widening participation and social class, relating these to data from working-class participants and non-participants. Chapter 1 introduced some key theoretical concepts and theories and Chapters 2 and 3 provided a historical overview to the widening participation policy agenda. Chapter 4 explored the characteristics of potential working-class participants and attempted to statistically model factors affecting participation.

Chapter 5 showed how working-class young people may be disadvantaged because they do not possess the same cultural capital as their middle-class peers. As a result, they may know less about what higher education entails and how to get there. Data revealed a widespread distrust of official information among working-class respondents, compared to a preference for 'hot', grapevine knowledge (Ball and Vincent 1998) which was linked to the construction of various cultural discourses, some of which positioned participation in HE as out of the question.

Chapter 6 argued that currently participation in higher education does not represent as good 'value' an investment for working-class groups because they are disproportionately disadvantaged by the high risks and costs of participation. In Chapter 7, attention was drawn to the longstanding academic/vocational divide between curricula, qualifications and institutions in the UK education system. This divide, and the differential value placed on different forms of knowledge and expertise, is one way in which middle-class privilege and dominance in (higher) education and employment is sustained.

Chapter 8 outlined how financial factors form crucially important barriers to the participation of working-class groups in higher education. It was argued that current student support systems disadvantage the less affluent student, and are highly complex and opaque.

Chapter 9 highlighted the importance of issues of identity within working-class negotiations around participation. It was argued that complex inequalities of 'race', class and gender are all key concerns within working-class men's and women's relationships to higher education participation.

We would like to conclude the book by raising a number of questions that need to be addressed through policy and practice in relation to widening participation in higher education.

Higher education for social inclusion?

The government has set a target of increasing participation in higher education to 50 per cent of under-30-year-olds by the year 2010. The current figure has been estimated from government figures as 41 per cent (34 per cent are 18–21-year-olds and 7 per cent who enter HE as mature students) (*THES* 2002a). But even if the target were achieved, would this necessarily mean that social inclusion and social justice have also been achieved? The answer to this question depends upon who would constitute the additional 20 per cent. The National Audit Office (2002a) and Woodrow *et al.* (2002) suggest that achievement of the government's target would not necessarily require greater inclusion of under-represented groups. For example, the 50 per cent target participation levels could be achieved almost entirely through additional recruitment of middle-class young and mature students, leaving working-class participation rates barely changed. Such a situation would result in an expanded, but not socially broadened/widened participation in HE. Thus the government's target does not *necessarily* address social justice concerns, although these are widely cited as reasons motivating the setting of the target.

The question might also be raised as to whether this target is realistically achievable. Participation rates for lower socio-economic groups remain lower in England than in most other western countries (including Scotland), although only two other European countries (Sweden and The Netherlands) having achieved significant changes to balance participation between social groups (HEFCE 2001b). Thus patterns of under-representation among working-class groups have remained relatively consistent across most countries, regardless of educational structures and vigorous policy initiatives (HEFCE 2001b). However, HEFCE also note that many OECD countries have now reached the saturation point for entrants from the most affluent social groups, meaning that further expansion will depend upon widened future participation.

The government's explicit commitment to an economic rationale underpinning current rhetoric on widening participation also raises concerns over the 'inclusion' agenda in relation to HE participation. Woodrow *et al.* (2002: 165) suggest, 'those with an interest in widening participation might need to keep a watchful eye on the way in which terminology is being used in debates about, and also the enactment of, policy in this area'. As Morgan Klein and Murphy (2002) have identified, a 'mixed bag' of contradictory discourses may underpin the motivation of various agencies, institutions and bodies to engage with widening participation. These differing motivations represent the range of competing agendas at work within various approaches to widening participation, for example with concerns over institutional competition and survival potentially at odds with more traditional social justice motivations.

The concepts of 'social exclusion' (and conversely 'social inclusion') are central to New Labour discourses, yet the usage of these terms has been criticized in a number of ways for doing little to help redress social inequalities. Levitas (1998), for example, argues that discourses of social exclusion contain the unquestioned assumption that inclusion is the best, most desirable state. She also argues that social exclusion rhetoric often obscures inequalities between the positions into which people are socially integrated. Furthermore, as they are currently used, notions of 'social exclusion' can have the effect of naturalizing unequal practices due to its close association with working-class 'failure' while ignoring middle-class self-exclusions from education (Whitty 2001). Gewirtz (2001) has also criticized the ways in which New Labour policy discourses have tended to normalize particular middle-class values and practices, which are offered as solutions or ideals to overcoming working-class social exclusion from education. This focus upon cultural exclusions, she argues, detracts from analysis of inequalities, because they are based upon 'a deficit model of working-class parents ... [and] may serve to perpetuate homogenizing assumptions about working-class communities that characterize working-class families' (Gewirtz 2001: 375).

Thus within the higher education context, the notion that working-class groups are 'socially excluded' from higher education has been linked to attempts to change or 'raise' working-class aspirations and attainment. Notwithstanding the implicit assumptions of deficit contained within the terminology of 'raising' aspirations, it can be argued that the government's focus upon changing working-class cultures and patterns of decision-making represents, at least implicitly, a desire to make working-class groups more like the middle classes (see Gewirtz 2001).

As has also been noted elsewhere in relation to our own research:

> 'Social exclusion' can also appear to reflect a static, homogenized position, ignoring multiple inequalities and relationships, positions and forms of participation. Respondents' stories in this research pointed to a diversity of routes in and out of educational sites and showed clearly that there were few who could be unambiguously positioned as either permanently 'included' or 'excluded' from education.
>
> (Archer 2001: 26)

As we shall also argue below, the notion of social inclusion as achievable through widened participation in HE is equally problematic.

The issue of who should be the target of widening participation efforts carries an important social justice agenda. If participation is only increased among certain sections of the population, rather than widened to include all groups, then the achievement of the 50 per cent target could be highly divisive. For example, it would be instrumental in creating even starker social inequalities between those who are 'complete', qualified people in comparison to 'incomplete' un-credentialled social groups (Reay 2001). Strategies such as the Excellence Challenge identification of special support for 'gifted and talented' young people from under-represented groups may also fail to tackle wider issues of structural inequalities between sections of the population (Woodrow *et al.* 2002). Furthermore, the high profile focus upon working-class representation may mean that other inequalities, such as by disability and 'race', remain hidden and unaddressed.

Walkerdine *et al.* (2001) have noted how changes within the modern economy, towards a more flexible, uncertain 'risk society' (Beck 1992) have been mirrored within prominent policy discourses. Thus lifelong learning rhetoric has displaced a previous discourse of 'jobs for life', which they suggest is 'in recognition of the inherent instability built into the system' (Walkerdine *et al.* 2001: 2). The emphasis upon training and retraining within the New Labour vision of lifelong learning (Marks 1999) is clearly grounded within an economic, rather than a social justice, rationale. This economic rationale does not necessarily fit easily with a social justice agenda because the easiest, most 'profitable' way of increasing participation to the target level might not be the way that will best tackle social inequalities.

What sort of 'inclusive' higher education?

It is also debatable as to whether it would ever be possible for widening participation strategies to achieve a socially inclusive higher education system while stark inequalities remain within the sector itself. The persistence of a two-tier system, and the current hierarchy of institutions, raise the question as to whether inclusion is really possible or achievable while this divide remains. It has been argued that the gap between bands of institutions is actually widening, as HE evolves into an increasingly complex and differentiated system (Gallacher 2002). Some 'elite' universities may in fact be recruiting decreasing numbers of the 'least deprived' social groups, yet government policy has awarded funds to these universities for widening participation, rather than to those who have achieved success already within the field (Woodrow *et al.* 2002).

Government plans for further increasing this binary divide between 'teaching' (post-1992, equality orientated) institutions and 'research' (pre-1992, elite) institutions would surely exacerbate current inequalities. We would argue that it is important to attempt to dismantle the 'myth of meritocracy' that currently protects and supports the privileges of the elite universities and which excuses them from addressing the widening participation agenda in any real or meaningful ways.

Another important question that we would like to pose concerns what 'type' or form of HE provision might be made more accessible. Often government rhetoric draws upon the notion of a singular, homogenized higher education experience. We would argue instead that, if access and participation of working-class students is only widened within less prestigious institutions, then this does not fulfil a social justice mission. Equally, social justice issues will remain un-addressed if the 50 per cent target is primarily achieved through an expansion of sub-degree level courses, such as foundation degrees and HNDs, as this would effectively create a separate (lesser valued) form of HE for working-class students. Indeed, traditional notions of what constitutes the 'HE experience' are already being contested and reworked within contemporary patterns of participation. For example, as Morgan Klein and Murphy (2002) suggest, HE study is increasingly being conducted within FE and/or at higher national levels.

Changing individuals or changing institutions?

As argued in the introductory section of this chapter, we assert that a solely individualistic focus on widening participation is inadequate. There is an important role to be played through the interrogation and challenging of institutional cultures. As argued elsewhere (Read *et al.* 2003), even within institutions with high proportions of 'non-traditional' students, the culture of the academy predominantly reflects a discourse of the student as young, white, male and middle class. Students should be able to feel that they can 'belong' in any institution, but this will not happen until the elite universities are no longer the preserve of 'traditional' students. Yet large-scale change remains unlikely while government funding protects and perpetuates elitism, while institutions are encouraged to pursue widening participation agendas for reasons of institutional growth and survival, rather than solely to work towards social justice.

In addition to addressing inequalities within institutional cultures, we would also call more generally for more accessible and equitable systems to be put in place to facilitate entry for working-class students. Such measures would include addressing the potential costs and risks of higher education study that are faced by working-class students. We would question whether working-class students currently get a 'good deal' (or more precisely, 'as good a deal') from higher education. As argued in Chapters 7 and 8, we would also strongly support an overhaul of the student finance system and qualification entry routes into HE.

Retention

Issues of retention have increasingly come to the fore within discussions concerning widening participation and working-class students (House of

Commons 2001a; National Audit Office 2002b). While English universities currently record overall rates of retention which compare very favourably internationally (around 77 per cent completion among full-time undergraduates, National Audit Office 2002b), it is widely acknowledged that the issue of retention is a crucial component within widening participation. Non-traditional students must be supported all the way through to completion, rather than concentrating resources only at the point of entry. The evidence in relation to completion rates among working-class students is rather unclear and contradictory. For example, it has been suggested that, at an institutional level, prior academic achievement (A-level point scores) is closely correlated with predicted retention (House of Commons 2001a; National Audit Office 2002b), although Thompson and Corver have also suggested that mature students experience lower rates of completion (around 70 per cent) than younger students (82 per cent) (2000). Yet it is popularly assumed that working-class students are more likely not to complete (this is presumably deduced from performance indicator tables, where institutions with higher proportions of 'non-traditional' students also have the lowest rates of completion). Thus, concerns have been raised from various quarters regarding the 'costs' (social justice and economic) of widening access.

Actual rates of non-completion and withdrawal are difficult to assess because of the difficulty in obtaining sufficiently detailed and good-quality data. For example, social class (or occupational code) is not recorded for many students in the UK HESA returns and retention rates can only really be determined after each entire cohort has had time to complete (this may entail allowing at least seven or eight years to cover part-time study). A methodology is used by (2001b) to predict retention rates from current 'year-to-year' transitions. Such predictions are estimates based upon an assumption that the pattern of year-to-year student progression will remain much the same over successive years. HEFCE calculate their predicted retention rates allowing for differences between students according to their qualifications on entry, subjects studied and age. One aim of these calculations is to inform 'benchmark' retention rates for each HE institution, although obviously not all the salient factors which may affect retention are built into these models. It has been argued however that institutions may be able to 'massage' their perceived retention rates. For example, the use of modular systems (packaged more innocently as 'bite-sized education for struggling students') may help to hide 'visible' wastage rates (Morgan Klein and Murphy 2002). Additionally, the definition of completion can be made to include the achievement of any form of accreditation (not necessarily the course or level of course originally undertaken). Thus estimates of retention rates will depend upon how retention is measured and defined within different institutions.

The implications of the current New Labour obsession with performance indicators and league tables thus carry important implications for widening participation and increasing access for working-class students. Low completion rates entail negative funding implications for institutions, thus complicating the widening participation agenda. It is generally recognized that the costs for supporting and retaining 'non-traditional' students are indeed higher than for 'traditional' students, but these costs are crucial to endeavours to create a more equitable higher education system. It should also be noted that the costs of non-completion are not merely monetary and do not only impact on institutions. As outlined earlier within the book, for individual working-class students and their families participation may entail considerable social and psychic burdens, and 'failure' (or withdrawal) may have serious personal, social and/or economic implications for (often already vulnerable) students (see also Hoy 2002).

After HE: employability and identity

Within current widening participation and social inclusion rhetoric, there often seems to be a conceptual endpoint after the point of graduation. Concerns around employability are, however, being increasingly raised and brought on to the agenda (see for example Knight and Yorke 2001). As outlined earlier, the government has positioned education as a key means for producing a highly qualified and employable workforce. Yet as Morgan Klein and Murphy (2002) point out, there are numerous barriers to achieving an appropriate fit between employers' needs and students' and institutions' learning objectives (which they suggest is symptomatic of the diverse vested interests that underlie HE). Moreover, as analyses of graduate earnings suggest (see for example Audas and Dolton 1999), structural inequalities of 'race', class and gender strongly impact on access to, and earnings within, the labour market, over and above the possession of a degree.

We might also question whether, even if working-class graduates do progress into careers comprising of stable and well-paid jobs, this indicates that the goal of social inclusion has been achieved. Or does the social justice mission 'end' at graduation? Writings, by feminist academics from 'non-traditional' class and ethnic backgrounds, suggest that even when 'others' are able to join the academy (as academics, lecturers and researchers), they may have painful experiences grounded in their identifications with 'deficit' and 'not belonging' (see Mahony and Zmroczek 1997). This reflects the importance of subjectivity, whereby 'class is lived as an identity designation and not simply as an economic relation to the means of production' (Walkerdine *et al.* 2001: 13).

Reay (2001) also discusses the ambivalence surrounding credentialism for the working classes, which arises from the contradiction between desire for social mobility and affluence (achieved through increased credentialism), and 'the alienation, cultural losses and subordination' that arises from occupying disadvantaged and unequal positions within educational spheres (Reay 2001: 336). Thus she suggests that 'in the twenty-first century growing numbers of the working classes are caught up in education either as an escape, as a project for maximizing and fulfilling the self or a complicated mixture of the two' (ibid.).

The future: changing higher education?

The discussions within this chapter may also lead us to question, what is, what should, and what could be meant in the future by the notion of a 'university'/universities'? We would suggest that the definition of a 'university' goes beyond the physical buildings and, indeed, should extend beyond the 'ivory tower' concept. It is our opinion that the attainment of 'real' widened participation for working-class groups may well require a shift away from current notions of a fixed university site, and may require de-centred learning that takes place within working-class communities, *but on their own terms*. This notion extends beyond outreach work (conceptual-ized as projects controlled from a central university base, in which the institution remains unchanged and merely extends its influence outwards). An alternative vision might require radical power shifts in relation to the provision, control and nature of higher education learning. Drawing upon the example of innovative work being undertaken at the Bromley-by-Bow Centre in East London, we would support a more emancipatory model within which communities are provided with the tools to shape their higher education experiences on their own terms. These notions of decentred learning also constitute more than current proposals for 'flexible' and 'e-learning', being part of a more radical, democratizing and community activist movement.

We would also argue, along with various others, that there is an impor-tant need within widening participation policy and practice for a movement away from short-term, marginalized projects, towards mainstream strategies (McGivney 2002). Widening participation agendas need to be fully inte-grated into HE sector agenda and they must be linked with other social and educational policies.

The mainstreaming of equality issues will, however, also require an over-haul of the 'quality' agenda within higher education. Without this, equality drives will inevitably meet resistance from quality arguments and will remain marginalized within an already differentiated system.

This point leads us to raise the question of whether higher education can ever be truly equitable? As already hinted at within this book, it is a system with an in-built necessity for failure because, were everyone to participate, then it would no longer be 'higher' education in the same sense. Furthermore, while higher education is only one possible post-compulsory option, it retains (and has persistently retained) a hegemony such that even an expanded system would retain structures of power and elitism. As Giddens suggested almost 30 years ago, the middle and upper classes will continue to dominate and defend elite routes within higher education in order to ensure the reproduction of class privileges.

> What influences elite recruitment is not that the aspirant recuit possesses a degree in Physics or in engineering, but that degree is conferred at Oxford or at Harvard ... ownership of wealth and property continues to play a fundamental part in facilitating access to the sort of educational process which influences entry to elite positions.
>
> (Giddens 1973: 263–4)

Conclusion

In one sense it is rather difficult to write a conclusion to the issues raised within this book because there is no single reason for, or solution to, the under-representation of working-class groups in higher education. Issues around widening participation in HE are complex and, as we have argued from our data, they are intermeshed with identities and inequalities of gender, ethnicity and social class. Attempts to redress the longstanding imbalances in university participation will require action at numerous levels, but substantial change will depend upon the tackling of multiple inequalities which currently permeate the entire HE sector, and indeed, wider society. This is, quite obviously, no mean feat.

We would suggest, however, that distributive policies will be invaluable to such endeavours. Universities alone cannot bear the sole responsibility for widening participation, they must be located within partnerships and networks of action. Strategies aimed at widening participation will need to be located within numerous sites, such as schools, colleges, workplaces, community groups and universities, and should be linked into numerous social, educational and welfare policy agendas, with the aim of redistributing power and privileges. As Diane Reay writes: 'The solution to class inequalities does not lie in making the working classes more middle class, but in working at dismantling and sharing out the economic, social and cultural capital which goes with middle-class status' (Reay 1997: 23). This goal may entail reworking and redefining the content and nature of the higher education experience in order to 'widen access to meaningful education for working-class [men and] women' (Zmroczek 1999: 99). The creation of 'meaningful' education will require appropriate levels of resourcing and a commitment to ensuring a system that challenges, rather than reinforces, classed, raced and gendered inequalities.

A greater 'joining up' of theory and policy and practice, as advocated within this book, should help to ensure that considered and equitable strategies are developed across sectors. Thus through holistic, rather than piecemeal and specialized approaches, the broader factors underlying working-class under-representation in higher education might begin to be addressed.

Glossary

11-plus   Examination at age 11 designed to allocate children to schools in the tripartite system (see below)

Anderson   Colin Anderson, chair of committee reporting on student maintenance, 1960

Barlow   Alan Barlow, chair of committee reporting on scientific manpower (Barlow 1946)

Board of Education   Government department with responsibility for education until August 1944

Crowther   Geoffrey Crowther, chair of committee for the Central Advisory Council's 15–18 (Crowther 1959)

Central Advisory Council on Education (England)   *Ad hoc* set of advisory councils widely used in the 1950s and 1960s to advise government (for example Plowden, Newson and Crowther)

Dearing   Ron Dearing, chair of the NCIHE, 1997

Department for Education and Science   Government department with responsibility for education April 1963–April 1992

Department for Education   Government department with responsibility for education April 1992–July 1994

Department for Education and Employment   Government department with responsibility for education July 1994–June 2001

Department for Education and Skills   Government department with responsibility for education June 2001–present

Fabian Society   Labour Party pressure group/think tank

Geddes   Eric Geddes, chair of public expenditure cuts in the 1920s

Grammar schools   State secondary schools designed to cater for the 'most able' portion of the school population (between 10 and 20 per cent)

Matriculation   End of compulsory schooling examination system prior to the 1944 Act

Ministry of Education   Government department with responsibility for education August 1944–March 1963

National Advisory Body   Public-sector colleges financial and planning regulator from 1979 to 1989, when it was replaced by the Polytechnics and Colleges Funding Council (PCFC)

Oakes   Gordon Oakes, chair of the Committee of Inquiry that established National Advisory Body for Public Sector Higher Education (Oakes 1978)

Percy   Eustace Percy, chair of committee reporting on higher technical education (Percy 1945)

Robbins   Lionel Robbins, chair of the Royal Commission on Higher Education

Taylor Committee   Labour Party Committee on higher education policy that published *The Years of Crisis* (Labour Party 1963)

Tripartite system   System, following the 1944 Education Act, for three parallel sets of secondary schools: grammar, technical and comprehensive

Bibliography

Ainley, P. (1994) *Degrees of Difference: higher education in the 1990s*, London: Lawrence and Wishart.

Aitkin, M.A., Anderson, D.A., Francis, B.J. and Hinde, J.P. (1989) *Statistical Modelling in GLIM*, Oxford: Oxford University Press.

Alexander, C. (1996) *The Art of Being Black: the creation of black British youth identities*, Oxford: Oxford University Press.

Alexander, T. (2000) *The Asian Gang*, Oxford: Berg.

Allatt, P. (1993) 'Becoming privileged: the role of family processes', in I. Bates and G. Riseborough (eds) *Youth and Inequality*, Buckingham: Open University Press.

—— (1996) 'Consuming schooling: choice, commodity, gift and systems of exchange', in S. Edgell, K. Hetherington and A. Warde (eds) *Consumption Matters*, Oxford: Blackwell.

Althusser, L. (1971) 'Ideology and ideological state apparatuses', in L. Althusser (ed.) *Lenin and Philosophy and Other Essays*, London: New Left Books.

Anderson, C. (1960) Ministry of Education and the Secretary of State for Scotland, *Grants to Students: Report of the Committee* (Chairman: Sir Colin Anderson), Cmnd 1051, London: HMSO.

Anthias, F. and Yuval-Davis, N. (1992) *Racialized Boundaries: race, nation, gender, colour and class and the anti-racist struggle*, London: Routledge.

Archer, L. (2001a) 'Detours, dead ends and blocked roads: inner city, working class adults' access to higher education', in L. West, N. Miller, D. O'Reilly, and R. Allen (eds) *Travellers' Tales: Proceedings of the 31st Annual Conference of SCUTREA*, Nottingham: Pilgrim College, University of Nottingham.

—— (2001b) '"Muslim brothers, black lads, traditional Asians": British Muslim young men's constructions of race, religion and masculinity', *Feminism and Psychology*, 11(1): 79–105.

—— (2001c) 'Appendix 10: Memorandum from the University of North London', in House of Commons Education and Employment Committee, *Sixth Report: Higher Education: Student Retention*, London: The Stationery Office.

Archer, L. and Hutchings, M. (2000) '"Bettering yourself": discourses of risk, cost and benefit in ethnically diverse, young working-class non-participants' constructions of higher education', *British Journal of Sociology of Education*, 21(4): 555–74.

Archer, L., Hutchings, M. and Leathwood, C. (2001) 'Engaging with commonality and difference: theoretical tensions in the analysis of working class women's educational discourses', *International Studies in Sociology of Education,* 11(1): 41–62.

Archer, L., Pratt, S. and Phillips, D. (2001) 'Working-class men's constructions of masculinity and negotiations of (non)participation in higher education', *Gender and Education,* 13(4): 431–49.

Association of Graduate Recruiters (1999) *Graduate Salaries and Vacancies: 1999 summer update survey,* London: The Association of Graduate Recruiters.

Association of Teachers in Technical Institutions (ATTI) (1965) *The Future of Higher Education within the Further Education System,* London: ATTI.

Audas, R. and Dolton, P. (1999) 'Fleeing the nest'. Paper presented at Royal Economics Society Annual Conference, Nottingham, 29 March –1 April.

Avis, J. (1991) 'Curriculum categories and student identities in FE', in C. S. Education Group II, Birmingam (ed.) *Education Limited: Schooling and Training and the New Right Since 1979,* London: Unwin.

Ball, C. (1990) 'More means different: widening access to higher education'. Paper presented at RSA, London.

Ball, S.J., (1990) *Politics and Policy Making in Education: explorations in policy sociology,* London: Routledge.

Ball, S.J. and Vincent, C. (1998) '"I heard it on the grapevine": "hot" knowledge and school choice', *British Journal of Sociology of Education,* 19: 377–400.

Ball, S.J., Maguire, M. and Macrae, S. (2000a) *Choice, Pathways and Transitions Post-16: new youth, new economies in the global city,* London: RoutledgeFalmer.

—— (2000b) 'Space, work and the "new urban economies"', *Journal of Youth Studies,* 3(3): 279–300.

Ballard, B. and Clanchy, J. (1988) 'Literacy in the university: an "anthropological" approach', in G. Taylor, B. Ballard, V. Beasley, H. Bock, J. Clanchy and P. Nightingale (eds) *Literacy by Degrees,* Milton Keynes: SRHE and Open University Press.

Barke, M., Braidford, P., Houston, M., Hunt, A., Lincoln, I., Morphet, C., Stone, I. and Walker, A. (2000) *Students in the Labour Market: nature, extent and implications of term-time employment among University of Northumbria undergraduates,* London: DfEE.

Barlow, A. (1946), *Scientific Manpower* (The Barlow Committee), Ministry of Education, Cmnd 6824, London: HMSO.

Barnett, R. (1990) *The Idea of Higher Education,* Buckingham: Open University Press.

Bartholomae, D. (1985) 'Inventing the university', in M. Rose (ed.) *When a Writer Can't Write,* New York and London: Guilford.

Bates, I. and Riseborough, G. (eds) (1993) *Youth and Inequality,* Milton Keynes: Open University Press.

Becher, T. and Kogan, M. (1980) *Process and Structure in Higher Education,* London: Heinemann.

Beck, U. (1992) *Risk Society: towards a new modernity,* Newbury Park, CA: Sage.

Beckett, J. (2001) 'Support and guidance for progression to higher education'. Paper presented at Curriculum 2000: Student Choice and Progression to Higher Education Conference, Institute of Education, London, 8 November.

Benn, C. and Simon, B. (1970) *Halfway There: a report on the British comprehensive school reform,* London: McGraw-Hill.

Blackburn, R.M. and Jarman, J. (1993) 'Changing inequalities in access to British universities', *Oxford Review of Education*, 19(2): 197–215.

Blackmore, J. (1997) 'The gendering of skill and vocationalism in twentieth-century Australian education', in A.H. Halsey, H. Lauder, P. Brown and A. Stuart Wells (eds) *Education: culture, economy, society*, Oxford: Oxford University Press.

Blunkett, D, (2000) Speech made by David Blunkett, Secretary of State for Education and Employment, at the University of Greenwich New Campus, 15 February 2000.

Bordo, S. (1990) 'Feminism, postmodernism and gender-scepticism', in L.J. Nicholson (ed.) *Feminism/Postmodernism*, London: Routledge.

Bourdieu, P. (1986) *Distinction: a social critique of the judgement of taste*, London and New York: Routledge and Kegan Paul.

Bourdieu, P. and Passeron, J.C. (1977) *Reproduction in Education, Society and Culture*, London: Sage.

Bowles, S. and Gintis, H. (1976) *Schooling in Capitalist America*, Boston and London: Rouledge and Kegan Paul.

Box, G.E.P. (1976) 'Science and statistics', *Journal of the American Statistical Association*, 71: 791–9.

Bradley, H. (1996) *Fractured Identities: changing patterns of inequality*, Cambridge: Polity Press.

Braverman, H. (1974) *Labor and Monopoly Capital*, New York: Basic Books.

Brosan, G., Carter, C., Layard, R., Venables, P. and Williams, G. (1971) *Patterns and Policies in Higher Education*, Harmondsworth: Penguin.

Brown, P. (1987) *Schooling Ordinary Kids*, London: Tavistock.

—— (1997) 'Cultural capital and social exclusion: some observations on recent trends in education, employment and the labour market', in A.H. Halsey, H. Lauder, P. Brown and A. Stuart Wells (eds) *Education: culture, economy, society*, Oxford: Oxford University Press.

Brown, R. and Piatt, W. (2001) *Funding Widening Participation in Higher Education*, London: CIHE/IPPR.

Burgess, T. (1999) 'Teaching in higher education: a warning', *Higher Education Review*, 31(3): 45–52.

Burman, E. and Parker, I. (1993) 'Discourse analysis: the turn to text', in E. Burman and I. Parker (eds) *Discourse Analytic Research: repertoires and readings of texts in action*, London: Routledge.

Burr, V. (1995) *An Introduction to Social Constructionism*, London: Routledge.

Bynner, J., Ferri, W. and Shepherd, P. (1998) *Twenty-Something in the 1990s*, Aldershot: Ashgate.

Byrne, D.S., Williamson, B. and Fletcher, B.G. (1975) *The Poverty of Education: a study in the politics of opportunity*, London: Martin Robertson.

Callender, C. (2001) 'Changing student finances in higher education: policy contradictions under New Labour', *Widening Participation and Lifelong Learning*, 3(2): 5–15.

Callender, C., and Kemp, M. (2000) *Changing Student Finances: income, expenditure and the take-up of student loans among full- and part-time higher education students in 1998/9*, London: DfEE.

Callender, C., and Kempson, E. (1996) *Student Finances: income, expenditure and take-up of student loans*, London: Policy Studies Institute.

Calvert, P. (1982) *The Concept of Class*, London: Hutchinson.

Clark, S., Sharpe, R., Palmer, A., Holmes, J. and Hill, E. (2001) 'Working with selected under-represented groups to assist their progression into and through higher education'. Paper presented at NATFHE From Access to Achievement Conference, London, 6 July.

Coffield, F. (1999) 'Breaking the consensus: lifelong learning as social control', *British Educational Research Journal*, 25(4): 479–99.

Coffield, F. and Vignoles, A. (1977) *Widening Participation in Higher Education by Ethnic Minorities, Women and Alternative Students*, Report 5 for the National Committee of Inquiry into Higher Education, London: HMSO.

Cohen, P. (1988) 'The perversions of inheritance: studies in the making of multi-racist Britain', in P. Cohen and H.S. Bains (eds) *Multi-Racist Britain*, London: Macmillan.

Cohen, P. and Haddock, L. (1994) *Anansi meets Spiderwoman: curriculum resources for tackling common-sense racism in pupil cultures*, London: British Film Institute (BFI).

Collier, T., Gilchrist, R. and Phillips, D. (2002 forthcoming) 'Who plans to go to university? Statistical modelling of working class participation', in *Educational Research and Evaluation*.

Confederation of British Industry (CBI) (1994) *Thinking Ahead: ensuring expansion of higher education into the twenty-first century*, London: CBI.

Connell, R. (1989) 'Cool guys, swots and wimps: the interplay of masculinity and education', *Oxford Review of Education*, 15: 291–303.

Connolly, P. and Neill, J. (2001) 'Boys' underachievement, educational aspirations and constructions of locality: intersections of gender, ethnicity and social class', *International Studies in Sociology of Education*, 11(2): 107–30.

Connor, H. and Dewson, S. with Tyers, C., Eccles, J., Regan, J. and Aston, J. (2001) *Social Class and Higher Education: issues affecting decisions on participation by lower social class groups*, Research Report 267, London: DfEE.

Connor, H., Burton, R., Pearson, R., Pollard, E. and Regan, J. (1999) *Making the Right Choice: how students choose universities and colleges*, London: IES/CVCP.

Crompton, R. (1993) *Class and Stratification*, Cambridge: Polity Press.

Crosland, C.A.R. (1956) *The Future of Socialism*, London: Jonathan Cape.

—— (1966) 'A speech at Woolwich College of Technology', in E. Robinson (ed.) *The New Polytechnics*, Harmondsworth: Penguin.

—— (1974) *Socialism Now and Other Essays*, London: Jonathan Cape.

Crosland, S. (1982) *Tony Crosland*, London: Jonathan Cape.

Crossman, R. (1975) *The Diaries of a Cabinet Minister*, vol. 1, London: Hamish Hamilton and Jonathan Cape.

Crowther, G. (1959) *15–19*, Central Advisory Council on Education (Chairman: Sir Geoffery Crowther), London: HMSO.

Cubie A. (1999) *Student Finance: fairness for the future* (The Cubie Report), Independent Committee of Inquiry into Student Finances, Edinburgh: Scottish Executive.

CVCP (1999) Briefing note: *Widening Participation*, London: Committee of Vice-Chancellors and Principals of the Universities of the UK.

Davies, P. (1995) 'Response or resistance? Access students and government policies on admissions', *Journal of Access Studies*, 10(1): 72–80.

Davies, P. and Adnett, N. (1999) 'Quasi-market reforms and vocational schooling in England: an economic analysis', *Journal of Education and Work,* 12(2): 141–56.

Davies, P., Osborne, M. and Williams, J. (2002) *For Me or Not for Me? That is the Question: a study of mature students' decision-making and higher education,* Research Report 297, London: DfES.

Davies, P., Williams, J. and Webb, S. (1997) 'Access to higher education in the late twentieth century: policy, power and discourse', in J. Williams (ed.) *Negotiating Access to Higher Education: the discourse of selectivity and equity,* Buckingham: SRHE and Open University Press.

Dearing, R.(1997) *Higher Education in the Learning Society: the report of the National Committee of Inquiry into Higher Education* (The Dearing Report), London: The Stationery Office.

Delamont, S. (2000) 'The anomalous beasts: hooligans and the sociology of education', *Sociology,* 34: 95–111.

Department for Education (1991) *Higher Education: A New Framework* (White Paper), Cm 1541, London: HMSO.

Department for Education and Employment (DfEE) (1998a) 'Blunkett welcomes Teaching and Higher Education Act', DfEE Press Release, 17 July.

—— (1998b) *Higher Education for the 21st Century: response to the Dearing Report,* London: DfEE.

—— (2000) 'Blunkett: New drive to widen access to higher education', DfEE Press Release, 10 May.

Department for Education and Science (DES) (1966) *Statistics of Education* vol. 2, London: HMSO.

—— (1972) *Education: A Framework for Expansion* (White Paper), Cmnd 5174, London: HMSO.

—— (1978) *Higher Education into the 1990s,* London: DES.

—— (1981) *Statistical Bulletin 6/81,* London: HMSO.

—— (1985) *The Development of Higher Education into the 1990s* (Green Paper), Cmnd 9524, London: HMSO.

—— (1987) *Higher Education: Meeting the Challenge* (White Paper), Cmnd 114, London: HMSO.

—— (1988) *Top-Up Loans for Students* (White Paper), Cmnd 520, London: HMSO.

—— (1990) *Statistical Bulletin 12/80,* London: HMSO.

—— (1991) *Education and Training for the 21st Century* (White Paper), London: HMSO.

DES/Scottish Office (1978) *Higher Education into the 1990s: A Discussion Document,* London: HMSO.

Department for Education and Skills (DfES) (2001a) GCSE/GNVQ and GCE A/AS/ VCE/Advanced GNVQ Results for Young People in England 2000/2001 (early statistics), London: Department for Education and Skills. Available online at <http://www.dfes.gov.uk> (accessed February 2002).

—— (2001b) 'Review of student support', DfES press notice, 4 October.

—— (2001c) *Youth Cohort Study: The Activities and Experiences of 21 Year Olds, England and Wales 2000,* London: HMSO.

—— (2002) *14–19: Extending Opportunities, Raising Standards* (White Paper), London: The Stationery Office.

Edgell, S. (1993) *Class*, London: Routledge.

Edley, N. and Wetherell, M. (1995) *Men in Perspective: practice, power and identity*, London: Prentice Hall/ Harvester Wheatsheaf.

Edwards, G. and Roberts, I.J. (1980) 'British higher education: long term trends in student enrolment', *Higher Education Review*, 12(2).

Egerton M. and Halsey A.H. (1993), 'Trends by socio-economic group and gender in access to HE in Britain', *Oxford Review of Education*, 19(2): 183–96.

Elias, P., McKnight, A., Pitcher, J., Purcell, K. and Simm, C. (1999). *Moving On: graduate careers three years after graduation*, Manchester: CSU.

Epstein, D., Elwood, J., Hey, V. and Maw, J. (1998) *Failing Boys? Issues in gender and achievement*, Buckingham: Open University Press.

Esland, G. (1996) 'Knowledge and nationhood: The New Right, education and the global market', in J. Avis, M. Bloomer, D. Gleeson and P. Hodkinson (eds) *Knowledge and Nationhood: education, politics and work*, London: Cassell.

Fanon, F. (1975) *Peau Noire, Masques Blancs*, Paris: Seuil; trans. Charles Lam Markmann (1986) *Black Skin, White Masks*, London: Pluto.

Farr, M. (2001) 'Home or away? A study of distance travelled to higher education 1994–1999', *Widening Participation and Lifelong Learning*, 3(1): 17–25.

FEFC (2001) *Qualifications and Curriculum Bulletin, No. 3, Coventry: Further Education Funding Council*.

Fidler, L. (2001) 'A complex challenge', *Times Higher Education Supplement*, 17 August.

Field, J. (2001) 'Adults in British higher education: explaining the decline'. Paper presented at UACE Equality Network Workshop, Institute of Education, London, 14 February.

Fletcher, M. (2001) 'The rates of return to vocational and academic qualifications', *College Research*, 4(2): 46–7.

Floud, J., Halsey, A.H. and Martin, F. (1956) *Social Class and Equal Opportunity*, London: Heinemann.

Forsyth, A. and Furlong, A. (2000) *Socioeconomic Disadvantage and Access to Higher Education*, Bristol: Policy Press and Joseph Rowntree Foundation.

Foster, P., Gomm, R. and Hammersley, M. (1996) 'Inequalities in educational outcomes', in P. Foster, R. Gomm and M. Hammersley (eds) *Constructing Educational Inequality*, London: Falmer Press.

Foster, V. (1998) 'Gender, schooling achievement and post-school pathways: beyond statistics and populist discourse'. Paper presented at Australian Association for Research in Education, Adelaide: University of Wollongong. Available online at <http://www.swin.edu.au/aare/98pap/fos98289.html> (accessed October 2001).

Fox, P. (1994) *Class Fictions: shame and resistance in the British working-class novel, 1890–1945*, Durham, NC: Duke University Press.

Franklin, A. (1999) 'Personal reflections from the margins: an interface with race, class, nation and gender', in P. Mahony and C. Zmroczek (eds) *Women and Social Class: international feminist perspectives*, London: UCL Press.

Freire, P. (1972) *Pedagogy of the Oppressed*, Harmondsworth: Penguin.

Fricker, M. (1994) 'Knowledge a construct: theorizing the role of gender in knowledge', in K. Lennon and M. Whitford (eds) *Knowing the Difference: feminist perspectives in epistemology*, London: Routledge.

Fulton, O. (1981) *Access to Higher Education*, Guildford: SRHE.

Furlong, A. and Biggart, A. (1999) 'Framing choices: a longitudinal study of occupational aspirations among 13–16-year-olds', *Journal of Education and Work,* 12(1): 21–36.

Furlong, A. and Cartmel, F. (1997) *Young People and Social Change: individualization and risk in late modernity*, Milton Keynes: Open University Press.

Gallacher, J. (2002) 'Has widening access been a priority in the education of adults?' Paper presented at SCUTREA seminar: The Research Base for Widening Participation – Past, Present and Future, Birkbeck College, London, 8 February.

Gergen, K. (1985) 'The social constructionist movement in modern psychology', *American Psychologist*, 40: 266–75.

Gewirtz, S. (2001) 'Cloning the Blairs: New Labour's programme for the re-socialization of working-class parents', *Journal of Education Policy*, 16(4): 365–78.

Gewirtz, S., Ball, S.J. and Bowe, R. (1993) 'Parents, privilege and the education market', *Research Papers in Education*, 9: 3–29.

—— (1995) *Markets, Choice and Equity in Education*, Buckingham: Open University Press.

Giddens, A. (1973) *The Class Structure of Advanced Societies*, London: Hutchinson.

—— (1991) *Modernity and Self-Identity: self and identity in the late modern age*, Oxford: Polity Press.

Gill, R. (1995) 'Relativism, reflexivity, and politics: interrogating discourse analysis from a feminist perspective', in S. Wilkinson and C. Kitzinger (eds) *Feminism and Discourse: psychological perspectives*, London: Sage.

Gillborn, D. (1995) *Racism and Antiracism in Real Schools*, Buckingham: Open University Press.

Gillborn, D. and Mirza, H.S. (2000) *Educational Inequality. Mapping Race, Class and Gender: a synthesis of research evidence*, Institute of Education, University of London and Middlesex University.

Gilroy, P. (1993a) *The Black Atlantic*, London: Verso.

—— (1993b) *Small Acts*, London: Serpent's Tail.

Glass, D.V. (ed.) (1954) *Social Mobility in Britain*, London: Routledge and Kegan Paul.

Goddard, A. (2001) 'Predicted grades causing offer bias', *The Times Higher Education Supplement*, November 23: 6.

Goldthorpe, J. (1996) 'Class analysis and the reorientation of class theory: the case of persisting differentials in educational attainment', *British Journal of Sociology*, 47(3): 481–505.

Gordon, P., Aldrich, R. and Dean, D. (1991) *Education and Policy in England in the Twentieth Century*, London: Woburn Press.

Gough, B. (1998) 'Men and the discursive reproduction of sexism: repertoires of difference and equality', *Feminism and Psychology*, 8(1): 25–49.

Gough, B. and Edwards, G. (1998) 'The beer talking: four lads, a carry out and the reproduction of masculinities', *Sociological Review*, 46(3): 409–35.

Gramsci, A. (1971) *Selections from the Prison Notebooks*, London: Lawrence and Wishart.

Grant, B. (1997) 'Discipling students: the construction of student subjectivities', *British Journal of Sociology of Education*, 18(1): 101–14.

Greed, C. (1991) 'Review symposium', *British Journal of Sociology of Education*, 14: 103–7.

Green, P. and Webb, S. (1997) 'Student voices: alternative routes, alternative identities', in J. Williams (ed.) *Negotiating Access to Higher Education: the discourse of selectivity and equity*, Buckingham: SRHE and Open University Press.

Grundy, S. (2001) 'A collaborative framework for widening participation in Islington, Haringey, Hackney and Tower Hamlets, qualitative research: summary report'. Unpublished paper, University of North London.

Guardian (2001) 'Student rents soaring', Guardian Higher, *The Guardian*, 10 April: 9.

—— (2002) 'The funding maze', Guardian Higher, *The Guardian*, 22 January.

Hall, J. (1969) 'The CNAA and the philosophy of polytechnic education', in *The Development of the New Polytechnics* (Coombe Lodge Study Conference Report), London: DES.

Halsey, A.H. (1993) 'Trends in access and equity in higher education: Britain in international perspective', *Oxford Review of Education*, 19(2): 129–40.

Halsey, A.H. and Gardner, L. (1953) 'Social mobility and achievement in four grammar schools', *British Journal of Sociology,* March.

Halsey, A.H., Heath, A. and Ridge, J. (1980) *Origins and Destinations: family, class and education in modern Britain*, Oxford: Clarendon.

Haraway, D. (1988) 'Situated knowledges: the science question in feminism and the privilege of partial perspective', *Feminist Studies*, 4: 575–99.

Harding, S. (1990) 'Feminism, science and anti-enlightenment critiques', in L. Nicholson (ed) *Feminism/Postmodernism*, London: Routledge.

Hatcher, R. (1998a) 'Class differentiation in education: rational choices?', *British Journal of Sociology of Education,* 19(1): 5–24.

—— (1998b) 'Labour, official school improvement and equality', *Journal of Education Policy*, 13(4): 485–99.

Hatton, E.J. (1999) 'Questioning correspondence: an Australian woman's account of the effects of social mobility on subjective class consciousness', in C. Zmroczek and P. Mahony (eds) *Women and Social Class – International Feminist Perspectives*, London: UCL Press.

Heathfield, M. and Wakeford, N. (1993) *They Always Eat Green Apples: images of university and decisions at 16*, Lancaster: Unit for Innovation in Higher Education.

HEFCE (2001a) Indicators of Employment, 01/21, Higher Education Funding Council for England. Available online at <http://www.hefce.ac.uk> (accessed January 2002).

—— (2001b) *Supply and Demand in Higher Education*, HEFCE.

HESA (1999) *Students in Higher Education Institutions*, Cheltenham: HESA.

Hey, V. (1997) 'Northern accent and southern comfort: subjectivity and social class', in P. Mahony and C. Zmroczek (eds) *Class Matters: 'working class' women's perspectives on social class*, London: Taylor and Francis.

Higginson, G. (1988) *Advancing A Levels*, London: HMSO.

Himmelweit, H. (1954) 'Social status and secondary education since the 1944 Act: some data for London', in D.V. Glass (ed.) *Social Mobility in Britain*, London: Routledge and Kegan Paul.

Hirsch, F. (1977) *Social Limits to Growth*, London: Routledge.

Hodkinson, P. (1998) 'Choosing GNVQ', *Journal of Education and Work*, 11(2): 151–65.

Hogarth, T., Maguire, M., Pitcher, J., Purcell, K. and Wilson, R. (1997) *The Partici-pation of Non-traditional Students in Higher Education: full report*, HEFCE Research Series, Bristol: HEFCE.

Hoggart, R. (1957) *The Uses of Literacy*, London: Chatto and Windus.

hooks, b. (1994) *Teaching to Transgress: education as the practice of freedom*, London: Routledge.

House of Commons Education, Sciences, Arts Committee (1980) Fifth Report, *The Funding and Organization of Courses in Higher Education*, London: HMSO, pp. 5–9.

House of Commons (1999) *A Century of Change: trends in UK statistics since 1900*, Research paper 99/111, London: The Stationery Office.

—— (2001) *Hansard: Written Questions*, 19 February 2001 Malcolm Wicks to Ruth Kelly, Question 148702, cols 765W, 766W.

House of Commons Education and Employment Committee (2001a) Sixth Report, *Higher Education, Student Retention*, London: The Stationery Office.

—— (2001b) Fourth Report, *Higher Education: Access*, London: The Stationery Office.

Howieson, C. and Semple, S. (1996) *Guidance in Secondary Schools*, Edinburgh: Centre for Educational Sociology, The University of Edinburgh.

Howieson, C., Raffe, D., Spours, K. and Young, M. (1997) *Unifying Academic and Vocational Learning: the state of the debate in England and Scotland*, London: Post-16 Education Centre, Institute of Education and Centre for Educational Sociology, University of Edinburgh.

Hoy, J. (2002) 'Widening participation and learning support coordinator'. Paper presented at SCUTREA seminar: The Research Base for Widening Participation – Past, Present and Future, Birkbeck College, London, 8 February.

Hudson, R. and Williams, A. (1989) *Divided Britain*, London: Belhaven Press.

Hughes, J. (1998) Review of Pratt, J. *The Polytechnic Experiment* (Open University Press, 1997), *Journal of Vocational Education and Training*, 50(1).

Humphrey, R. (2001) 'Working is a class issue', *Times Higher Education Supplement*, 19 January.

Hutchings, M. and Archer, L. (2001) '"Higher than Einstein": constructions of going to university among working-class non-participants', *Research Papers in Education*, 16(1): 69–91.

Hutton, W. (1996) *The State We're In*, London: Vintage.

Independent (2001) 'Blair's tax solution stuns universities', *The Independent*, 11 October.

James, O. (2001) 'Holding on? The effect of student funding on retention in higher education in the UK', *Widening Participation and Lifelong Learning*, 3(2): 29–33.

Jary, D. and Thomas, E. (1999) Editorial: initiatives in widening participation and lifelong learning', *Widening Participation and Lifelong Learning*, 1(3): 2–5.

Kearney, H. (1970) *Scholars and Gentlemen: university and society in pre-industrial Britain 1500–1700*, London: Faber and Faber.

Keen, C. and Higgins, T. (1990) *Young People's Knowledge of Higher Education*, Leeds: HEIST/PCAS.

—— (1992) *Adults' Knowledge of Higher Education*, Leeds: HEIST/PCAS.

Keep, E. and Mayhew, K. (1996) 'Economic demand for higher education: a sound foundation for further expansion?', *Higher Education Quarterly,* 50(2): 89–109.

Kelsall, R.K. (1962) *Report of a Subcommittee on University Entrance Requirements in England and Wales,* London: CVCP.

Kelsall, R.K., Poole, A. and Kuhn, A. (1972) *Graduates: the sociology of an elite,* London: Methuen.

Kennedy, H. (1997) *Learning Works: widening participation in further education,* Coventry: FEFC.

Kenway, J. (1987) 'Left right out: Australian education and the politics of signification', *Journal of Educational Policy,* 2(3): 189–203.

Kenway, J. and Willis, S. (1995) *Critical Visions: policy and curriculum rewriting the future of education, gender and work,* Canberra: Australian Government Publishing Service.

Kidd, J. and Wardman, M. (1999) 'Post-16 course choice: a challenge for guidance', *British Journal of Guidance and Counselling,* 27(2): 259–74.

Knight, P.T. and Yorke, M. (2001) 'Employability through curriculum'. Available online at <http://www.open.ac.uk/vqportal/Skills-Plus/documents/PubPaper1.pdf> (accessed February 2002).

Knowles, J. (2000) 'Access for few? Student funding and its impact on aspirations to enter Higher Education', *Widening Participation and Lifelong Learning,* 2(1): 14–23.

Kogan, M. (1971) *The Politics of Education,* Harmondsworth: Penguin.

Labour Party (1963) *The Years of Crisis Report of the Labour Party Study Group on Higher Education* (Chair, W. Taylor), Labour Party.

Lawler, S. (1999) 'Getting out and getting away: women's narratives of class mobility', *Feminist Review,* 63: 3–23.

—— (2000) 'Escape and escapism: representing working class women', in S. Munt (ed.) *Cultural Studies and the Working Class: subject to change,* London: Cassell.

Layard, R., King, J. and Moser, C. (1969) *The Impact of Robbins,* Harmondsworth: Penguin.

Lea, M. and Street, B. (1998) 'Student writing in higher education: an academic literacies approach', *Studies in Higher Education,* 23(2): 157–72.

Leathwood, C. (2001) 'The road to independence? Policy, pedagogy and "the independent learner" in higher education', in L. West, N. Miller, D. O'Reilly, and R. Allen (eds) *Travellers' Tales: Proceedings of the 31st annual conference of SCUTREA,* Nottingham: Pilgrim College, University of Nottingham.

Leathwood, C. and Hayton, A. (forthcoming) 'Educational inequalities in the UK: a critical analysis of the discourses and policies of New Labour', *Australian Journal of Education.*

Levitas, R. (1998) *The Inclusive Society? Social exclusion and New Labour,* Basingstoke: Macmillan Press.

Lloyd, T. (1999) *Young Men, the Job Market and Gendered Work,* York: York Publishing Services.

Lynch, K. and O'Neill, C. (1994) 'The colonisation of social class in education', *British Journal of Sociology of Education,* 15(3): 307–24.

Lynch, K. and O'Riordan, C. (1998) 'Inequality in higher education: a study of class barriers', *British Journal of Sociology of Education,* 19(4): 445–78.

Mac an Ghaill, M. (1988) *Young, Gifted and Black*, Milton Keynes: Open University Press.

—— (1994) 'The making of black English masculinities', in H. Brod and M. Kaufman (eds) *Theorizing Masculinities*, London: Sage.

—— (1996a) '"What about the boys?": schooling, class and crisis masculinity', *Sociological Review*, 44: 381–97.

—— (1996b) *Understanding Masculinities: social relations and cultural arenas*, Buckingham: Open University Press.

McClelland, K. (1991) 'Masculinity and the "representative artisan" in Britain, 1850–80', in M. Roper and J. Tosh (eds) *Manful Assertions*, London: Routledge.

McGivney, V. (2002) 'Future strategy and research needs'. Paper presented at SCUTREA seminar: The Research Base for Widening Participation – Past, Present and Future, Birkbeck College, London, 8 February.

McPherson, A. and Willms, J.D. (1997) 'Equalization and improvement: some effects of comprehensive reorganization in Scotland', in A.H. Halsey, H. Lauder, P. Brown and A. Stuart Wells (eds) *Education: culture, economy, society*, Oxford: Oxford University Press.

Maguire, M., Ball, S.J. and Macrae, S. (1999) 'Promotion, persuasion and class-taste: marketing (in) the UK post-compulsory sector', *British Journal of Sociology of Education*, 20(3): 291–308.

Mahony, P. and Zmroczek, C. (eds) (1997) *Class Matters: 'working class' women's perspectives on social class*, London: Taylor and Francis.

Mama, A. (1995) *Beyond the Masks: race, gender and subjectivity*, London: Routledge.

Marks, A. (1999) 'Really useful knowledge: the new vocationalism in higher education and its consequences for mature students', *British Journal of Educational Studies* 47(2): 157–69.

Marton, F. (ed.) (1997) *The Experience of Learning: implications for teaching and studying in higher education*, Edinburgh: Scottish Academic Press.

Marx, K. (1976) *Capital*, vol. 1, Harmondsworth: Penguin.

Melville, D. and Macleod, D. (2000) 'The present picture', in A. Smithers and P. Robinson (eds) *Further Education Re-formed*, London: Falmer.

Metcalf, H. (1997) *Class and Higher Education: the participation of young people from lower social classes*, London: CIHE.

Ministry of Education (1956) *The Organisation of Technical Colleges*, London: HMSO.

Mirza, H.S. (1995) 'Black women in higher education: defining a space/finding a place', in L. Morley and V. Walsh (eds) *Feminist Academics: creative agents for change*, London: Taylor and Francis.

—— (1992) *Young, Female and Black*, London: Routledge.

Modood, T. (1993) 'The number of ethnic minority students in British higher education: some grounds for optimism', *Oxford Review of Education* 19(2): 167–82.

Modood, T. and Shiner, M. (1994) *Ethnic Minorities and Higher Education: why are there differential rates of entry?*, London: Policy Studies Institute.

Moodie, G. (1959) *The Universities: A Royal Commission?* Fabian Society Research Series no. 209, London: Fabian Society.

Morgan, D.H.J. (1992) *Discovering Men*, London: Routledge.

Morgan, D.L. (1997) *Focus Groups as Qualitative Research*, Thousand Oaks, CA: Sage.

—— (1998) *The Focus Group Guidebook*, Thousand Oaks, CA: Sage.

Morgan Klein, B. and Murphy, M. (2002) 'The transformation of access: the changing nature of policies on access, research findings from a national study in Scotland'. Paper presented at SCUTREA seminar: The Research Base for Widening Participation – Past, Present and Future, Birkbeck College, London, 8 February.

Morgan, M., Roberts, C. and Powdrill, P. (2001) 'More money than sense? Investigating student money management', in A.J. Scott, A. Lewis and S.E.G. Lea (eds) *Student Debt: the causes and consequences of undergraduate borrowing in the UK*, Bristol: Policy Press.

Mortimore, P. and Whitty, G. (1997) *Can School Improvement Overcome the Effects of Disadvantage?*, London: Institute of Education, University of London.

Mudie, G. (1998) Keynote address presented at From Elitism to Inclusion Conference, London, 2 November.

National Audit Office (2002a) *Improving Student Achievement in English Higher Education*, London: The Stationery Office.

—— (2002b) *Widening Participation in Higher Education in England*, London: The Stationery Office.

Newman, J.H. (1873) *The Idea of a University Defined and Illustrated*, New York: Holt, Rinehart and Winston.

Nixon, N. (1987) 'Central control of the public sector', in T. Becher (ed.) *British Higher Education*, London: Allen and Unwin.

NUS (1995) *Students at Work: a report on the economic conditions of students in employment*, London: National Union of Students.

—— (1999) *Student Hardship Survey*, London: National Union of Students.

Oakes, G. (1978) *Report of the Working Party on the Management of Higher Education in the Maintained Sector* (The Oakes Report), Cmnd 7130, London: HMSO.

OECD (1988) *Alternatives to Universities in Higher Education Country Study: United Kingdom*, Paris: mimeo.

—— (2001) *Economics and Finance of Lifelong Learning*, Paris: Organization for Economic Co-operation and Development.

OFSTED (1996) *Part 1 GNVQs: Pilot Interim Report 95–96*, London: The Stationery Office.

Office of Population, Censuses and Surveys (OPS) (1978) *Census 1971: Household Composition*, London: HMSO.

Ozga, J. and Sukhnandan, L. (1997) 'Undergraduate non-completion: a report for the Higher Education Funding Council for England', Report 2 in *Undergraduate Non-Completion in Higher Education in England*, Bristol: HEFCE.

Paczuska, A. (1996) 'Research study at South Bank University on progression to HE'. Unpublished paper, London: South Bank University.

Paechter, C. (1998) *Educating the Other: gender, power and schooling*, London: Falmer.

Parry, G. (1997) 'Patterns of participation in higher education in England: a statistical summary and commentary', *Higher Education Quarterly*, 51(1): 6–28.

Paterson, L. (1997) 'Trends in higher education in Scotland', *Higher Education Quarterly*, 51: 29–48.

Payne, J. (2001) *Student Success Rates in Post-16 Qualifications: data from the England and Wales Youth Cohort Study*, Nottingham: DfEE.

Payne, J. and Callender, C. (1997) *Student Loans: who borrows and why?*, London: Policy Studies Institute.

Percy, E. (1945) *Board of Trade: Report of the Committee on Higher Technical Education* (Chairman: Lord Eustace Percy), London: HMSO.

PEP (Political and Economic Planning) (1950) *University Students: a pilot study*, London: PEP.

Peters, H. (2001) 'The "Trojan Horse": can recognition of prior learning be used as a means of bringing about change from within traditional institutions of higher education?', in L. West, N. Miller, D. O'Reilly, and R. Allen (eds) *Travellers' Tales: Proceedings of the 31st Annual Conference of SCUTREA,* Nottingham: Pilgrim College, University of Nottingham.

Peterson, A.D.C. (1966) 'English higher education: the issues involved', in E.J. McGrath (ed.) *Universal Higher Education*, Chicago: McGraw-Hill.

Phoenix, A. (1994) 'Practising feminist research: the intersection of gender and race in the research process', in M. Maynard and J. Purvis (eds) *Researching Women's Lives from a Feminist Perspective*, London: Taylor and Francis.

Piper, D.W. (ed.) (1981) *Is Higher Education Fair?*, Guildford: SRHE.

Pokorny, H. and Pokorny, M. (2001) 'Numeracy and student progression in higher education: a case study'. Paper presented at the Society for Research into Higher Education Annual Conference, Cambridge, 17–21 December.

Popkewitz, T. and Lindblad, S. (2000) 'Educational governance and social inclusion and exclusion: some conceptual difficulties and problematics in policy and research', *Discourse,* 21(1): 5–44.

Pratt, J. (1997) *The Polytechnic Experiment 1965–1992*, Buckingham: Society for Research into Higher Education/Open University Press.

—— (2000) 'The emergence of colleges', in A. Smithers and P. Robinson (eds) *Further Education Re-formed*, London: Falmer.

—— (2001) 'Protecting a binary system: why and how'. Paper presented at Colloquium on Change and Challenge in the Technological Sector, The Cork Institute of Technology, October.

Pratt, J. and Burgess, T. (1974) *Polytechnics: a report*, London: Pitman.

Prest, A.R. (1966) *Financing University Education* (Occasional paper of the Institute for Economic Affairs), London: Institute for Economic Affairs.

Pugsley, L. (1998) '"Throwing your brains at it": higher education, markets and choice', *International Studies in Sociology of Education,* 8(1): 71–90.

QCA (2001) *Review of Curriculum 2000*, London: QCA.

Quinn, J. (2001) 'Commentary: recent reports about higher education from the UK Select Committee on Education and Employment: Fourth Report: Higher Education Access', *Widening Participation and Lifelong Learning,* 3(1): 5–6.

Raggatt, P. and Williams, S. (1999) *Government, Markets and Vocational Qualifications: an anatomy of policy*, London: Falmer.

Ramsden, B. (2001) *Patterns of Higher Education Institutions in the United Kingdom: a report for the longer term strategy group of Universities UK*, London: Universities UK.

Rawls, J. (1971) *A Theory of Justice*, Oxford: Oxford University Press.

Read, B., Archer, L. and Leathwood, C. (2003) 'Challenging cultures: student conceptions of "belonging" and power at a post-1992 university', *Studies in Higher Education*, 28: 3.

Reay, D. (1996a) 'Dealing with difficult differences: reflexivity and social class in feminist research', *Feminism and Psychology*, 6: 443–56.

—— (1996b) 'Insider perspectives or stealing the words out of women's mouths: interpretation in the research process', *Feminist Review*, 53: 57–73.

—— (1997) 'The double-bind of the "working-class" feminist academic: the success of failure or the failure of success?', in P. Mahony and C. Zmroczek (eds) *Class Matters: 'working-class' women's perspectives on social class*, London: Taylor and Francis.

—— (1998) '"Always knowing" and "never being sure": familial and institutional habituses and higher education choice', *Journal of Education Policy*, 13(4): 519–29.

—— (1999) 'Class acts: educational involvement and psycho-sociological class processes', *Feminism and Psychology*, 9(1): 89–106.

—— (2001) 'Finding or losing yourself: working-class relationships to education?', *Journal of Education Policy*, 16(4): 333–46.

Reay, D. and Ball, S.J. (1998) '"Making their minds up": family dynamics of school choice', *British Educational Research Journal*, 24(4): 431–48.

Reay, D. and Lucey, H. (2001) 'Stigmatised choices: social class and local secondary school markets'. Paper presented at Addressing Issues of Social Class and Education: Theory into Practice Conference, University of North London, 26 June.

Reay, D. and Wiliam, D. (1999) '"I'll be a nothing": structure, agency and the construction of identity through assessment', *British Educational Research Journal*, 25(3): 343–54.

Reay, D., Davies, J., David, M. and Ball, S.J. (2001) 'Choice of degree or degrees of choice? Class, "race" and the higher education choice process', *Sociology*, 35(4): 855–74.

Rees T. (2001) *Investing in Learners: coherence, clarity and equity for student support in Wales* (The Rees Report), Independent Investigation Group on Student Hardship and Funding in Wales, Cardiff: National Assembly for Wales.

Reid, I. (1989) *Social Class Differences in Britain*, 3rd edn, Glasgow: Fontana.

Reynolds, T. (1997) 'Class matters, "race" matters, gender matters', in P. Mahony and C. Zmroczek (eds) *Class Matters: 'working-class' women's perspectives on social class*, London: Taylor and Francis.

Rich, A. (1986) 'Compulsory heterosexuality and lesbian existence', *Signs: Journal of Women in Culture and Society*, 5(4): 631–60.

Robbins, L. (1963a) *Higher Education: Report of a Committee* (Chairman: Lord Robbins), Cmnd 2154, London: HMSO.

—— (1963b) *Higher Education: Report of a Committee. Appendix 1: The demand for places in Higher Education* (Chairman: Lord Robbins) Cmnd 2154–1, London: HMSO.

Robbins, L. and Ford, J. (1965) 'Report on Robbins' (address to Gulbenkian Conference on Higher Education), *Universities Quarterly*, 20(1).

Robbins, Y.J. (1991) 'A "model" idea for recruitment and retention', *AARC Times* 15(4): 62.

Roberts, D. and Allen, A. (1997) *Young Applicants' Perceptions of Higher Education*, Leeds: Heist.

Robertson, D. (1995) 'Aspiration, achievement and progression in post-secondary and higher education', in J. Burke (ed.) *Outcomes, Learning and the Curriculum*, London: Falmer.

Robertson, D. and Hillman, J. (1997) *Widening Participation in Higher Education for Students from Lower Socio-Economic Groups and Students with Disabilities*. Report 6 for the National Commission of Inquiry into Higher Education, London: The Stationery Office.

Robinson, E. (1968) *The New Polytechnics*, Harmondsworth: Penguin.

Rose, D. and O'Reilly, K. (1997) *Constructing Classes: towards a new social classification in the UK*, Swindon: ESRC/ONS.

Salter, B. and Tapper, T. (1994) *The State and Higher Education*, London: Woburn.

Sawyer, B. and Carroll, L. (2000) 'Attitudes to student financial support systems', Annex N Research Report, vol. II, *Student Finance for the Future* (The Cubie Report), Edinburgh: Scottish Executive.

Schön, D.A. (1987) *Educating the Reflective Practitioner: toward a new design for teaching*, San Francisco: Jossey-Bass.

Schuman, J. (1999) 'The ethnic minority populations of Great Britain – latest estimates', *Population Trends,* 96: 33–43.

Sennett, R. and Cobb, J. (1977) *The Hidden Injuries of Class*, Cambridge: Polity Press.

Sewell, T. (1997) *Black Masculinities and Schooling: how black boys survive modern schooling*, Stoke-on-Trent: Trentham Books.

Shain, F. (2000) 'Culture, survival and resistance: theorizing young Asian women's experiences and strategies in contemporary British schooling and society', *Discourse,* 21(2): 155–74.

Shaw, G.B. (1903) *Man and Superman* (2000 edn, Weintraub, S. (ed.), London: Penguin.

Silver, H. (1990) *A Higher Education: The CNAA and British Higher Education*, London: Falmer.

Simon, B. (1985) 'The Tory Government and education 1950–60: background to breakout', *History of Education,* 14(4).

Skeggs, B. (1997) *Formations of Class and Gender: becoming respectable*, London: Sage.

Smith, J. (1997) 'From FE to HE: the experience of GNVQ students', *College Research,* Summer: 10–11.

Smith, J. and Naylor, R. (2001) 'Dropping out of university: a statistical analysis of the probability of withdrawal for UK university students', *Journal of the Royal Statistical Society Series A,* 164(2): 389–405.

Smith, R. and Eddison, R. (1963) *Talent for Tomorrow* (Bow Group pamphlet), London: Bow Group.

Smithers, A. (2000) 'The qualifications framework', in A. Smithers and P. Robinson (eds) *Further Education Re-formed*, London: Falmer.

Snow, C.P. (1959) *The Two Cultures and the Scientific Revolution*, Cambridge: Cambridge University Press.

Soskice, D. (1993) 'Social skills from mass higher education: rethinking company-based initial training paradigm', *Oxford Review of Economic Policy,* 9(3): 101–13.

Spours, K. and Young, M. (1988) *Beyond Vocationalism*, London: Institute of Education.

Squirrell, G. (1999) *Widening Participation into HE : Issues for Inner Cities*, Bristol: University of Bristol.

Steedman, C. (1986) *Landscape for a Good Woman: the story of two lives*, London: Virago.

Stone, L. (1994) 'The educational revolution', *Past and Present*, 41–80.

—— (1994) *The Education Feminism Reader*, London: Routledge.

Tawney, R.H. (1931) *Equality*, London: Allen and Unwin.

Tett, L. (1996) 'Making a difference? Including excluded groups in higher education: a case study'. Paper presented at European Conference on Lifelong Learning, Bremen, Germany: October.

—— (2000) '"I'm working class and proud of it": gendered experiences of non-traditional participants in higher education', *Gender and Education,* 12(2): 183–94.

THES (2000) 'Loans – rent = misery', Student Matters supplement, *Times Higher Education Supplement*, 31 March: iv.

—— (2001) 'Give students back grants urge voters', *Times Higher Education Supplement*, 4 May: 1.

—— (2002a) 'GCSEs are route to HE expansion', *Times Higher Education Supplement*, 22 February.

—— (2002b) 'Poor face a steep climb', *Times Higher Education Supplement*, 18 January.

—— (2002c) 'Debts grow ever bigger and more painful' (findings from the MORI Unite Student Living Survey), *Times Higher Education Supplement*, 1 February: 6–7.

Thomas, E. (2001) *Widening Participation in Post-Compulsory Education*, London: Continuum.

Thompson, A. (1997) 'Gatekeeping: inclusionary and exclusionary discourses and practices', in J. Williams (ed.) *Negotiating Access to Higher Education: the discourse of selectivity and equity*, Buckingham: SRHE and Open University Press.

Thompson, J. and Corver, M. (2000) 'Measuring participation and achievement'. HEFCE presentation and paper for CVCP Higher Education conference Mature Students: Encouraging Participation and Achievement, October 2000.

Tolson, A. (1977) *The Limits of Masculinity*, London: Tavistock.

Trotman, C. (1998) 'How can HEIs effectively target and recruit young people from low-income/socio-economic groups?'. Paper presented at From Elitism to Inclusion Conference, London, 2 November.

TUC (1956) *Higher Education*, London: Trades Union Congress.

UCAS (1999) *Statistical Bulletin on Widening Participation*, Cheltenham: UCAS.

—— (2000) *Ethnic Origin Of Home Applicants 1996–1999*. Cheltenham: UCAS.

—— (2002) *Annual Statistical Tables: 1994 to 2000 entry*. Available online <http://www.ucas.ac.uk/figures/archive/download/index.html> (accessed March 2002).

UCCA (1979) *Annual Report and Statistical Supplement 1978–79*. Cheltenham: UCCA.

UGC (1948) *Report on University Development 1935–1947*, London: HMSO.

—— (1952) *University Development: interim report on the years 1947–51*, Cmnd 8473, London: HMSO.

—— (1953) *University Development: report on the years 1947–1952,* Cmnd 8875, London: HMSO.

—— (1958) *University Development 1952–1957,* Cmnd 534, London: HMSO.

Venables, P. (1978) *Higher Education Developments: the technological universities, 1956–1976,* London: Faber.

Wagner, L. (1989) 'Access and standards: an unresolved (unresolvable?) debate', in C. Ball and H. Eggins (eds) *Higher Education into the 1990s: new dimensions,* Buckingham: SHRE and Open University Press.

Wakeford, N. (1993) 'Beyond *Educating Rita*: mature students and access courses', *Oxford Review of Education,* 19(2): 217–29.

Walkerdine, V. (1990) *Schoolgirl Fictions,* London: Verso.

Walkerdine, V., Lucey, H. and Melody, J. (1999) 'Class, attainment and sexuality in late twentieth-century Britain', in P. Mahony, and C. Zmroczek (eds) *Women and Social Class: international feminist perspectives,* London: UCL Press.

—— (2001) *Growing Up Girl: psychosocial explorations of gender and class,* Hampshire: Palgrave.

Weaver, T. (1994) 'Knowledge alone gets you nowhere: a memoir', *Capability,* 1(1).

Webb, S. (1997) 'Alternative students? Conceptualizations of difference', in J. Williams (ed.) *Negotiating Access to Higher Education: the discourse of selectivity and equity,* Buckingham: SRHE and Open University Press.

Weber, M. (1938) *The Protestant Ethic and the Spirit of Capitalism,* London: Unwin.

Weiner, G. (1994) *Feminisms in Education: an introduction,* Buckingham: Open University Press.

Wetherell, M. and Potter, J. (1992) *Mapping the Language of Racism: discourse and the legitimation of exploitation,* London: Harvester Wheatsheaf.

White, C., Stratford, N., Thomas, A. and Ward, K. (1996) *Review of Qualifications for 16–19 year olds: young people's perceptions of 16–19 qualifications,* London: Social and Community Planning Research.

Whitehead, A.N. (1929) *The Aim of Education,* London: Ernest Benn.

Whitty, G. (2001) 'Education, social class and social exclusion', *Journal of Education Policy,* 16(4): 287–95.

Williams, J. (1997) 'The discourse of access: the legitimation of selectivity', in J. Williams (ed.) *Negotiating Access to Higher Education: the discourse of selectivity and equity,* Buckingham: SRHE and Open University Press.

Williams, S. (1999) 'Knowledge of the university, its provision and its procedures: dispelling ignorance, inside and outwith the institution', *Widening Participation and Lifelong Learning,* 1(3): 20–5.

Williamson, B. (1981) 'Class bias', in D.W. Piper (ed.) *Is Higher Education Fair?,* Guildford: SRHE.

Willis, P. (1977) *Learning to Labour: how working class kids get working class jobs,* Farnborough: Saxon House.

Wolf, A. (1997) *The Tyranny of Numbers,* London: Institute of Education.

Wolffensperger, J. (1993) '"Science is truly a male world": the interconnectedness of knowledge, gender and power within university education', *Gender and Education,* 5(1): 37–54.

Woodrow, M. (1999) 'Student finance: access opportunity'. Paper for the Independent Committee of Inquiry into Student Finance, Edinburgh: Scottish Executive.

Woodrow, M. and Crosier, D. (1996) *Access for Under-Represented Groups*, vol. II: *Report on Western Europe*, Strasbourg: Council of Europe.

Woodrow, M., Yorke, M., Lee, M., McGrane, J., Osborne, B., Pudner, H. and Trotman, C. (2002) *Social Class and Participation: from elitism to inclusion 2*, London: Universities UK.

Woodward, W. (2001) 'Brighter pupils could skip GCSE exams', *The Guardian*, 15 November.

Wymer, K. (1994) 'Equal opportunities and further education', in C. Flint and M. Austin (eds) *Going Further*, Blagdon: The Staff College and the Association for Colleges.

Yorke, M., Bell, R., Dove, A., Haslam, L., Hughes Jones, H., Longden, B., O'Connell, C., Typuszak, R. and Ward, J. (1997) 'Undergraduate non-completion in England: Final report of a research project commissioned by HEFCE', Report 1 in *Undergraduate Non-Completion in Higher Education in England*, Bristol: HEFCE.

Yuval-Davis, N. and Anthias, F. (eds) (1989) *Woman- Nation- State*, London: Macmillan.

Zera, A. and Jupp, T. (2000) 'Widening participation', in A. Smithers and P. Robinson (eds) *Further Education Re-formed*, London: Falmer.

Zmroczek, C. (1999) 'Class, gender and ethnicity: snapshots of a mixed heritage', in P. Mahony and C. Zmroczek (eds) *Women and Social Class: international feminist perspectives*, London: UCL Press.

Index

A levels: drop-out rate 143; and
  employability 152; fall in standards
  150; gold standard 139, 150, 153;
  and student retention 198; university
  entrance 138, 149, 151; vocational
  (AVCEs) 144
academic culture, and working-class
  students 178
academic failure, and institutional
  culture 133
academic success, and racism 132
Access funds, student funding 162
adult education, and social justice 122
Advanced Further Education Pool,
  polytechnic funding 55–7
Afro-Caribbean men, masculinity 182
Afro-Caribbean women, attitudes to
  higher education 125, 146, 147
age, admission to higher education
  76–9
Australia, educational policies 142

Bengali men, masculinity 182
binary system: demise 64–5; higher
  education 46–55; origins 47–9;
  purpose 49
black students, university choice 130
black women students, class mobility 127
books, costs 162
boys, performance at school 40

careers advisers, value 107, 108
charitable trusts, student funding 161–2
class differences, and functionalism 8
class identity: social markers 177; threat
  from higher education 94, 176–9
class imbalance, student recruitment
  58–62

class mobility: black women students
  127; and higher education 124,
  126–7, 134, 170, 183
CNAA (Council for National Academic
  Awards): creation 47; polytechnic
  policy 57, 63
college funding, and student numbers
  106–7
Colleges of Advanced Technology
  (CATs) 30, 47
Colleges of Education: attendance of
  women 54–5; class distribution
  61–2; decline 54–5; and local
  authorities 46
common sense, lack in graduates 125
community education, and social justice
  122
comprehensive schools, higher
  education information 102–3
compulsory education, and social class 7
cost, higher education 112, 114
CSE (Certificate of Secondary
  Education) 139
cultural discourses, working-class
  people 111–16
culture, and social class 8–9, 16–17
Curriculum 2000 144, 153
curriculum, unified 143–4

Dearing Report 67–73, 97; economic
  benefits of higher education 168–9;
  principal recommendations 68–9;
  student funding 156
decentred learning 200
decision making: application for
  higher education 97–8; and
  information 98
degrees: Council for National Academic